# THE ROOSEVELT READER

## SELECTED SPEECHES, MESSAGES, PRESS CONFERENCES AND LETTERS OF

## FRANKLIN D. ROOSEVELT

*Edited and with an introduction by*
BASIL RAUCH

To read this carefully edited selection from the writings, speeches, and conferences of the late Franklin D. Roosevelt is to finally understand the "powerful rapport that grew up between him and his supporters, which reduced his enemies to ever more helpless tantrums." Mr. Rauch has successfully selected — from a vast amount of material — those letters, speeches, etc., which best display the unique qualities of Roosevelt's mind, character and personality, those which stand today as clues to the leadership which made him — and these documents — so important.

These selections range from very early childhood through Yalta; some of them have never been published before and give quite an amazing

*(continued on back flap)*

licies and
k is not
political

items —
address,
ech, etc.
iar ones.
articular
atesman-
is the
the best
at an
to read
elatively
osevelt's
tion can
ultimate
cannot

essor of
ge and
merican
ng his
story of
osevelt:
or."

# The Roosevelt Reader

SELECTED SPEECHES, MESSAGES,

PRESS CONFERENCES, AND LETTERS OF

FRANKLIN D. ROOSEVELT

*EDITED AND WITH AN INTRODUCTION*
*BY BASIL RAUCH*

NEW YORK *Rinehart & Co., Inc.* TORONTO

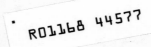

# INTRODUCTION

Technicians of free government have generally assumed that a heroic leader will be the enemy of liberty. They have exercised much ingenuity to prevent such a leader from leading. The American creed is very dogmatic on the point that the leader is not to be trusted with much power because he may develop ambition and destroy the people's liberty. It is a great paradox of our history that, in spite of this dogma, the United States of America has produced a matchless array of hero-leaders who actually strengthened our liberties. Our pantheon is not merely tribal. George Washington, Abraham Lincoln, and others in lesser degree have entered the legendry of all humanity. Almost all of them were civilian or military war chiefs but, alone among major republics of history, ours produces heroes who are not guilty of caesarism. The embarrassment that the existence of these heroes presents to our dogma is so keen that we scarcely dare to place the two things side by side.

The Framers of the Federal Constitution of 1787 knew and dreaded the ancient pattern of the people's hero become the destroyer of the people's liberties. They also knew that free government in America since the overthrow of British rule was in danger of expiring for lack of the vitality which might be infused into it by a leader with power. They did not solve the great dilemma. They incorporated it intact in the office of President of the United States. This office, on the one hand, beckons for heroes to fill it more urgently than any in the Old World, where executive power is divided between a ceremonial head of state and a political head of government who is subject to parliamentary majorities. On the other hand, the American Presidency is surrounded with opportunities for Congress and the Courts to frustrate for years on end any Chief Executive who tries to develop a policy of his own.

The absurdity of some of the arrangements whereby Americans have learned to live with this dilemma bothers outside observers and political scientists more than the American people. These arrangements truly express the ambivalence of our love-hate of the hero-leader. Every four years we conduct a frenzied search for a hero to lead us, and we drive the candidates to fight each other like brutal gladiators. The victor is allowed a few months' honeymoon during which he is assured of the people's united love and urged to do his will. If he shows no particular desire to do anything, popular disappointment is veiled by praise of his respect for Congress, the Courts, and the people's liberties, and the honeymoon declines into a comfortable marriage modulated by small squabbles. Such a President is admired while alive and then forgotten by all but historians.

But if during his honeymoon a President shows that he has the will and the force to use his power to effect large purposes, the paradox of his role puts him on a throne-rack unknown to any other system of government. Popular love and popular hatred for him boil up together. Even George Washington, for whose universal prestige the office of President was in the first place created, could not finish his eight years of great accomplishment without suffering contumely. The animosities directed against Jefferson, Jackson, the two Roosevelts, and Wilson are well known. Less clearly understood is the fact that Lincoln, in our pantheon the saintliest of Presidents, is the man who was so hated and feared that his mere election, before he had been allowed a day's honeymoon in the White House, led some of his defeated opponents to quit the Union and get ready for war. That he should today replace Washington in the hearts of his countrymen as their supreme hero is a manifestation of the strange character of the Presidential office. One reason for Lincoln's apotheosis is that he had the peculiar faculty of sharing with the people their fear of the Executive power even while he used it to the hilt. Like the scapegoat-saviors of primitive religions, his heroism was itself his true martyrdom.

Lincoln most thoroughly demonstrates the rule that the greatly loved and greatly hated Presidents make the creative additions to American policy which stand the test of time. Fear and hatred die out as the successors consolidate the achievements of the hero, and then he is ready for the pantheon. Meditating on the incidence of hero-Presidents in our history, we may be tempted to conclude that some mechanism produces a hero in the White House to match and master the crises of our history whenever they occur. But it is well to avoid mysticism, and even the doctrine that the opportunity provided by the crisis creates the great man makes as much difficulty as it solves. Our great Presidents have too often appeared too late to deal with crisis before disaster occurred. Had President Buchanan been a man of heroic character, the crisis of 1860 might have been solved without civil war. Had Presidents Harding or Coolidge or Hoover been great heroes, the Depression and the Second World War, one or both, might have been avoided.

The normal state of the American political psyche is one of fear of heroic leadership slightly dominating the desire for it. That we have found Presidents to pull us through disaster without ruin is our luck. For a President to foresee in ordinary times the approach of crisis and take forehanded measures to avert it is deeply irritating to the American people. Our unwillingness to submit to strong leadership until disaster has struck is our gravest weakness. It gives to our political history its odd tone of extreme alternations between passive utopia and creative hellfire.

Franklin D. Roosevelt foresaw the likelihood of depression before Herbert Hoover entered the White House. He knew the American habit well enough to expect that it would require collapse of the economic boom before voters would listen to reform. He also foresaw the danger to the United States of a second world war before the isolationist majority in Congress and the country would believe it. He begged Congress for various measures of cooperation with peaceful nations against the rising aggressions of the Axis leaders in time to try to prevent the Second World War, but he got them only in time to help win it. He went so far as to sacrifice the principle of anti-imperialism as a concession to Russia at the Yalta Conference not only to make sure of winning the War but also to secure forehanded measures to prevent a third world war, and he has been bitterly criticized for sacrificing too much. The disasters he had to deal with were second in gravity throughout our history only to the one Lincoln faced. The people twice gave him unified support for a few months to help him surmount the domestic crisis of 1933 and the Axis attack of 1941. During the rest of his twelve years in the White House he faced hatred which was also second only to that of Lincoln. His death, too, at the apparent moment of fulfillment, but actually when the cause he led was falling into internal dissension reducing the value of victory, was strongly reminiscent of the Emancipator's.

These parallels are not matched by parallels in their natures. Roosevelt loved the exercise of power, Lincoln regretted it. Roosevelt used his own self-confidence, gaiety, and charm as instruments of leadership. Lincoln loved jokes in which he found private relief, but could not conceal the sorrow he felt in his public role. Roosevelt's spiritual perceptions were rather shallow; he lived by a facile optimism enriched by very broad human sympathies. Lincoln's hope for mankind was chastened by tragic insight; the depth of his vision placed such utterances as the Gettysburg Address and the Second Inaugural in the canon of humanity's sacred literature. The generations for whom reading the printed word left behind by these two men will be the most vivid experience of their qualities may decide very unfavorably to Roosevelt. Only the creativity of Roosevelt in action, the sheer quantity of work he accomplished for the country and the world, will balance the judgment of his inferiority in the written word.

As if aware that quantity was his forte, Roosevelt was singularly careful that the written evidences of his life, and shoals of interesting and trivial memorabilia besides, should all be preserved. The acreage of paper now stacked in the Franklin D. Roosevelt Library at Hyde Park is so vast that it baffles the most laborious scholars. The present selection is designed to reduce the hazard of quantity to proportions reasonable enough to appeal to general readers as well as to more specialized students of American history. The selections are not intended to relate the story of his life or the political history in which he took part, although leading events of both are represented. Rather the selections are intended to reveal the qualities of Roosevelt's mind, character, and personality, as clues to the leadership which made them important.

The transcripts of his press conferences give us the most intimate perceptions of his leadership. They show his ability to bring an astonishing range of facts and ideas to bear on the decisions of the day, his virtuosity in making publicity hay out of his sunny method of dealing with the correspondents, and his humanity in reading events and statistics not as abstractions but as matters deeply involving people he actually knew and millions more whom he could imagine each as an individual with a name, a face, and private hopes and fears. His tremendous talent for statesmanship by improvisation shows to advantage in these records while his weakness for disorderly administration is not on display. Out of the monumental pile of transcripts of nine hundred and eighty-six Presidential press conferences, a generous lot of culled passages is offered. Most of his letters are disappointing as they convey more information external to himself than individuality, and they are sparely represented. His Messages to Congress are far more readable than the run of such literature. Very frequently they really announced new determinations of policy, and some of the Special Messages are among the most dramatic of American state papers. But he will probably live in the printed word chiefly in his great political speeches, and they are given the most space in this book.

They were his supreme acts of leadership. All his intellectual penetration, all his activism in the cause of social improvement, all the warmth of his feeling for human beings, and also the passion with which he countered his opponents, were poured into these speeches. Those drawn from his early years demonstrate that his style and his political philosophy were never dependent on the brains trusters and assistants he later used to help organize policies and prepare addresses. Even though his magic failed on several great occasions, the massive accomplishments of his Presidency in renovating the domestic and foreign policies of the nation were in very large part the result of his superlative power as a political orator.

Readers of the younger generation may be surprised to discover that this legendary oratory is not commemorated in a great prose style. But Roosevelt was so great a master of oral delivery that he transmitted emotion that was not in the composition itself. He could even make great music out of the rather mechanical literary devices he favored. As the years passed, the style of his speeches was sharpened and simplified, but it underwent no deepening into literary greatness comparable to the maturation of Lincoln's style.

How could he move so many millions so deeply in campaign speeches and fireside chats? The answer is not in the manner or meaning of any particular words but in the total sense of the man which his listeners absorbed over the years in a thousand conscious and unconscious ways. The accumulation of causes he spoke for and policies and laws he fought for steadily strengthened the belief of most Americans that he was a very great man, there grew up a powerful rapport between him and his supporters, and his enemies were reduced to ever more helpless tantrums. During the War some of his speeches took on the character of national epiphanies with traffic stopped in the great cities, every radio leaned over by rapt faces, and many listening in abroad who were hiding from Nazi bombs or boots.

Hatred of Roosevelt is now, more than a decade after his death, dying away. Except as a treasured personal phobia, this hatred could hardly outlive the adoption by a Republican Administration of every one of his important policies. The younger generation of readers of American history all too automatically accord Roosevelt a place in the national pantheon alongside the very greatest Presidents. For them historical background is necessary to understand why he was once widely and deeply feared and hated.

The curious reader can delve into such materials as the many anti-Roosevelt syndicated newspaper columnists of the period, but he will probably think them more maniacal than comprehensible. They were certainly balanced in the press by fairly objective and extremely thorough news coverage. Roosevelt liked to complain about his treatment at the hands of columnists and publishers, and they did build many a fire under him, but he seemed to forget that he knew how to make his own news, prodigiously in both quantity and impact, which no publisher could possibly keep off his front page. Quite well-rounded and more available source materials are the memoirs so many of his alienated as well as loyal associates wrote. Biographies and histories can hardly be expected to provide so soon the balanced perspective we demand of great work. Those listed below should be read as reflections of the convictions or prejudices of their authors while bearing in mind the interesting fact that the great majority of authorities in the fields of history and political science were and are pro-Roosevelt. They can afford to be the more objective in tone because they dominate the situation. The reader should be warned of this because it may prove no more about any specific issue than that Roosevelt is winning the battle for history as he won the battle for opinion during his lifetime. Still that is a great deal: all that remains is that he should become a hero to businessmen and Republicans as Lincoln has become a hero to Southerners and Democrats.

The very best procedure if one wishes to arrive at an independent judgment is to read Roosevelt's own words. Relatively free of the passions of those days, the new generations can gain insights from this ultimate source which their elders cannot equal. They can relate paradoxical Rooseveltian phenomena to the fact that human society in general and the American form of government in particular, although they need heroes as leaders, also dread and resist them, because conservatism is a real necessity of life and because the man who molds history into new forms may really be an enemy of liberty. The editor professes his belief that study of Roosevelt's words and of all his actions will confirm the instinct of the younger generation that another hero-President has lately been added to the company of George Washington, Thomas Jefferson, Andrew Jackson, Abraham Lincoln, Theodore Roosevelt, and Woodrow Wilson. Like all of them, Franklin D. Roosevelt was a great and successful progressive with respect to the abolition of evils, and a great and successful conservative with respect to the ideals for which liberty is our oldest and still our most precious word.

A number of these documents have never before been published in any form. Some were reported in the press at the time, and others have been published in the large collections listed below. Whether or not this is their first publication, the texts in virtually all cases are those of the original manuscripts in the Franklin D. Roosevelt Library at Hyde Park.

The work of exploring the Library's stores to make a fresh selection was vastly eased by the help of many kinds provided in truly generous measure by Dr. Herman Kahn, the Director, Dr. George W. Roach, Mr. William J. Nichols, and the others of that excellent institution's staff. The Director has given permission to publish all the materials in this book except those copyrighted selections for which permission has been obtained from the publishers (see page iv).

I am grateful to Mrs. Franklin D. Roosevelt and Mr. Joseph P. Lash for their efforts to assist me. For the ideas and work of Roberta Brown Rauch my debt is greatest of all.

BASIL RAUCH

Barnard College
Columbia University

# SELECTED BIBLIOGRAPHY

COLLECTIONS:

*The Public Papers and Addresses of Franklin D. Roosevelt;* Special Introductions and Explanatory Notes by President Roosevelt (New York: Random House, Inc., 1938), 5 volumes, 1928-1936; (New York: The Macmillan Company, 1941), 4 volumes, 1937-1940; Compiled with Special Material and Explanatory Notes by Samuel I. Rosenman (New York: Harper & Brothers, 1950), 4 volumes, 1941-1945.

*F. D. R.: His Personal Letters: Early Years,* Foreword by Eleanor Roosevelt (New York: Duell, Sloan & Pearce, Inc., 1947); *1905–1928,* Foreword by Eleanor Roosevelt, Edited by Elliott Roosevelt assisted by James N. Rosenau (Duell, Sloan & Pearce, Inc., 1948); *1928–1945,* Foreword by Eleanor Roosevelt, edited by Elliott Roosevelt assisted by Joseph P. Lash (New York: Duell, Sloan & Pearce, Inc., 1950), 2 volumes.

BOOKS BY PEOPLE WHO KNEW HIM:

James A. Farley, *Behind the Ballots* (New York: Harcourt, Brace & Co. Inc., 1938) and *Jim Farley's Story: The Roosevelt Years* (New York: Whittlesey House, 1948).

Harold L. Ickes, *Secret Diary* (3 vols.; New York: Simon & Schuster, 1953, 1954).

Raymond B. Moley, *After Seven Years* (New York: Harper & Brothers, 1939).

Frances Perkins, *The Roosevelt I Knew* (New York: The Viking Press, Inc., 1946).

Eleanor Roosevelt, *This Is My Story* and *This I Remember* (New York: Harper & Brothers, 1937, 1949).

Samuel I. Rosenman, *Working with Roosevelt* (New York: Harper & Brothers, 1952).

Robert E. Sherwood, *Roosevelt and Hopkins* (New York: Harper & Brothers, 1948).

Edward R. Stettinius, Jr., *Roosevelt and the Russians* (New York: Doubleday & Co. Inc., 1949).

BOOKS BY HISTORIANS AND JOURNALISTS:

Charles A. Beard, *American Foreign Policy in the Making: 1932-1940* and *President Roosevelt and the Coming of the War, 1941* (New Haven: Yale University Press, 1946, 1948).

Denis W. Brogan, *The Era of Franklin D. Roosevelt* (New Haven: Yale University Press, 1950).

John T. Flynn, *The Roosevelt Myth* (New York: Devin-Adair Company, 1948).

Frank Friedel, *Franklin D. Roosevelt: The Apprenticeship, The Ordeal,* and *The Triumph* (Boston: Little, Brown & Company, 1952, 1954, 1956).

Harold F. Gosnell, *Champion Campaigner, Franklin D. Roosevelt* (New York: The Macmillan Company, 1952).

John Gunther, *Roosevelt in Retrospect* (New York: Harper & Brothers, 1950).

William L. Langer and S. E. Gleason, *The Challenge to Isolation: 1937-1940* and *The Undeclared War: 1940-1941* New York: Harper & Brothers, 1952, 1953).

Basil Rauch, *The History of the New Deal: 1932-1938* and *Roosevelt: From Munich to Pearl Harbor* (New York: Creative Age Press of Farrar, Straus & Cudahy, Inc., 1944, 1950).

Arthur M. Schlesinger, Jr., *The Age of Roosevelt: The Crisis of the Old Order* (Boston: Houghton, Mifflin Company, 1957).

# CONTENTS

PART TWO / September, 1921 - March 4, 1933

*Poliomyelitis / Governor of New York /*
*First Presidential Campaign*

PART THREE / March 4, 1933 - January 1, 1935

*The First New Deal / End of the Honeymoon*

PART FOUR / January 1, 1935 - January 1, 1937

*The Second New Deal / Landslide Election*

PART FIVE / January 1, 1937 - September 1, 1939

*"Court Packing" Fight / Primaries "Purge" Campaign /
Fight to Repeal Arms Embargo*

CONTENTS

PART SIX / September 1, 1939 - December 7, 1941

*Disaster in Europe / Third Term Campaign /*
*The Great Arsenal of Democracy / Battle of the Atlantic*

## PART SEVEN / December 7, 1941 - January 1, 1944

*Disaster in the Pacific / Invasion of North Africa*

---

# PART EIGHT / January 1, 1944 - April 12, 1945

*World Leader / D-Day / Fourth Term Campaign / Yalta*

*Part
One*

Childhood
Groton and Harvard
State Senator
Assistant Secretary of the Navy
Vice Presidential Candidate

SPRING, 1888 — OCTOBER 18, 1920

## LETTER TO SARA DELANO ROOSEVELT

*Hyde Park. Spring, 1888*

*Living on his elderly father's beautiful Hudson River estate, the only child of his young mother, Franklin Delano Roosevelt enjoyed a very happy childhood.*

My dear Mama.

Thank you so much for the lovly soldiers. Brother Rosy may take a pictuer of our gardans because it looks so nice. We are going to have a big bush in our gardans and it's nearly two feet high. I take my rest evry day but I am not out much We have battles with the soldiers evry day. and they are so nice. Good bye dear Mama    Your loving little

FRANKLIN

P. S. Give my love to papa and Uncle Frank and Aunt Laura.


## EARLIEST NEWSPAPER ARTICLE

*January 1, 1891*

*Just before his ninth birthday, Franklin decided to start the New Year right by publishing a newspaper. All his life he liked the idea of becoming a newspaperman. The Hyde Park Daily Herald was written, published, and edited by him.*

THE HYDE PARK DAILY HERALD.

*January 1, 1891*

The Graphic has arrived this morning.
It snowed this morning.
The thermometer is 14 degrees. Probae [probable] it will freeze to morrow. Good coasting at Hyde Park on the Hudson N.Y. Jas. Roosevelt upset a large bob with 6 ladies and 1 boy. The boy scraped his leg a little, but it is not a very bad wound. Mrs Jas. Roosevelt and Miss Anna Roosevelt both hurt their hips. They probably will be well in two weeks.

2

Miss A. Roosevelt is staying with Mr. and Mrs Jas. Roosevelt. Miss Sands has left Mr. and Mrs. Rogers. There was a coasting party at Mr. . . . place today.

Hard rain tomorrow.

Mr and Mrs J. Roosevelt will probably not go to New. York tomorrow.

Not much snow melted . . Hard rain in New York day before yesterday. A boy was kicked in the head by a horse while he was coasting.

## LETTER TO JAMES AND
## SARA DELANO ROOSEVELT

*Groton School, Groton, Massachusetts. September 27, 1896*

*He had been prepared for Groton entirely by governesses and tutors and a good deal of travel abroad. All this produced a boy whose interests were extremely normal.*

Dear Papa and Mama

I am getting on very well so far. Thanks very much for your letters; the more the better.

I have not had any blackmarks or latenesses yet and I am much better in my studies.

I got the best mark in Algebra yesterday morning and the day before I got the best in English Composition. Yesterday afternoon our 1st Eleven played the Brookline High School team, a lot of toughs, and beat them quite badly, the score was 16–0 and for the first game of the season it was very good.

I cheered myself hoarse so that I was quite croaky at choir practice.

I like Greek very much, it is very easy so far, and Mr. Abbott, a young Englishman just come to the school, gives us very short lessons. I am going to try for the punctuality prize, but it will be hard work, as one lateness will spoil.

The Biddle boy is quite crazy, fresh and stupid, he has been boot-boxed once and threatened to be pumped several times. Our 4th twenty-two play four times a week, and we have had some very desperate battles. My head is a little bunged up, but otherwise I am all right. Mr. Peabody read to us in his study several evenings in the week after supper. I eat a great deal and I have gained several pounds.

I am going to Groton on Wednesday for the second time. A number of boys have fruit sent them and it is kept in the fruit closet and given out three or four times a week. Could you send me some grapes or other small fruit? It would be very nice.

With lots of love to Muriel and Warren and papa and yourself

affectionately

## LETTER TO JAMES AND SARA DELANO ROOSEVELT

*Groton. January 12, 1898*

*He became a school team manager and a debater. Was he a convinced anti-imperialist? His father was a Democrat, and he always identified himself with that Party, which opposed the imperialist adventures in which his distant cousin Theodore won fame.*

My dear Mama and Papa

I was much excited when I got your letter telling of the runaway and I am only too thankful that neither you nor Papa were in it, and that no one was hurt. . . .

You will be surprised to hear that I am to debate next Wednesday the 19th. We are not to debate alphabetically this year but by lot & I fell in the first debate with Blagden, Harold Peabody and Krumbhaar. I debate with Blagden against the other two. We have chosen for our subject: "Resolved, that Hawaii be promptly annexed." Krumbhaar & Peabody are for it, Pro, & we are Con. . . .

If you see any articles in the papers or the Spectator against the annexation of Hawaii I wish you could send them to me.

With a great deal of love to you both   I am your affec son

## LETTER TO SARA DELANO ROOSEVELT

*Cambridge, Massachusetts. January 6, 1902*

*After Groton, Harvard. His kinsman entered the White House, and Franklin went to Washington for the greatest social event of the day, the debut of the President's daughter, Alice.*

Dearest Mama—

I got here all right this a.m. at 8, & have been unpacking most of the day. To go back—On Thursday evening the Groton dinner was a great success, good speeches by the Rector & some of the older graduates. On Friday Aunt Kassie, P. C. & M. D. R. & I took the train at 10.50 & had a very comfortable journey to Washington. I went straight to the Kean's, & from there, in obedience to Cousin Bammie's note to Mrs. Townsend's tea, which was interesting & filled with New Yorkers whom I knew. I dined at the Keans, (old Mrs.) & there were 40 there. Then to the dance, which was most glorious fun. The Washington people weren't in it with the New Yorkers & from start to finish it was glorious. I am sure M. D. R. had a good time. We left at 2 a.m. & I slept till 12 on Saturday. After lunch Mr. Kean took me over the new Congressional Library, & at 4 I went to the White House for tea & stayed till 6. All most interesting. We dined quietly, & at 10 went to the Austrian ambassador's reception, where I saw many diplomats. On Sunday I went to Church with the old Keans, & afterwards went again to the White House. Lunched at Cousin Bammie's & left on the 4.50 train for here. On the whole it was one of the most interesting & enjoyable three days I have ever had. Found every thing all right here. Your 2 notes have come. It is time to go to bed.

Ever

## LETTER TO SARA DELANO ROOSEVELT

*Interlaken, Switzerland. August 12, 1903*

*Family connections also permitted him to enter some of the great houses of England, but there, during a European tour following his graduation from Harvard, he enjoyed asserting rather aggressively his Americanism.*

Dearest Mamma—

. . . After luncheon we played fives on the billiard table, & at three Sir Hugh, Aline & I drove over to the place of the Lord-Lieutenant of the County—beyond Grantham. The place is called Belton I think & *his* name was as near as I could gather *Brownel* or something like it. It is a most perfect place & house & there was a large house party there besides lots of neighbors—all having tea on a heavenly terrace. As a large detachment of volunteers were encamped in the park there were officers there too—among them Gen. Gatacre of South African war fame. As I knew the uncivilized English custom of never introducing people I had about three fits when we arrived & got at once separated from Aline & her Father—but I walked up to the best looking dame in the bunch & said "howdy?" Things at once went like oil & I was soon having flirtations with three of the nobility at the same time. I had a walk with the hostesses' niece over the entire house which was really perfect in every way—I mean the house—although the walk wasn't bad—I will have to wait to tell you about it in person— again I mean the house. Then I inspected the gardens with another 'chawmer' & ended up by jollying the hostess herself all by her lonesome for ten minutes while a uniformed Lord stood by & never got in anything except an occasional "aw" or an "I sy." We stayed about an hour and I made about 15 bosom friends & got on so well with about 10 of these that I found out their names! After our return I fished for a half-hour—had dinner (*and some port* of about A.D. 1800 that made me almost weep for joy) & then played bridge again. . . .

There you have it all & I will be home a few days after this letter—It has been perfect so far & great fun but I wont be sorry to get home—though I could have a good time right here for a month—

Ever dear mum    Lovingly

## LETTER TO SARA DELANO ROOSEVELT

*Cambridge, Massachusetts. December 4, 1903*

*That fall he returned to Harvard for a fifth year because he had been elected editor of the daily* Crimson. *He had to break the news gently to his mother, now a widow, that he was engaged to marry his fifth cousin, Anna Eleanor Roosevelt.*

Dearest Mama—

I have been absolutely rushed to death since I came back, with a thousand things to attend to. . . .

Dearest Mama—I know what pain I must have caused you and you know I wouldn't do it if I really could have helped it —mais tu sais, me voilà! Thats all that could be said—I know my mind, have known it for a long time, and know that I could never think otherwise: Result: I am the happiest man just now in the world; likewise the luckiest— And for you, dear Mummy, you know that nothing can ever change what we have always been & always will be to each other—only now you have two children to love & to love you—and Eleanor as you know will always be a daughter to you in every true way—

I shall be here over Sunday working all the time but will write you a longer letter then—

Excuse this hurried scrawl, it doesn't express anything but you know what I mean

Your ever loving

## LETTER TO SARA DELANO ROOSEVELT

*Venice. June 26, 1905*

*On his honeymoon trip, he wrote what seems to be the only record of an interest in art other than naval pictures and Hudson Valley Dutch architecture.*

Dearest Mama,

Here we are, quite overcome by the wonders of Venice, and settled comfortably for ten days. . . .

We saw the [Milan] Cathedral which is fine and well proportioned, though rather ornate in style. Also we saw the Church of Santa Maria della Pietà, an interesting basilica with fascinating cloisters by Bramante which are being restored from rather rough usage as barracks by the Austrians. Unfortunately the "Last Supper" of Leonardo da Vinci is not open till the afternoon, so we had to miss it. We left Milan at 1 p.m. passing through Verona, Vicenza and Padua, and got here at seven, stepping from the station into a gondola, and got to the hotel which is on the Grand Canal and but a block from the Piazza di San Marco. I had telegraphed ahead for an excellent gondolier recommended by Cousin Julia Delano and this morning at ten we went out with him and explored the Piazza and the buildings around it. After lunch we went the whole length of the Grand Canal, examining the wonderful palaces along it and came back through the small canal, visiting three of the churches en route. Then we had tea on the Piazza and found Charlie Forbes soon after our return. We are to lunch with him on Wednesday and tomorrow go to his studio.

I think I had expected to be disappointed in Venice, but the reality is far more wonderful than the pictures I had made. . . .

Ever your devoted
Loads of love from us both.

# NEW YORK TIMES *INTERVIEW*

*January 22, 1911*

*After some legal training at Columbia University and a few
years as a lawyer in New York City, he performed the feat of
winning election to the State Senate as a Democrat in traditionally Republican Dutchess County. Immediately, he began
to make news as the leader of a successful revolt against Tammany control of the New York Democratic Party.*

## SENATOR F. D. ROOSEVELT,
## CHIEF INSURGENT AT ALBANY

He's a Fifth Cousin of the Colonel, and He Stepped Into the Spot-
light the First Day He Took His Seat as Leader
of the Independent Democrats.

. . . Senator Roosevelt is less than 30. He is tall and lithe.
With his handsome face and his form of supple strength he
could make a fortune on the stage and set the matinee girl's
heart throbbing with subtle and happy emotion. But no one
would suspect behind that highly polished exterior the quiet
force and determination that now are sending cold shivers
down the spine of Tammany's striped mascot. . . .

For a few days Senator Roosevelt went about the Capitol
unobtrusively enough. Then came the day when the scene of
the Senatorial contest shifted to the Capitol. Rumors that he
might stay out of Mr. Murphy's caucus last Monday night had
reached Albany from Hyde Park, where the young lawmaker
spent the recess with his family. These rumors made the more
seasoned lawmakers who knew what it meant to defy a boss
smile. Then Senator Roosevelt came to the Capitol himself.
On the Sunday prior to the caucus he told his friends that he
was going out to get some fresh air. He buttoned up his coat
and started on a long, lone walk. Before he returned to the
Hotel Ten Eyck, then the throbbing centre of the biggest game
of politics in a generation, he had paid a visit to the Executive
Mansion.

"Nobody has been authorized to say that I would stay out of the caucus," he declared in answer to questions. But when the next day came and the caucus with it Senator Roosevelt was the leader of twenty-one Democratic lawmakers who were willing to take their political future in their hands in order to register their independence and strike a blow for the freedom of conscience in public life.

Since then Senator Roosevelt has been the head and front of the insurgent movement that has caused Boss Murphy and his candidate for the Senate sleepless nights and riveted the attention of the entire country on Capitol Hill.

"Gee!" said a Tammany "regular," in discussing Senator Roosevelt's hurry in creating a disturbance in the ranks of the legislative majority, "the other Roosevelt didn't lose much time in making trouble once he got here, but this fellow 'beat him' to it. His seat in the Senate wasn't warm before he became a bolter. Ain't it fierce?"

It was at the headquarters of the anti-Sheehan movement at the Hotel Ten Eyck that Senator Roosevelt consented to tear himself away from an insurgent conference long enough to talk for a few minutes to a representative of the Sunday *Times*.

"Shoot away quick," he urged. "I must be back with my friends in about five minutes."

The words did not come with the explosive force that would have propelled them had they come from the centre of volcanic energy with which the name of Roosevelt is usually associated. The young lawmaker said it rather quietly, and in a softly modulated voice. . . .

The people through the boss-ridden counties Senator Roosevelt represents have not been slow in showing their appreciation of his efforts to resist Murphy's dictatorial methods at the capital.

"I got all these today," he said, displaying a great stack of letters. "They come by every mail, and between mails I receive telegrams and telephone communications. I could pursue no other course in justice to my constituents, and these letters are the best evidence that the people at home feel that I am doing my duty."

"Have you heard from your uncle-in-law?" I asked the Senator.

He smiled quietly.

"No," he said. "I have had no word from uncle in a long time. But I will hear from him some time when this is over, I have no doubt. I am sure that any fight for principle would have his blessing and approval.

"Funny," the Senator added after a moment of silence. "When I was a candidate people would write me almost every day and ask if I was in any way related to Col. Roosevelt. It was very embarrassing at times, and I do not know at this moment whether the relationshp helped or hurt in the campaign."

"Are you an admirer of your uncle-in-law?" I asked the Senator.

"Why, who can help but admire him?" he replied. "I differ with him on a great many questions, but they are the differences between men who both are seeking to do their best for the public good. Only he is doing it in the Republican way while I am trying to do it in a Democratic way. It is a difference in method growing out of fundamental difference in party faith, that's all." . . .

"Do you believe that political conditions are on the verge of undergoing a change for the better?"

"I most decidedly do," he replied. "'But one thing should be emphasized. More people should take an interest in politics. It is everybody's business. Especially do I think more young men should take an active part, though it is difficult to see how public life and political work can afford any attraction to those who are young and ambitious as long as the name 'politician' is a by-word." . . .

## LETTER TO ELEANOR ROOSEVELT

*Albany, New York. July 18, 1911*

*Senator Roosevelt did not go very far in favor of progressive social and economic reforms, but he championed political progressivism, and he loved the battle.*

Dearest Babby—

Here I am back again in Albany for what I hope is the final week. I raised a riot this a.m. in the Senate when the Governor's message in favor of direct primaries was read by moving to instruct the Judiciary Committee to report a bill conforming with the message. It upset the plans of the organization and precipitated a 3-hour angry debate, and although beaten the motion has served to wake people up about Direct Nominations and may help to give us a good law, though we have only three days more.

I am feeling stronger and had my sinuses washed out yesterday for the last time. Dr. Dobson wants to poke the tonsils once more before I go away, so I will have to go to Poughkeepsie once for a very short time. . . .

A call of the house is ordered.

Ever your devoted

## SPEECH TO THE PEOPLE'S FORUM

*Troy, New York. March 3, 1912*

*In the climactic year of Progressivism, Roosevelt broadened and deepened his political philosophy.*

. . . If we go back through history, or rather through the history of the past thousand years, we are struck by the fact that as a general proposition the Aryan races have been struggling to obtain individual freedom. For nearly one thousand years and in almost every European and American country this has been the great and fundamental question in the economic life of the people. The Reformation, for instance, and the Renaissance in Europe are too commonly regarded as religious or educational struggles and have not, by teachers of history, been sufficiently explained as efforts on the part of the various peoples affected to obtain individual liberty. In the same way the American revolution, the French revolution and at a later date the general European uprisings of 1848.

Almost every struggle of representative government has been in reality an attempt to secure individual freedom and almost everywhere one turns today, can be found a form of government, which to a great degree, guarantees this personal liberty. There are exceptions of course, like Russia. It is a sweeping statement to make but taking the nations as a whole today, in Europe and America, the liberty of the individual has been accomplished.

On my assumption that this liberty of the individual has been largely accomplished and that it has been until now the main object of human research, I come to the next step in the search for the cause of the conditions of unrest today, and I find the cause in the growth of what is in modern civilization a new way of looking at things, a new economic theory. It is new because there never has been any immediate need for such a theory in the past. When men are serfs or are ruled by tyrants they need first of all, individual freedom. They do not need to go beyond that, but when this freedom has been acquired they have not yet got to Utopia.

During the past century we have acquired a new set of conditions which we must seek to solve. To put it in the simplest and fewest words I have called this new theory the struggle for liberty of the community rather than liberty of the individual. When all is said and done every new doctrine which had been advanced for the last fifty years comes under this definition. Every new star that people have hitched their wagon to for the past half century, whether it be anti-rebating, or anti-trusts, or new fashioned education, or conservation of our natural resources or State regulation of common carriers, or commission government, or any of the thousand and one other things that we have run after of late, almost without any exception come under the same heading. They are all steps in the evolution of the new theory of the liberty of the community.

The Socialist has at times called this same thing 'community interest' and some sounding orators have called it the 'brotherhood of man.' Neither of these expressions is possible to use anywhere outside of heaven for community of interest at once suggests to the mind a kind of happy condition where everybody wants the same thing and everybody gets it. This is comparatively recent doctrine, but at least the liberty of the individual has been obtained, and we must face new theories.

To state it plainly, competition has been shown to be useful up to a certain point, but co-operation, which is the thing that we must strive for today, begins where competition leaves off. This was what the founders of the republic were groping for and it is precisely today along every possible walk of life.

Let us take some examples of this—for instance what we call today, conservation. We are taking merely a theory which began to be developed in other countries many years ago. It was recognized in Germany for instance a hundred years ago that the trees on the land were necessary for the preservation of the water power and indeed for the general health and prosperity of the people. One hundred and fifty years ago in Germany the individual was not restricted from denuding his lands of the growing trees. Today he must cut only in a manner scientifically worked out, which is calculated to serve the ends of the community and not his ends.

They passed beyond the liberty of the individual to do as he pleased with his own property and found it was necessary to check this liberty for the benefit of the freedom of the whole people. So it is in New York State today. We are beginning to see that it is necessary for our health and happiness that the rights of individuals that lumber companies may not do as they please with the wooded growths in the Catskills and the Adirondacks.

There are, however, many persons who still think that individuals can do as they please with their own property even

though it affects a community. The most striking example of
what happens in such a case that I know of, was a picture
shown me by Gifford Pinchot last week. It was a photograph of
a walled city in northern China. Four or five hundred years
ago this city had been the center of the populous and prosperous district, a district whose mountains and ridges were covered with magnificent trees, its streams flowing without interruption and its crops in the valleys prospering. It was known
as one of the richest provinces in China, both as a lumber ex-
porting center and as an agricultural community.

Today the picture shows the walled town, almost as it stood
500 years ago, but there is not a human being within the walls,
and but few in the whole region. Rows upon rows of bare
ridges and mountains stretch back from the city without a
vestige of life. Everything is in a dilapidated condition, and
this is all due to the liberty of the individual. This is what will
happen in this very State if the individuals are allowed to do
as they please with the natural resources to line their own
pockets during their life. With them the motto is 'After us the
deluge.' They do not care what happens after they are gone
and even do not care what happens to their neighbors. . . .

There is, to my mind, no valid reason why the food supply
of the nation should not be put on the most economical and at
the same time the most productive basis by carrying out cooperation. If we call the method regulation, people hold up
their hands in horror and say 'Unamerican,' or 'dangerous,'
but if we call the same identical process co-operation these
same old fogies will cry out 'well done.' It may seem absurd to
call the rebating formerly done by railroads, and the great
trusts so-called, minor issues, but after all rebating was discrimination and the doctrine of co-operation came with it. The
same with trusts, they were and are run on the theory of monopoly, but co-operation puts monopoly out of date and we
now understand that the mere size of a trust is not of necessity
its evil. The trust is evil because it monopolizes for a few and
as long as this keeps up it will be necessary for a community to
change its features.

And here I come to the final point. How must the liberty of the community be obtained? It will not be obtained at once, whether the Democrats, Republicans or Socialists say so or not. It must be worked out by keeping ever in view the cause of the condition and we must also keep in view the other essential point: Law and order.

## LETTER TO ELEANOR ROOSEVELT

*Washington. August 2, 1914*

*He supported Woodrow Wilson as Democratic candidate for President, and was appointed Assistant Secretary of the Navy in the new Administration. Procurement and labor relations were his immediate responsibilities, but the outbreak of the First World War made him see his job in a more brilliant light.*

My own Dearest—

At last I have time to write you a real letter. I posted a line on the train last night, and on arrival went straight to the Department, where as I expected, I found everything asleep and apparently utterly oblivious to the fact that the most terrible drama in history was about to be enacted. . . .

To my astonishment on reaching the Dept. nobody seemed the least bit excited about the European crisis—Mr. [Secretary of the Navy Josephus] Daniels feeling chiefly very sad that his faith in human nature and civilization and similar idealistic nonsense was receiving such a rude shock. So I started in alone to get things ready and prepare plans for what *ought* to be done by the Navy end of things. Friday I worked all day on these lines, and actually succeeded in getting one ship north from Mexico.

These dear good people like [Secretary of State William Jennings Bryan] and J. D. have as much conception of what a general European war means as Elliott has of higher mathematics. They really believe that because we are neutral we can go about our business as usual. To my horror, *just for example,* J. D. told the newspaper men he thought favorably of sending our fleet to Europe to bring back marooned Americans!

Aside from the fact that tourists (female etc.) couldn't sleep in hammocks and that battleships haven't got passenger accommodations, he totally fails to grasp the fact that this war between the other powers is going inevitably to give rise to a hundred different complications in which we shall have a direct interest. Questions of refugees, of neutrality, of commerce are even now appearing and we should unquestionably gather our fleet together and get it into the highest state of efficiency. We still have 12 battleships at Vera Cruz—their "materiel" has suffered somewhat, their "personnel" a great deal! The rest of the fleet is scattered to the four winds—they should be assembled and prepared. Some fine day the State Department will want the *moral* backing of a "fleet in being" and it *won't be there.*

All this sounds like borrowing trouble I know but it is *my* duty to keep the Navy in a position where no chances, even the most remote, are taken. Today we are taking chances and I nearly boil over when I see the cheery "mañana" way of doing business.

Two hours ago a telegram from Badger came in asking for information about the war and instructions as to neutrality. Nobody had thought it necessary to keep him in touch! And yet he has a German, a French and an English cruiser off Vera Cruz! . . .

There seems no hope now of averting the crash. Germany has invaded France according to this afternoon's report. The best that can be expected is either a sharp, complete and quick victory by one side, a most unlikely occurrence, or a speedy realization of impending bankruptcy by all, and cessation by mutual consent, but this too is I think unlikely as history shows that money in spite of what the bankers say is not an essential to the conduct of a war by a determined nation.

Rather than long drawn-out struggle I hope England will join in and with France and Russia force peace *at Berlin!* . . .

Your devoted

## SPEECH ON PREPAREDNESS

*Flushing, New York. December 21, 1915*
*He made himself a leader of the Preparedness movement.*

. . . My friends, I am very sorry that this is not a Baptist church, because I won't be able to give any particular point in the greetings the Secretary of the Navy told me to convey to you if the meeting were held in a Baptist church. "Tell them," he said, "how fond I am of other churches, the Congregational, Reformed, Methodist, Episcopalian—they are the Army of the Lord, but I love the Baptists because they are the Navy of the Lord."

I want to talk tonight quite informally if you will let me. I am not in any way an orator, as a good many audiences in this State have had occasion to find out. All I hope to do tonight is present a few thoughts which have come to me, gradually perhaps, especially since I have been down in Washington and had a chance to study at first hand the events of the past few years—events that transcend in importance as they effect the destiny of nations and of peoples, any in all history.

I have had the privilege of being somewhat in the vortex of a great problem that has seemed to come home to the American people in the last six months with greater force than at any time since the men in front of me to the left [the Secretary was referring to the Grand Army men] did their part for the preservation of this nation.

We are confronted with a unanimity of public interest on the question of national defense. For that reason it is an excellent thing to have a full and free discussion of the question so the people of this country will make up their minds the right way, just as in the past where there has been a full and free discussion of a question of vital importance affecting the wel-

fare of the nation the people have always made up their mind
the right way.

I don't believe that my friend [the editor of *The Nation,*
Oswald Garrison] Villard has any right to try to gain any advantage over me by speaking on Sunday night. As a matter of
fact, his subject of "Peace" is no more proper for a Sunday
night discussion than is my subject of "Preparedness." Both, I
take it, are good Christian doctrines. We have recently had a
great many quotations by eminent men from the Bible. It is
possible to prove almost anything by taking a literal text from
somewhere in the Bible, if you are satisfied with that kind of
proof. . . .

The point is clear that national jealousies and national ambitions do exist and that a great many nations and peoples are
jealous of us, either of something we have or of some influence
we exert or of some possession in the way of trade outside our
borders, and which they would be glad to take away from us.
. . . The question comes down to this: if you believe there is
any possibility of an attack upon our country, whether upon
our shores or our island possessions or our trade with foreign
lands, then you become at once a believer in adequate national defense.

If we were to take a poll of this country upon the mere
words there would scarcely be a handful of people, I believe,
to oppose adequate national defense. All parties have en-
dorsed it, we all believe in it in a vague sort of way. But what
is adequate national defense? We have heard it defined as
that condition of preparedness which would be capable of repelling an invasion of the Atlantic seaboard or the Pacific seaboard. We have seen in movies and read in books and newspapers and magazines pictures and articles depicting a foreign
fleet outside Sandy Hook knocking over the Woolworth Building and doing a few other choice things like that; and foreign
troops marching up Broadway, and there is a certain element
of possibility in it. Certainly, if an enemy were to land on our
shores at present we would have nothing to oppose him with
practically. Our excellent Army (I am speaking now of our

mobile troops) is just three times the size of New York City's police force, that is about 35,000 men.

But adequate national defense is more than the mere repelling of an invasion of our shores. We have seen many examples of a nation hemmed in for a certain length of time; at first self-supporting and self-sufficient, that is raising sufficient food for its people to live upon, but cut off from external communication they have suffered economic death in the end. It is perfectly clear economically that if you cut off the United States from all trade and intercourse with the rest of the world, you would have economic death in this country before long. Think of what the foreign trade of this country amounts to every year and how it affects every individual more or less in this church; think of the industries dependent upon keeping up that trade; think what would happen if our foreign trade were suddenly cut off for a period of four or five years, and you begin to get an idea of what adequate national defense means. Then there are, of course, our possessions outside the States. Alaska will some day be a place of natural resources of inestimable value to every citizen of this country. Then there is the great humanitarian work almost completed at Panama, done with our money for the benefit of all mankind; and Hawaii and Porto Rico, and our relations with other Americans, with the countries of Central and South America which we have regarded as cherishing the same ideals of liberty as we since they made themselves free. And thinking of these things you come down to what adequate national defense means. . . .

If adequate defense means we want to protect that trade of ours so that in case of attack we can continue to live economically; if it means that we are determined to defend the Panama Canal and Alaska and our ideals and aspirations elsewhere beyond our borders, then we must have a navy which, to employ the simplest terms, will give us control of adjacent seas. . . .

## LETTER TO ELEANOR ROOSEVELT

*Washington. November 9, 1916*

*With Theodore Roosevelt (who Franklin thought should have been a Democrat anyway) out of the Presidential race in 1916, the Assistant Secretary's support of President Wilson became more partisan in spirit. He wrote to his wife while the election result was still in doubt.*

Dearest Babs,

Another day of the most wild uncertainty. . . .
If Wilson is elected I shall wire as follows:
"W. Delano
Barrytown"

The Republican party has proved to its own satisfaction I hope that the American people cannot always be bought.

I hope to God I don't grow reactionary with advancing years.

## MEMORANDUM FOR SECRETARY OF THE NAVY JOSEPHUS DANIELS

*Washington. October 29, 1917*

*United States entry into the War gave new scope to Roosevelt's activism. Besides his regular duties he concerned himself with the highest questions of inter-Allied strategy. He was by no means alone in urging a mine barrage against German submarines, but after this Memorandum was written the plan was adopted. Its enforcement was one of the great feats of the United States Navy.*

SUBJECT: Proposed measures to close English Channel and North Sea against submarines by mine barrage.

1. This is, of course, nothing more nor less than a resurrection of my proposition, which, with all earnestness possible, I

called to the attention of the President, the Secretary of the Navy, the Chief of Operations, the General Board, Admiral Sims (and through him the British Admiralty), Admiral de Chair (and through him also the British Admiralty) and Admiral Chocheprat (and through him the French Ministry of Marine) during the months of May and June past.

2. While I have never claimed that the proposed plan was an infallible one, and while, quite properly, I have never attempted to lay down the exact location or the exact type of mines, etc., to be used in the barrage, I did state, and still state, that every consideration of common sense requires that the attempt be made, first in the English Channel and then in the North Sea.

3. But above all, starting when the Balfour and Viviani Missions were here in May, I reiterated the need for haste. I know how unseemly it is to seem to say "I told you so," but it is a literal fact that, while the British Admiralty may be blamed in part, our own Navy Department is at least largely responsible for failing to consider this proposition seriously during all of these months—May, June, July, August, September and October—which have gone over the dam beyond recall.

4. Now, this is the milk in the cocoanut: The powers that be seem at last willing to take up this proposition seriously. Unless we are willing to throw up our hands and say it is too late, we must admit that the same need for immediate haste exists today as existed last May. We have done altogether too much amiable "consideration" of this matter. If it is to be carried out at all it must be carried out with a different spirit from any of the operations up to now. It will require prompt decision all along the line and an immediate carrying out of the procurement of the material—mines and ships.

5. To accomplish the above it should be placed in the hands of one man on our part and one man on the part of the British. These two men should receive orders from their governments, not as to details, but simply orders to carry out the plan. *And most important of all, these men should have all the authority*

*requisite to do this.* This is a bigger matter than sending destroyers abroad or a division of battleships, or building a bunch of new destroyers—it is vital to the winning of the war. Its success cannot be guaranteed. No military or naval operation can be guaranteed. But if it works it will be the biggest single factor in winning the war. I have seen something during the past four and a half years of how our present Navy Department organization works and it so happens that I am also fairly familiar with the way the British Admiralty works. If the suggested plan is carried out solely under the present organizations its chance of success will, in my judgment, be seriously diminished. You need somebody with imagination and authority to make the try.

6. I know you will not mind my sending a copy of this to the President, as I have discussed it with him several times.

## DIARY

*London. July 30, 1918*

*Many Democratic leaders in New York wanted him to run for governor in 1918, but he wanted to get into uniform and settled for an official inspection trip to United States naval bases in Europe. Often in his life he set about keeping a diary; this trip was the only time he kept the resolution for more than a few days. The crossing on a new destroyer, meetings with Allied leaders, and a trip to the front were to him magnificent adventures.*

*1918, July 30 — London, England.*

A very interesting day yesterday, came in from Cliveden in the morning, dressed and went to Buckingham Palace at 10:30 and had forty minutes all alone with the King. We drove to the "new front" of Buckingham Palace, which has been pasted on since I was here in 1905. I say "pasted" on because from almost any angle you see the other sides of Buckingham Palace, and the new façade is obviously an unsuccessful attempt to hide the earlier style. I was accompanied by Admiral Everett and Captain McCauley and we passed through several corridors lined with paintings of naval actions that I would have given anything to stop and look at; thence up a half flight to a charming little room with some very good Chinese lacquer ornaments, etc. I hope they were presents from the Chinese Imperial Family, and not acquired as a result of the expedition of 1900. I am moved to make this remark by a story I have just heard about the wife of an American official in Peking. A year after the Boxer trouble she gave a formal dinner for one of the Imperial Princes and after dinner in the drawing room asked the Prince how the Chinese all seemed able to tell the difference between really good jade and the commoner varieties. The Prince said that to a Chinaman jade showed the same difference of quality as precious stones would to an American or European. The hostess insisted on pursuing the topic and finally said—"Now, Prince, I wish you would tell me whether that piece of jade on the mantel-piece is really good or not." The Prince's face did not change and though ten feet away from the mantel-piece he replied—"That is a truly excellent piece." The American woman said—"But how can you tell without examining it?", and he answered—"Because I gave it to my Aunt, the Empress, on her last birthday."

A gentleman in a frock coat soon conducted us up another half flight to the King's study. I was then introduced, shook hands and presented Captain McCauley, who also shook hands and then retired with the gentleman-in-waiting. The King has a nice smile and a very open, quick and cordial way of greeting one. He is not as short as I had expected, and I think his face is stronger than photographs make it appear. This is perhaps because his way of speaking is incisive, and later on when he got talking about German atrocities in Belgium his jaws almost snapped. We talked for a while about American war work in general and the Navy in particular. He seemed delighted that I had come over in a destroyer, and said his one regret was that it had been impossible for him to do active naval service during the war. Then the subject switched to the Germans and he told me a lot about the atrocities in Belgium and northern France—many examples which had been proved true but

which were too horrible to be placed even in the French official report or the report of Lord Bryce. Our troops had just
reoccupied Château-Thierry and had found examples of wan-
ton destruction of property by the Germans before they left,
such as the smashing of pictures, breaking of furniture, etc.
The King said he hoped that this at least would persuade the
American people that the stories of outrageous destruction
were true, and I agreed with him that there had been a singular unwillingness in the United States to accept even the official reports of England and France.

I then remarked something about having been to school in
Germany and having seen their preparation for the first stages
of the war machine. The King said he went to school in Germany, too, for a year; then with a twinkle in his eye—"You
know I have a number of relations in Germany, but I can tell
you frankly that in all my life I have never seen a German gentleman."

The King said he had just had a nice letter from Uncle Ted,
thanking him for one he had sent at the time of T. R.'s illness
last spring. We had just received news of Quentin's probable
death, and the King expressed much sympathy.

He was a delightfully easy person to talk to, and we got going so well that part of the time we were both talking at the
same time. I understand that this type of interview is supposed
to last only fifteen minutes, but it was nearly three-quarters of
an hour before the King made a move. I said—"Good-bye"—
and went back to the Chinese room, where I found McCauley
and the gentleman-in-waiting looking at each other hopelessly.

Luncheon was given to Sir Eric Geddes and me by the Anglo-
American Luncheon Club, a big affair at the Savoy and we
both spoke. In my speech I took occasion to give the British
Navy due credit for what they had done in transporting and
escorting American troops to Europe in the greatly increased
numbers of the past few months and I gave, for the first time,
the official figures showing that during the month of June over
60% of our troops came over in British transports and under
British escort. Slightly over 30% were in American transports

and 5% in French and Italian. I much hope these figures will be telegraphed home, but I doubt it as the representatives of the Committee on Public Information over here have done nothing. In the afternoon I went down to the Liberty Hut, a Y.M.C.A. building for our troops and spoke to a great gathering of American soldiers, with a sprinkling of Canadians, Anzacs and our Blue-jackets. Last night one of the famous Gray's Inn dinners, a really historic occasion in honor of the War Ministers. Lord Curzon spoke most wonderfully for an hour. A defense of the War Cabinet, or rather a résumé of what England has done and is doing. Sir Robert Borden responded for Canada, General Smuts for South Africa and to my horror the Italian Ambassador and I were called on without warning at the close to speak for the Allies. Today a luncheon for me at the Embassy, Lloyd George, Mr. Balfour and various Navy people and Mrs. Page, the only woman. She sent her love to Mama. I had a very good time with Lloyd George. Lloyd George is just like his pictures; thick set; not very tall; rather a large head; and rather long hair; but what impressed me more than anything else was his tremendous vitality. There is no question that the great majority of Englishmen are standing solidly behind him on the sole issue of winning the war. The Conservatives who used to despise him as a demagogue; the Liberals who used to fear him as a radical; and most of the Labor people who now look on him as a reactionary, may hate him just as much as ever and be unwilling after the war to trust reconstruction to his hands, but they will stand by him just as long as his administration keeps the winning of the war as its only political aim. Strikes are threatened at the present time at a number of munition plants and shipyards. Mr. Lloyd George and I talked over the labor situation here and at home. He said of course the weakness of the British Government's position has all come from the failure to adopt conscription at the outbreak of the war and I suggested to him that in the same way we should have had vastly more trouble if we had not had the selective draft law as the final lever to insure continuation of work. I ventured to suggest that in my opinion the

British Unions would obtain no sympathy from our Federation of Labor in any action involving a tie-up of war work and that on the contrary a firmer attitude on the part of the British Government would receive hearty applause from the United States. He seemed very greatly pleased and intimated that he had decided on a firmer stand in the future. Tea with Lady Edward; nice reminiscent time; and to end off, a dinner at the House of Commons by Sir Ian Malcolm, Mr. Balfour, Lord Robert Cecil, Dawson of the Times, Lord Londonderry, Sykes, M.P., who drew a picture for me on the dinner card, Sir Auckland Geddes, the First Lord's brother, and Minister of National Service, and two others. A long talk with Mr. Balfour afterwards while we walked up and down the terrace in the dark. What has pleased me more than anything else is the apparent determination of the British Cabinet to go through with the war to a definitely successful end. The past month has I think clearly marked the turning point of the war. June marked the high tide of the German advance, although the Channel Ports may still be considered in danger. The latest German offensive along the Marne and in the Château-Thierry salient has been not only broken up but during the past ten days has developed into what is apparently a definite retirement to the original lines. For the first time people realize that the American troops are to be the deciding factor. Mr. Balfour said that everyone understands that it was the American Second Division with the Brigade of Marines which stopped the rush at Château-Thierry and which opened the definite counter-offensive at Soissons, which has pinched the salient into untenability. We also talked about the Italian Naval situation; he said that he had discussed with the Cabinet the advisability of my going to Italy in a further attempt to get some action and that they had heartily approved. I am to see Geddes in the morning to discuss the matter further. We are off in the morning, all of us, for France and should have a wonderfully interesting time. Calais and Dunkirk on the way, and motor all the way behind the lines. I will not add to this as it is late and I have not finished packing. . . .

## SPEECH ON LEAGUE OF NATIONS

*New York. March 1, 1919*

*After the Armistice he went to Europe again to supervise naval demobilization. He watched the Paris Peace Conference in action and returned on the* George Washington *with President Wilson. He became an ardent advocate of the League of Nations in speeches like this one reported in the New York* Tribune.

". . . President Wilson said to me very recently that unless this League goes through in some form or other it will break the heart of the world. . . .

"The same arguments that have been advanced against this League were advanced against the Constitutional Convention, and that proved to be very satisfactory in the end. Unless the United States comes in, this League will be a new form of European alliance, but if we do come in I take it for granted the League will not demand what the United States does not want." . . .

Earlier in his address, Mr. Roosevelt said that while once a "big navy" advocate, he no longer was one. When the League of Nations was proposed last summer, he was a bit skeptical, thinking it a bit illusory and vague, but he had swung around to the opinion that it was possible and necessary.

Knowing as they do, said Mr. Roosevelt, that the United States is the most disinterested of all nations participating in the Peace Conference, the peoples of Europe look to America trustingly.

Mr. Roosevelt said while some people were playing politics over the League, he was sure that in time Senator Lodge, who, he was certain, was honest in his objections, would come over to the principle of the League, if not to the actual words.

Discussing the objection of internationalism that has been directed against the League, Mr. Roosevelt said it depended on what sort of internationalism was meant. If it is meant, he said, that the League will promote an internationalism that will prevent future wars, as the people of the world are anxious to avoid, then the League was an attempt at internationalism. If, however, the internationalism of the "red flag and the black flag" was meant, he was sure hundreds of thousands of supporters could be found to stamp that sort out. . . .

## SPEECH ACCEPTING THE DEMOCRATIC VICE PRESIDENTIAL NOMINATION

*Hyde Park. August 9, 1920*

*Believing that the mood of the people indicated a conservative reaction in the 1920 elections, he nevertheless identified himself with the Wilsonian-Progressive wing of his Party and won the Vice Presidential nomination. As the running mate of James M. Cox of Ohio he made United States entry into the League of Nations his chief proposal.*

I accept the nomination for the office of Vice-President with humbleness, and with a deep wish to give to our beloved country the best that is in me.—No one could receive a higher privilege or opportunity than to be thus associated with men and ideals which I am confident will soon receive the support of the majority of our citizens.

In fact, I could not conscientiously accept it if I had not come to know by the closest intimacy that he who is our selection for the Presidency, and who is my chief and yours, is a man possessed of ideals which are also mine. He will give to America that kind of leadership which will make us respect him and bring further greatness to our land. In him I recognize one who can lead this nation forward in an unhalting march of progress. Such a man is James M. Cox.

Two great problems will confront the next administration; our relations with the world and the pressing need of organized progress at home. The latter includes a systematized and intensified development of our resources and a progressive betterment of our citizenship. These matters will require the guiding hand of a President who can see his country above his party, and who, having a clear vision of things as they are, has also the independence, courage and skill to guide us along the road to things as they should be without swerving one footstep at the dictation of narrow partisans who whisper "party" or of selfish interests that murmur "profits".

In our world problems, we must either shut our eyes, sell our newly built merchant marine to more far-seeing foreign powers, crush utterly by embargo and harassing legislation our foreign trade, close our ports, build an impregnable wall of costly armaments and live, as the Orient used to live, a hermit nation, dreaming of the past; or, we must open our eyes and see that modern civilization has become so complex and the lives of civilized men so interwoven with the lives of other men in other countries as to make it impossible to be in this world and not of it. We must see that it is impossible to avoid, except by monastic seclusion, those honorable and intimate foreign relations which the fearful-hearted shudderingly miscall by that Devil's catch word "international complications".

As for our home problem, we have been awakened by this war into a startled realization of the archaic shortcomings of our governmental machinery and of the need for the kind of re-organization which only a clear thinking business man, experienced in the technicalities of governmental procedure, can carry out. Such a man we have. One who has so successfully reformed the business management of his own great State is obviously capable of doing greater things. This is not time to experiment with men who believe that their party can do no wrong and that what is good for the selfish interests of a political party is of necessity good for the nation as well. I as a citizen believe that this year we should choose as President a proved executive.—We need to do things; not to talk about them.

Much has been said of late about good Americanism. It is right that it should have been said, and it is right that every chance should be seized to repeat the basic truths underlying our prosperity and our national existence itself.—But it would be an unusual and much to be wished for thing, if, in the coming presentation of the issues a new note of fairness and generosity could be struck. Littleness, meanness, falsehood, extreme partisanship—these are not in accord with the American spirit. I like to think that in this respect also we are moving forward.

Let us be definite. We have passed through a great war,—an armed conflict which called forth every effort on the part of the whole population.—The war was won by Republicans as well as by Democrats. Men of all parties served in our armed forces.—Men and women of all parties served the government at home. They strived honestly as Americans, not as mere partisans. Republicans and Democrats alike worked in administrative positions, raised Liberty loans, administered food control, toiled in munition plants, built ships.—The war was brought to a successful conclusion by a glorious common effort —one which in the years to come will be a national pride. I feel very certain that our children will come to regard our participation as memorable for the broad honor and honesty which marked it, for the absence of unfortunate scandal, and for the splendid unity of action which extended to every portion of the nation. It would, therefore, not only serve little purpose,— but would conform ill to our high standards if any person should in the heat of political rivalry seek to manufacture political advantage out of a nationally conducted struggle. We have seen things on too large a scale to listen in this day to trifles, or to believe in the adequacy of trifling men.

It is that same vision of the bigger outlook of national and individual life which will, I am sure, lead us to demand that the men who represent us in the affairs of our government shall be more than politicians or the errand boys of politicians —that they shall subordinate always the individual ambition and the party advantage to the national good. In the long run the true stateman and the honestly forward looking party will prevail.

Even as the Nation entered the war for an ideal, so it has emerged from the war with the determination that the ideal shall not die. It is idle to pretend that the war declaration of April 6th, 1917, was a mere act of self-defense,—or that the object of our participation was solely to defeat the military power of the Central Nations of Europe. We knew then as a Nation, even as we know today, that success on land and sea could be but half a victory. The other half is not won yet. To the cry of the French at Verdun; "They shall not pass"; the cheer of our own men in the Argonne; "We shall go through"—we must add this; "It shall not occur again". This is the positive declaration of our own wills; that the world shall be saved from a repetition of this crime.

To this end the democratic party offers a treaty of peace, which, to make it a real treaty for a real peace MUST include a League of Nations; because this peace treaty, if our best and bravest are not to have died in vain, must be no thinly disguised armistice devised by cynical statesmen to mask their preparations for a renewal of greed-inspired conquests later on. "Peace" must mean peace that will last. A practical, workable, permanent, enforcible kind of a peace that will hold as tightly as the business contracts of the individual. We must indeed be, above all things, businesslike and practical in this peace treaty making business of ours. The League of Nations is a practical solution of a practical situation. It is no more perfect than our original Constitution, which has been amended 18 times and will soon, we hope, be amended the 19th, was perfect. It is not anti-national, it is anti-war. No super-nation, binding us to the decisions of its tribunals, is suggested, but the method and machinery by which the opinion of civilization may become effective against those who seek war is at last within the reach of humanity. Through it we may with nearly every other duly constituted government in the whole world throw our moral force and our potential power into the scale of peace. That such an object should be contrary to American policy is unthinkable; but if there be any citizen who has HONEST—and I emphasize the word honest—fears that it may be perverted from its plain intent so as to conflict with our established form of government, it will be simple to declare to him and to the other nations that the Constitution of the United States is in every way supreme. There must be no equivocation, no vagueness, no double dealing with the people on this issue. The League will not die. An idea does not die which meets the call of the hearts of our mothers.

So, too, with peace. War may be "declared"; peace cannot. It must be established by mutual consent, by a meeting of the minds of the parties in interest. From the practical point of view alone a peace by resolution of Congress is unworkable. From the point of view of the millions of splendid Americans who served in that whirlwind of war, and of those other millions at home who saw, in our part of the conflict, the splendid hope of days of peace for future generations, a peace by resolution of Congress is an insult and a denial of our national purpose.

Today we are offered a seat at the table of the family of nations to the end that smaller peoples may be truly safe to work out their own destiny, to the end that the sword shall not follow on the heels of the merchant, to the end that the burden of increasing armies and navies shall be lifted from the shoulders of a world already staggering under the weight of taxation. We shall take that place. I say so because I have faith—faith that this nation has no selfish destiny, faith that our people are looking into the years beyond for better things, and that they are not afraid to do their part.

The fundamental outlook on the associations between this Republic and the other Nations can never be very different in character from the principles which one applies to our own purely internal affairs. A man who opposes concrete reforms and improvements in international relations is of necessity a reactionary, or at least a conservative in viewing his home problems. . . .

Some people have been saying of late: "We are tired of progress, we want to go back to where we were before; to go about our own business; to restore 'normal' conditions of 'normalcy.'" They are wrong. This is not the wish of America! We can never go back. The "good old days" are gone past forever; we have no regrets. For our eyes are trained ahead—forward to better new days. In this faith I am strengthened by the firm belief that women of this nation, now about to receive the

National franchise, will throw their weight into the scale of progress and will be unbound by partisan prejudices and a too narrow outlook on national problems. We cannot anchor our ship of state in this world tempest, nor can we return to the placid harbor of long years ago. We must go forward or founder.

America's opportunity is at hand. We can lead the world by a great example, we can prove this nation a living, growing thing, with policies that are adequate to new conditions. In a thousand ways this is our hour of test. The Democratic program offers a larger life for our country, a richer destiny for our people. It is a plan of hope. In this, chiefly let it be our aim to build up, not to tear down. Our opposition is to the things which once existed, in order that they may never return. We oppose money in politics, we oppose the private control of national finances, we oppose the treating of human beings as commodities, we oppose the saloon-bossed city, we oppose starvation wages, we oppose rule by groups or cliques. In the same way we oppose a mere period of coma in our national life. . . .

It is the faith which is in me that makes me very certain that America will choose the path of progress and set aside the doctrines of despair, the whispering of cowardice, the narrow road to yesterday. May the Guiding Spirit of our land keep our feet on the broad road that leads to a better tomorrow and give to us strength to carry on.

## CAMPAIGN SPEECH

*San Francisco. August 23, 1920*

*Roosevelt made an exceptionally vigorous campaign. Starting early, he reached the West Coast on a "whistle stop" tour.*

My friends: . . . So far, it has been somewhat difficult for us to find out exactly what the foreign policy of our opponents is going to be. I remember just before I left New York the situation in the Republican ranks. Just after Senator

Harding's speech of acceptance, in fact the very next morning, the two great New York Republican dailies, the *Sun* and the *Tribune*, came out editorially commenting on Senator Harding's speech. They had been looking, of course, for what they considered the principal point they were to make clear, the Republican foreign policy. The *Tribune* came out with an editorial, half hearted editorial, but still it said, "We are glad to know where Senator Harding stands. We were a little bit mystified by the Republican platform; it seems to have cut both ways. It could be interpreted in several different ways, but at last we believe Senator Harding has made it clear. We believe he has come out definitely in favor of the United States going into the League of Nations with the Lodge amendments." The same morning the *Sun* came out with a glittering editorial: "We know now just what the Republican foreign policy is going to be. We know, at last, that Senator Harding and the Republican party will never go into the League of Nations under any condition."

It has been a little bit difficult to answer that kind of campaigning. We do see though, as the days go by, that Senator Harding, a very old friend of mine and a very nice gentleman, is squarely on top of the fence with his legs curled under him. But we know also that he has not a definite foreign policy; that he has no workable theory for bringing to an end the war which we entered on April 6, 1917. He has given us some very difficult and glittering phrases about some day having this country with the other nations of the world establish some kind of an association of nations which will, at least, tend to prevent future wars. That is as far as he goes. That must make it perfectly clear to any thinking person; must mean opposition to the definite plan, the definite remedy of the definite situation. It must mean opposition to the perfectly definite stand taken by the Democratic platform and by the Democratic candidates that if we are elected we will go into the League of Nations. . . .

In the old days of civilization in small towns and communities there were people who when they saw their neighbor's house on fire sat still on their own front porch and did not help. But after a while that type of man and woman discovered something; discovered that the fire in their neighbor's house was apt to spread to their own houses. The result was that communities of that kind pretty soon organized fire departments. Today nations of the world have what might be called a fire department, and they are all contributing to its upkeep. But the trouble is that the fire department of the nations of the world just now lacks a chief. It has apparatus; it has a pole for the firemen to slide down, and it has uniforms, but it has not any chief. And what the League of Nations needs today is a chief—a man who knows how to fight fire—a man who knows how to keep fire from spreading —and that man is the United States. . . .

## CAMPAIGN SPEECH

*Manchester, New Hampshire. September 13, 1920*

*His arguments against the ideas of his rival for the Vice Presidency, Calvin Coolidge of Massachusetts, were prophetic of their different ways of conducting themselves as Presidents of the United States.*

My friend, Governor Coolidge, made an excellent address here in Manchester last Saturday night on the subject of autocracy in Government. Any American who is not an anarchist can agree with his patriotic sentiments in favor of a continuation of our Government with its three-fold branches, the Executive, Legislative and Judicial.

But it is on statements of historical fact and the conclusions therefrom that my thought must differ from his. His whole argument is based on the assumption that the great accomplishments of our history are due to the preponderating wisdom and power of the Congress of the United States, and that the leadership of the Nation should during the next four years devolve on the leaders of the Legislative Branch. This is in line with the theory of Senator Harding that the Presidency itself should be a kind of Chief Clerkship to carry out the policies announced by a syndicate or coterie of old line party leaders. We are told that war powers still vest in the Executive, and that extravagance, not specified, results. We are told that the present Republican Congress has saved the day.

There is so little that is constructive in the Republican campaign that one wonders how long the people are going to be satisfied with criticizing words. Here is their campaign in a nutshell:

1. Charging that President Wilson is an autocrat.
2. Charging waste by his Administration.
3. Offering to have the Government run by a Republican House and Senate through a subservient Administration.
4. Trying to take out an exclusive patent on the American flag and on all the great accomplishments of our history in favor of the Republican Party.

As I recall history, most of our great deeds have been brought about by Executive Leaders, by the Presidents who were not tools of Congress but were true leaders of the Nation, who so truly interpreted the needs and wishes of the people that they were supported in their great tasks. Washington would not have led us to victory in the Revolution if he had merely followed the actions or lack of action of the Continental Congress. Lincoln would not have issued the Emancipation Proclamation if he had heeded the leaders of the Senate. Cleveland would not have maintained the Monroe Doctrine in the Venezuela affair if he had first asked the advice of mere party leaders. Roosevelt would not have kept the Government out of the clutches of predatory interests if he had bowed to Mark Hanna and Foraker and Boss Platt. Wilson's Administration would not have been successful in the War if he had not adopted the policy of calling in the experts of the Nation, without regard to party affiliations, in order to create and send across the seas that great Army in record-breaking time. . . .

## CAMPAIGN SPEECH

*Grand Rapids, Michigan. Ocotber 18, 1920*

*Fighting hard to the end of a hopeless campaign, Roosevelt made serious accusations against the Republican candidate for the Presidency.*

. . . It is hardly conceivable how the more progressive element among the Republican Party Leaders can continue their support of Senator Harding. Were he even a standpatter—a conservative of conservatives, it seems to me it would be easier for them to follow him. His apparent inability to say what he means, or to mean what he says, should make him absolutely hopeless as a standard bearer from a progressive point of view. Day after Day his indecision and vacillation become more apparent. Since the time he first yielded openly to Borah's threats and came out flatly against the League of Nations, the Senator's troubles have been increasing daily and his task of keeping the pro and anti-leaguers of his own party in line has become a desperate problem—in fact so desperate has it become that there are signs that near panic reigns in the Republican camp. Desertions from the Republican ranks by independent thinking voters, disgusted with the straddling policy of their standard-bearer, has brought a forceful realization to the Republican Leaders of the tremendous spread of sentiment from Coast to Coast for Cox and the League. So marked is this turn in the tide as reports come in from all parts of the country, the leaders in desperation have taken a new tack and are making a frantic appeal to the hundreds of thousands of pro-leaguers in their ranks to stand firm for Harding. This is illustrated by the statement a couple of days ago of thirty-one prominent Republicans in reiterating their intention to support Harding. On record as being unalterably opposed to the League of Nations, Senator Harding last night, evidently under pressure from another source, tried to hedge a little on his "irreconcilable" stand, but so deeply has he committed himself to an open support of Borah and his "scrap the League" plan that it is impossible for him to again fool his followers by meaningless phrases that can be interpreted any way the reader desires. . . .

Were we willing even for a moment to sidetrack the great issue of the campaign now so clean cut there can be no more question about it, whether the United States shall enter the existing League of Nations or not, it seems that the paramount question that the American voting public then would have to decide would be—Is Senator Harding fitted for the Presidency of the United States? Is a man who reverses his position on the most vital issue before the American public twelve times in as many days the type of man the American public wants as its Chief Executive? Is a man who after eight years in the United States Senate and two years a member of the Foreign Affairs Committee admits that he has no definite constructive foreign programme, though he aspires to the highest office in the land, fitted to be the people's choice? Is a man who has proven before election vacillating and weak enough to yield to the importunities of the last influence brought to bear upon him, fitted to be chosen to guide the destinies of a hundred million people? . . .

# Poliomyelitis
# Governor of New York
# First Presidential Campaign

## SEPTEMBER, 1921 — MARCH 4, 1933

# LETTER TO WALTER CAMP

*New York. September 28, 1921*

*In August, 1921, at the family summer home on Campobello Island, New Brunswick, Roosevelt was struck by poliomyelitis. Mental depression is a great hazard of this disease, and Roosevelt was very fond of outdoor sports as well as ambitious for a career that had scarcely begun. But his buoyancy and will power seemed to gain from the desperate struggle. Before anyone could be certain, he assured well-wishers like the famous Yale football coach, Walter Camp, that he would recover.*

Dear Mr. Camp:

Thank you for your nice little note.

There were days in the old "Flying Squadron" when I felt that "double-quicking" around Potomac Park came very near [the] classification of hard work, but I can assure you that if I could get up this afternoon and join with Messrs. McAdoo, Davis and Delano in a sprint for the record, I would consider it the greatest joy in the world.

However, the doctors are most encouraging and I have been given every reason to expect that my somewhat rebellious legs will permit me to join in another course of training sometime in the future.

Very sincerely yours,

# LETTER TO ELEANOR ROOSEVELT

*Warm Springs, Georgia. October, 1924*

*His mother insisted that he should retire to Hyde Park as a permanent invalid. With his wife's support, Roosevelt refused. His return to public life began in the summer of 1924 when he achieved a personal triumph at the Democratic National Convention by delivering the nominating speech for his friend, Governor Alfred E. Smith of New York, whom he called "the 'Happy Warrior' of the political battlefield." Then in October he found an encouraging new method of therapy.*

42

Dearest E,

It is just a week since you left, but the time has passed almost without our realizing it, as the life is just the same day after day and there is no variety to give landmarks. The mornings are as you know wholly taken up with the pool and four of the afternoons we have sat out on the lawn or as Roy calls it the "yard," and I have worked at stamps or cheques or accounts or have played rummy. . . .

The legs are really improving a great deal. The walking and general exercising in the water is fine and I have worked out some special exercises also. This is really a discovery of a place and there is no doubt that I've got to do it some more.

Various people came over Sunday. The Harts to stay with the Hudsons a block away, and today the pool was very gay, at least twenty people.

Thank Louis for the papers and tell him I hear nothing of interest.

I have a hunch that [Democratic Presidential nominee John W.] Davis' strength is really improving, but I still think the election will go into the house. Anyway, I am philosophic enough to think that even if Coolidge is elected we shall be so darned sick of conservatism of the old money-controlled crowd in four years that we [will] get a real progressive landslide in 1928.

Much love, take care of yourself.

Your devoted

## "IS THERE A JEFFERSON ON THE HORIZON?"

New York Evening World. *December 3, 1925*

*He had plenty of time now to read and to think. This review of Claude G. Bowers' Jefferson and Hamilton in the leading liberal newspaper of the period revealed a deepening understanding of political history and a hope for the future which he himself would try to fulfill.*

I felt like saying "At last" as I read Mr. Claude G. Bowers' thrilling "Jefferson and Hamilton." Perhaps this feeling is influenced by my personal experiences, but, in the broader sense, I am convinced that it would be a supreme contribution to current thought if the simple historic facts of this book could be learned in the newspaper editorial rooms as well as in the homes and schools of America.

Let me explain the personal side of it. A year ago I took occasion in a letter addressed to more than a thousand Democratic leaders throughout the country to refer in passing to the difference between the Jeffersonian and Hamiltonian ideals for an American method of government, and to apply their fundamental differences to present-day policies of our two great parties. Immediately many editors, including even some of the metropolitan press, launched sneers at the mere suggestion that Jeffersonianism could, in any remote manner, bear upon the America of 1925. A materialistic press reflects a materialistic age, but I still boil inwardly when I think of these smug writers who, wish being father to the thought, deny that the forces hostile to control of government by the people which existed in the crisis of 1790-1800 could still be a threat in our day and land.

The other personal reason is that for some years I have been, frankly, fed up with the romantic cult which has, since the publication of an historical novel, surrounded the name of Alexander Hamilton; and I have longed to write this very book, which now so much more ably comes from the delightful pen and untiring research of Mr. Bowers.

What is more valuable, however, is that in this study of a period which was, in every way, as important to the preservation of the Union as was the Civil War itself, a spirit of fairness and calm judgment is shown which makes the book not merely convincing to the general reader but of permanent value to the advanced student.

For Hamilton emerges still a romantic and fascinating figure, albeit in his true character of aristocrat and convinced opponent of popular government. And in Jefferson we see not only the savior of the deeper ideals of the Revolution, but also the man with human failings, the consummate politician.

The history of the United States may be interesting to some for the mere fact of events or personalities, but it is of value to us as a whole because of the application we make of these facts to present problems. It is in this spirit in which the book must be read: if we obtain from its pages only the knowledge of the definite establishment of a democratic republic because of the leadership of Jefferson and his associates, we fail unless we in addition apply the basic ideals of those days to the later events in American history and to the often essentially similar problems that still lie unsolved before us.

In fact what is the chief revelation is not the day by day contest of the first ten years of the constitutional United States, but the constantly recurring thought of parallel or at least analogous situations existing in our own generation.

Mr. Bowers' book enters into the midst of the organization of the Government in 1789 after the ratification of the Constitution and the election of President Washington. . . .

There were no political parties, yet the line of demarcation was drawn before ever Washington was inaugurated. It is the little things which germinate. The World War had its murder of Sarajevo; the birth of American party battles had rise in the problem of the titles by which the President, the Cabinet and the Congress should be addressed. Next the social climbers, the snobbery, the appointment of Hamilton and Jefferson to the Cabinet, the rise of Hamilton to a position of supremacy and with it the control of the infant Government by the moneyed class. All still in the stage of experiment, and who, even to-day, can say that immediate success did not lie in the establishment of the Republic's finances and commercial credit? Alexander Hamilton we honor because of his master stroke for sound money, his genius for finance. Yet we must take into account the scandal of the day, the unconscionable profiteering of his followers—even some in Congress—in that same moneyed class who made veritable fortunes from the stupidity or the need or the lack of inside information on the part of the thousands of veterans, tradesmen, farmers or frontier settlers away from the larger seaport towns.

Slowly the lines were being formed. Within the Cabinet itself Jefferson, a veritable Westerner of his day, mistrusting the fondness of Hamilton for his Chambers of Commerce and his contempt for the opinion of the masses; Hamilton, confident of his power, confident of the power of his leaders among merchants and aristocrats, wholly lacking in understanding or in fear of the rights of what he thought of as the rabble—the poor, the uneducated, the average human being who, even then, made up the mass of his countrymen.

The scene changes to Philadelphia, the next temporary capital. More display, greater snobbery, an increased assurance on the part of the men and women of wealth, of family, of commercial prestige; and, most important, a growth of the pro-British sentiment on the part of these, and an abhorrence for the successes and excesses of the onrushing French Revolution.

It is natural that in this environment the demarcation into parties grew apace. Jefferson, eclipsed in the Cabinet by Hamilton, the natural democrat against the natural aristocrat, began then the mobilization of the masses against the autocracy of the few. It was a colossal task. With Hamilton were the organized compact forces of wealth, of birth, of commerce, of the press. With him at heart was Washington, the President. Jefferson could count only on the scattered raw material of the working masses, difficult to reach, more difficult to organize.

So began a warfare by press and pamphlet, skillfully forced by Jefferson and Madison and Freneau; bitterly answered by Hamilton and Ames and Fenno. A drawn battle of wits, perhaps, but every new reader a step toward the goal of Jefferson. A true public opinion was being made possible. . . .

So the ten years' drama drew to its curtain. Through all the mud-slinging, the abuse of power, the deliberate misrepresentation, Jefferson remained the calm philosopher. When troops were asked, it was Jefferson's followers who were the readiest to fall in on country's call. When grave questions of domestic policy arose, it was reserved for certain Federalists of New England to be the first to talk of the dissolution of the Union. Jefferson's faith in mankind was vindicated; his appeal to the intelligence of the average voter bore fruit; his conception of a democratic republic came true. . . .

I have a breathless feeling as I lay down this book—a picture of escape after escape which this Nation passed through in those first ten years; a picture of what might have been if the Republic had been finally organized as Alexander Hamilton sought. But I have a breathless feeling, too, as I wonder if, a century and a quarter later, the same contending forces are not again mobilizing. Hamiltons we have to-day. Is a Jefferson on the horizon?

## LETTER TO DEAN GREENOUGH OF HARVARD UNIVERSITY

*Marion, Massachusetts. August 15, 1926*

*Among the pleasures and perplexities of fatherhood, Roosevelt found particularly disturbing the fear that wealth might spoil his children. His son James persuaded him not to send this letter.*

My dear Dean Greenough:

This is a more or less personal note in reply to yours of August 11th regarding my oldest boy James who is about to enter the Freshman Class.

He goes to Harvard with the usual advantages and handicaps of having spent six years at Groton. He did very well there in athletics and leadership, rather poorly in studies— lower half of the form—but passed all his College Board Examinations, two with honors.

He is clean, truthful, considerate of others, and has distinct ambition to make good. He has at the same time, I think, too much of a love of "social good times" (like the rest of his crowd), and for that reason, although a former Overseer, etc., I hesitated for some time before letting him go to Cambridge at all. In other words, I know enough of the club and Boston life of the average private school freshman to fear the lack of individuality and the narrowness which comes to so many of them.

One of the principal troubles with most of these private school undergraduates of yours is, I am convinced after a good deal of investigation, that their parents give them a great deal too much money to go through college on. To this is added in most cases, automobiles, and all sorts of expensive toys in the holidays.

You people in authority have done and are doing a great work in aiming at greater simplicity of college life, and incidentally your fine efforts for higher scholarship, i.e., more work, is bearing good fruit.

I, as one graduate among many, want to cooperate with you in this. During this past summer my boy has worked as a laborer in a Canadian pulp and paper mill. Most of the Groton boys will have college allowances well over $2,000 a year. James and his room mate Harrison Parker, Jr. will have only $1500 or $1600.

I should like them in addition to find some sort of employment while at college so that they could earn part of their education, even if it covered only the $300 tuition. In my own days such a thing was rare and difficult. Waiting on table at Memorial was about the only method, and the college office made very little effort to encourage boys to find jobs. I hope this phase is better handled now.

Concretely in regard to my boy I feel that the following should be the objectives:
1. Better scholarship than passing marks. 2. Athletics to be a secondary not a primary objective. 3. Activity in student activities such as debating, Crimson, etc. to be encouraged. 4. Acquaintance with the average of the class, not just the Mt. Auburn Street crowd to be emphasized. 5. Opportunity to earn part of his education.

I hope to get up to Cambridge this autumn and to have a chance to see you.

Very sincerely yours,

## LETTER TO ANNA ROOSEVELT COWLES

*New York. June 29, 1927*

*Warm Springs by a standard Rooseveltian mutation became a cause as well as a cure.*

Dearest Auntie Bye:

. . . I am sending you some of our folders about Warm Springs. The work of starting a combined resort and therapeutic center has been most fascinating for it is something which, so far as I know, has never been done in this country before.

We have already 30 patients there this summer and our total capacity for this coming year will be only 50, a figure I think we shall reach in a few weeks.

Most of the patients are suffering from infantile paralysis though we have two arthritis cases at the present time and expect several others, and also hope to have a good many people come there next winter for a few weeks of after-cure succeeding operations or serious illness. It ought to be a success as the doctors are most enthusiastic and, at the same time, the climate is a delightful one all the year round. The elevation of 1000 feet makes it cool enough even in summer and it is far enough south to make it dry and bracing, and yet warm enough during the winter.

Aside from the therapeutic value, we have so many natural resources for the families or patients that the swimming, golf, riding and quail shooting ought to appeal to those in perfect health. The whole property I have put under the Georgia Warm Springs Foundation and am now busily engaged in trying to raise two or three hundred thousand dollars to carry out the improvements and pay the mortgage on the property.

Oh, I do wish that you could be wafted down there and placed gently in a chair and slid gracefully down a ramp into the water. You would love the informality and truly languid southern atmosphere of the place! My one fear is that this gentle charm will appeal to some of our rich friends who are suffering from nervous prosperity and that they will come down there and ruin our atmosphere. Cousin Susy Parish talks of a visit there, but I am not certain that she could endure our southern cooking.

Do send me some nice souls this coming winter, but not the kind who would insist on full dress for dinner every evening.

Always affectionately yours,

## *"OUR FOREIGN POLICY: A DEMOCRATIC VIEW."*

Foreign Affairs Quarterly. *July, 1928*

*Working for Al Smith's nomination in 1928, in consultation with Sumner Welles and others, he wrote an article to strengthen his friend's and his Party's position on foreign relations. It amounted to a preview of his own Good Neighbor Policy.*

In our century and a half of national life there have been outstanding periods when American leadership has influenced the thought and action of the civilized world towards international good will and peace; and there have been moments —rare ones, fortunately—when American policy either has been negative and sterile, or has earned for us dislike or fear or ridicule.

I believe many millions of citizens in the United States share my conviction that the past nine years must be counted on the debit side of the ledger.

Since the summer of 1919 our country has had to face the charge that in a time when great constructive aid was needed in the task of solving the grave problems facing the whole earth, we have contributed little or nothing save the isolated Naval Conference of 1921. Even here the ground gained was not held. The definite sacrifices we made were not productive because we assumed that a mere signature was enough; no machinery was set up to finish the work. This is a negative charge. On the positive side, we must admit also that the outside world almost unanimously views us with less good will today than at any previous period. This is serious unless we take the deliberate position that the people of the United States owe nothing to the rest of mankind and care nothing for the opinion of others so long as our seacoasts are impregnable and our pocketbooks are filled. . . .

The present position of the United States in world affairs dates from 1919, for during the last two years of the Wilson Administration a bitterly hostile opposition in the Senate prevented any constructive action, and further, this nation, free as Europe was not from post-war penury, turned to internal industrial development and did its best to forget international subjects.

When, therefore, the Harding Administration was organized in 1921 it interpreted the temper of the nation as being weary of international leadership and uninterested in further efforts to follow the vision of a new era which it had so enthusiastically welcomed three years before. The new President was in no sense a leader; the Presidency he thought of as essentially a routine political job. So vague were his ideas that his campaign and his years in office gave constant evidence, particularly in the field of international relations, that citizens of diametrically opposite opinions could join in his support and praise. He was given at least lip-service by League of Nations supporters, by the bitterest League opponents, and by those who talked of the creation of some entirely new association of nations. It will always be a regret to fair-minded Americans that, except in one instance, the Secretary of State, Charles Evans Hughes, allowed his great ability and high ideals to be wholly smothered by the caution and smallness of the President's mind and the provinciality and ignorance of most of his professional political advisers.

That exception was the Washington Conference for limitation of naval armaments. . . .

What has happened to other efforts to establish and maintain the principles of peace? The United States has taken two negative steps. It has declined to have anything to do with either the League of Nations or the World Court. It is beside the point at this time to agitate the question of our membership in the League. There is no doubt that a majority of American voters has been opposed to membership on the conditions under which the other nations have joined. We see other great nations making use of the League without loss of national sovereignty, but we are opposed to any official participation in purely European affairs or to committing ourselves to act in unknown contingencies.

Nevertheless we see more and more the great effectiveness of the League in many matters which do concern us,—international health work, improvement of labor conditions, aid to backward peoples, the improving of education, the clarification of international law, assistance to world trade. Best of all, it offers a common round table where threats against the peace of the world can be discussed and divergent views compromised. Even without full membership we Americans can be generous and sporting enough to give to the League a far larger share of sympathetic approval and definite official help than we have hitherto accorded.

More and more people here are coming to see that the League has taken a leaf from the note-book of modern industry. A generation ago capital and labor were at each other's throats. Strike or lock-out was the remedy. Today each side realizes that at least there is another side. Today, friendly conference has in large measure superseded riot. Sitting around a table works better than issuing hostile statements. Why does not this rather obvious fact of human nature, first applied successfully to relations between individuals and then to relations between aggregations called companies or unions, apply with equal truth to larger organizations called nations? . . .

Last of all, and in many ways most important of all, is the subject of the Americas. The Wilson Administration started splendidly by eliminating "Dollar Diplomacy," and by the Mobile speech to which I have already referred. It helped the cause of better feeling on the part of the Central and South American nations by its ready acceptance of the offer of Argentine, Brazil and Chili to be of friendly assistance in Mexico. But intervention as we practiced it in Santo Domingo and Haiti was not another forward step. It is not that assistance of some sort was not necessary; it was the method which was wrong. I had a slight part in these actions. As they are excellent illustrations of circumstances which may recur it is worth while to summarize them.

In the case of Santo Domingo we had had for several years by treaty an American Customs Receiver in that Republic, principally to insure the payment of the external debt. Serious political disturbances endangered economic life and threatened anarchy, and when a revolution left the country without a president, a cabinet or a legislature, or even any form of government, American marines and sailors were landed. They remained until last year. Peace was insured, good roads, railroads, sanitation, honest taxes and honest expenditures were introduced, and the government was handed back to the citizens of Santo Domingo after a stewardship of about twelve years. We accomplished an excellent piece of constructive work, and the world ought to thank us.

In Haiti a worse situation faced us. That Republic was in chronic trouble, and as it is close to Cuba the bad influence was felt across the water. Presidents were murdered, governments fled, several times a year. We landed our marines and sailors only when the unfortunate Chief Magistrate of the moment was dragged out of the French Legation, cut into six pieces and thrown to the mob. Here again we cleaned house, restored order, built public works and put governmental operation on a sound and honest basis. We are still there. It is true, however, that in Santo Domingo and especially in Haiti we seem to have paid too little attention to making the citizens of these states more capable of reassuming the control of their own governments. But we have done a fine piece of material work, and the world ought to thank us.

But does it? In these cases the world is really the Latin American world, for Europe cares little about what goes on in Santo Domingo or Haiti or Nicaragua. The other republics of the Americas do not thank us, on the contrary they disapprove our intervention almost unanimously. By what right, they say, other than the right of main force, does the United States arrogate unto itself the privilege of intervening alone in the internal affairs of another Sovereign Republic?

The net result of these instances, and recently of the far less justified intervention in Nicaragua, is that never before in our history have we had fewer friends in the Western Hemisphere than we have today. We are certainly far from popular in Canada; we are slightly better off than last year in Mexico, thanks to the individual efforts of Mr. Morrow and Col. Lindbergh; and in the sixteen Republics of Central and South America the United States Government by its recent policies has allowed a dislike and mistrust of long standing to grow into something like positive hate and fear.

The time has come when we must accept not only certain facts but many new principles of a higher law, a newer and better standard in international relations. We are exceedingly jealous of our own sovereignty and it is only right that we should respect a similar feeling among other nations. The peoples of the other Republics of this Western world are just as patriotic, just as proud of their sovereignty. Many of these nations are large, wealthy and highly civilized. The peace, the security, the integrity, the independence of every one of the American Republics is of interest to all the others, not to the United States alone.

It is possible that in the days to come one of our sister nations may fall upon evil days; disorder and bad government may require that a helping hand be given her citizens as a matter of temporary necessity to bring back order and stability. In that event it is not the right or the duty of the United States to intervene alone. It is rather the duty of the United States to associate with itself other American Republics, to give intelligent joint study to the problem, and, if the conditions warrant, to offer the helping hand or hands in the name of the Americas. Single-handed intervention by us in the internal affairs of other nations must end; with the coöperation of others we shall have more order in this hemisphere and less dislike. . . .

## CAMPAIGN SPEECH

*Buffalo. October 20, 1928*

*He nominated Al Smith again in 1928 and this time the Happy Warrior carried the Convention. Then Smith and many others insisted that Roosevelt run for Governor of New York to assure a Democatic sweep of the state for the national ticket. Although he wanted more time to strengthen his legs at Warm Springs, Roosevelt consented. He won, while Smith lost New York and the Presidency. Roosevelt scribbled on the back of the last page of this campaign speech one of his many appeals against the religious intolerance that helped to defeat Smith.*

In a pigeon hole in the desk of the Republican leaders of New York State is a large envelope, soiled, worn and bearing a date that goes back twenty-five years. Printed in large letters on this envelope are the words "Promises to Labor". Inside the envelope are a series of sheets dated two years apart and representing the best thought of the best minds of the Republican leaders over the succession of years. Each sheet of promises is practically a duplicate of every other sheet. Nowhere in that envelope is there a single page bearing the title "Promises Kept".

I ought to know something about it personally, because I had the good fortune to be a member of the State Senate in that famous year of 1911 when the Democratic Party, coming into control of the State government for the first time in a generation, started on its way a program, not of promises but of accomplishments.

The set-up in 1911 was exactly the same as it is in 1928. The Democratic administration and the Democratic leaders in the legislature began at that time a series of practical measures in the interest of the men and women of this State who work with their hands. That session of the legislature was the "Godfather" of the Workmen's Compensation Law, of the first law limiting the hours of women in industry, of the Factory Investigation Committee, and of a series of important measures strengthening the provisions of the existing labor law and building up the effective strength of the Labor Department.

It is worthwile to go back as far as 1911 because we get at that time a definite picture of the attitude of the leaders of the two parties—an attitude which has continued down to the present day.

I remember well that the position of the Democratic Party was at that time severely criticized by the reactionary element in this State as being socialistic and radical, and if the term Bolshevist had been then in existence it would undoubtedly have been applied to Assemblyman Alfred E. Smith, Senator Robert Wagner and many others, including myself, because of our ardent support for the whole program.

Arrayed against us was the silent, powerful pressure of the old school of thought, which held to the theory that when an employer hired working men or working women, that employer became the master of the fate of his employees; that when a worker entered the factory doors it was nobody's business as to how he worked, how long he was worked or how much he was paid.

It is most difficult seventeen years later for this generation to understand the attitude of the old conservative element towards employment back in 1911, but it is a fact that this attitude was subscribed to sometimes silently sometimes openly but always definitely by the Republican leaders of this State at that time.

During the years 1911 to 1915, the splendid record of definite accomplishment made by the Democratic Party in this State was fought and blocked and criticized at every turn by the Republican legislative leaders.

The best example of the difference in attitude between the two parties is the fact that during the four years of Governor Whitman, constructive labor legislation in the State of New York came to an end. The progress was not resumed until Govenor Smith went back to Albany as the Chief Executive in 1919.

In this year of 1928 it would have been possible to forecast last May with absolute exactitude what the Republican leaders and the Republican candidate would say during this autumn's compaign. First of all, they would trot out the old envelope, dust it off and copy into their platform the same old words which had been used every two years for a generation back. Let me read you the labor plank of the Republican Party:

"The Republican Party in this State has done more for labor than any other party. The Labor Law and the Workmen's Compensation Law, conceded by labor to be the best in all the states, almost every line has been written in these laws by or with the approval of our party."

How dare they say that?

How do grown up and ostensibly sane political leaders perjure themselves that way? For a statement of that kind is so openly and flagrantly dishonorable that it comes pretty close to the border line of perjury. These same leaders know perfectly well that the Republican Party has consistently fought against almost every progressive measure in the interests of labor that the State of New York has added to its statute books during the past seventeen years. . . .

Let us take the practical example of the principle of limiting the hours of work of women and children in industry.

Back in that session of 1911 the Democratic leaders brought forward what was then regarded as the "radical" "socialistic" proposal limiting the hours to fifty-four a week. The record shows that the opposition came from the Republican leaders, but after a long fight the proposal became law.

When Alfred E. Smith went back to Albany as Govenor in 1919 progressive thought had advanced to the point of demanding a further limitation for the women and children to a maximum of forty-eight hours a week. Through six years the demand for action increased and in 1924 the Republican State platform for the first time came out definitely in favor of a forty-eight hour week. It is almost needless to say that the Democratic platform again and yet again supported that demand.

It seemed, therefore, that the workers were definitely assured by both parties of the passage of the proposed law. Definite assurance was given to the voters of this State by Theodore Roosevelt, Jr., and the Republican leaders that they would carry out that pledge. What happened? The Republican legislature of 1925 failed utterly to carry out this plan, in spite of the demand for it by every Democratic member and by the Govenor of the State. As a deliberate subterfuge, the Republican legislature passed the Joiner Bill, which was unanimously opposed by Labor and was characterized by the Governor as a "fraud upon the people of the State." Another promise gone bad! . . .

I want to add only one additional fact about myself. For seven and one-half years, as the Assistant-Secretary of the Navy, I had full charge of all matters relating to the subject of labor in the navy yards of the United States. The Navy was the direct employer of more than twenty thousand civilians during the peace period, and of more than one hundred thousand civilians during the war period. Up to 1913 the relations between the Government and its civilian employees had been precarious and filled with constant disputes. I shall always be very proud of the fact that from 1913 to the time I left the Navy Department in 1920, the United States Navy never had a single strike or a single serious dispute with the civilians in the Navy Yards, and the whole system of Navy Yard civilian employment was brought up to a far higher standard than ever before. . . .

If I am elected Govenor, it will of course be difficult to carry out the present splendid program of the Democratic Party, unless at the same time our party is in control of the Senate and of the Assembly. At least you can feel confident that I would use every effort to obtain legislation from a hostile legislature. . . .

And now one final word—the last time I expect to speak it in this campaign. Some misguided people in every section of the land have been violating by written or spoken word the Sixth Amendment to the Constitution of the United States, that great charter which forbids any religious test for the holding of public office. I hope and believe that as election day approaches this question will be left out of the decision of the electorate. Just as I have begged up and down the land that no vote be given to Hoover because his opponent is a member of another church of God, so I plead that no vote be given to me because my opponent is a member of a different church of God.

## LETTER TO HERBERT C. PELL

*Albany. January 28, 1929*

*Shortly after his inauguration, Governor Roosevelt wrote to a friend a succinct appraisal of the country's economic and political future.*

My dear Bertie:

Thanks for your mighty nice letter of January fourth. I am sending you herewith my inaugural speech, and first message to the Legislature.

You are right that the business community is not much interested in good government and it wants the present Republican control to continue just so long as the stock market soars and the new combinations of capital are left undisturbed. The trouble before Republican leaders is that prevailing conditions are bound to come to an end some time. When that time comes, I want to see the Democratic party sanely radical enough to have most of the disgruntled ones turn to it to put us in power again.

I will send you a copy of a special message on water power within a few weeks.

Sincerely yours,

## LETTER TO ROBERT F. WAGNER

*Hyde Park. September 9, 1930*

*Facing the campaign for re-election as Governor, Roosevelt sent United States Senator Wagner a summary of his achievements during his first term. On the same day he publicly announced that he favored repeal of the Prohibition Amendment.*

Dear Bob:

I want to tell you how very happy I am that you are slated to be the temporary chairman of the Democratic State Convention, and further to tell you of some of the matters which I think should be stressed at the Convention.

On the matter of the serious unemployment situation, I regret to say that my trips to practically every part of the state this summer confirm the fear that the depression exists not only in a few of the larger cities but extends to all the smaller cities and even to the villages and rural districts. You know this situation so thoroughly through your excellent work in the Senate, that I will not attempt to point out to you the primary causes of this depression, or that it is nationwide as well as state-wide. I will, however, send you data showing the very important practical steps which have been taken by the state government to improve conditions in our state and also my suggestions for an immediate study of the broad subject of unemployment relief by a contributory system and not dole methods.

Also, I will send you a brief outline showing the very important steps which have been taken during the past two years for social welfare, notably the prison and hospital programs, the organization of the parole system, etc., etc.

You are also familiar with the great strides which have been taken this year in relation to the development of state-owned water power and a closer control over public utilities in general. . . .

The very notable achievements in farm relief and in the development of a permanent farm policy are described in my various messages to the Legislature, and I hope that you will read them. The farm population has been relieved of paying approximately thirty million dollars a year of highway tax, real estate tax and school burdens, and we are definitely working out a state program for dirt road improvement.

Old age security against want is provided for by the first measure along this line ever adopted by the state. It goes into effect on January first next, and applications are now actually being received.

These are only a few of the high points, and it is worth while to note that all this progress has been made only after determined opposition by the Republican legislative leaders. . . .

So widespread in this state is the resentment against the results of the Eighteenth Amendment, that the time has come to stop talking and to seek action.

Very sincerely yours,

## LETTER TO ELLIOTT ROOSEVELT

*Warm Springs. November 29, 1930*

*The Governor was re-elected by a huge majority. His vote-getting power made him interesting to Democratic politicians throughout the country. Deepening depression following the Wall Street Crash of 1929 discredited the Republican Party and created the opportunity for new leadership. People racked their brains to solve the anomaly of hunger in the cities while farmers could not dispose of their crops. One idea came to the Governor from his son.*

Dear Elliott:

I have thought about that plan of flying provisions from up-state farms to New York City, but I am convinced it is not practicable because of the great weight of things like apples or other fruits or vegetables. Five hundred pounds or even a thousand pounds of any raw food stuffs would be a mere drop in the bucket in the food supply of New York City and the cost of getting it there would be approximately five hundred times as much as if it came in a freight car or even in a motor truck. Also, the State has no possible fund for paying any of the expense—even the organization work in the farming communities.

## MESSAGE TO THE LEGISLATURE

*Albany. August 28, 1931*

*While the Hoover Administration denied federal responsibility for unemployment relief, Governor Roosevelt formulated a far-reaching policy for state action.*

What is the State? It is the duly constituted representative of an organized society of human beings, created by them for their mutual protection and well-being. "The State" or "The Government" is but the machinery through which such mutual aid and protection are achieved. The cave man fought for existence unaided or even opposed by his fellow man, but today the humblest citizen of our State stands protected by all the power and strength of his Government. Our Government is not the master but the creature of the people. The duty of the State toward the citizens is the duty of the servant to its master. The people have created it; the people, by common consent, permit its continual existence.

One of these duties of the State is that of caring for those of its citizens who find themselves the victims of such adverse circumstance as makes them unable to obtain even the necessities for mere existence without the aid of others. That responsibility is recognized by every civilized Nation.

For example, from the earliest days of our own country the consciousness of the proper relationship between the State and the citizen resulted in the establishment of those often crude and unscientific but wholly necessary institutions known as the county poor houses.

In many messages to your Honorable Bodies I have pointed out that this earlier exemplification of the State's responsibility has been sustained and enlarged from year to year as we have grown to a better understanding of government functions. I have mentioned specifically the general agreement of today, that upon the State falls the duty of protecting and sustaining those of its citizens who, through no fault of their own, find themselves in their old age unable to maintain life.

But the same rule applies to other conditions. In broad terms I assert that modern society, acting through its Government, owes the definite obligation to prevent the starvation or the dire want of any of its fellow men and women who try to maintain themselves but cannot.

While it is true that we have hitherto principally considered those who through accident or old age were permanently incapacitated, the same responsibility of the State undoubtedly applies when widespread economic conditions render large numbers of men and women incapable of supporting either themselves or their families because of circumstances beyond their control which make it impossible for them to find remunerative labor. To these unfortunate citizens aid must be extended by Government, not as a matter of charity, but as a matter of social duty.

It is true beyond question that aid must be and will be given in large measure through the agencies of private contributions; and in normal times these contributions should be regarded as sufficient to meet normal conditions. However, even here the appeal is not alone on the basis of charity, but is laid on the foundation of the civic duty of all good citizens.

I would not be appearing before you today if these were normal times. When, however, a condition arises which calls for measures of relief over and beyond the ability of private and local assistance to meet—even with the usual aid added by the State—it is time for the State itself to do its additional share.

As my constitutional duty to communicate to your Honorable Bodies the condition of the State, I report to you what is a matter of common knowledge—that the economic depression of the last two years has created social conditions resulting in great physical suffering on the part of many hundreds of thousands of men, women and children. Unless conditions immediately and greatly change, this will, we fear, be aggravated by cold and hunger during the coming winter.

The many reports which I have received from municipal officials, from the Governor's Commission on the Stabilization of Employment, from the State Department of Social Welfare, and from many private organizations for relief and charity, agree that the number of our citizens who, this coming winter, will be in need will, so far as it is possible to estimate, be nearly, if not quite, twice as many as during the winter of 1930-1931.

There are many causes. Many individuals and families, because of prolonged unemployment, have exhausted their savings and their credit. Many who were at work last winter and were enabled to take care of their relatives and friends are now themselves out of work. In the same way, many employers who, up to recently, with fine public spirit have continued to use their resources to prevent the laying-off of workers, are finding that they can no longer do so. . . .

There is no escaping the simple conclusion that very large additional funds must be looked for this winter to supplement the lines of assistance given last year. . . .

# LETTER TO ROBERT W. BINGHAM

*Albany. September 29, 1931*

*The publisher of the Louisville* Courier-Journal *was one of many influential Democrats who urged Roosevelt to run for President.*

My dear Judge Bingham:

Many thanks for your nice note. I am reminded of President Wilson, who said to me early in his first term something to this effect:

"It is only once in a generation that a people can be lifted above material things. That is why conservative government is in the saddle two-thirds of the time."

I am fully convinced that the cycle has swung again after twelve years and that it is our turn next.

It was delightful to see you the other day and I hope you will surely let us know the next time you come this way.

Always sincerely yours,

# THE "FORGOTTEN MAN" RADIO SPEECH

*Albany. April 8, 1932*

*This was probably the most successful of Roosevelt's pre-convention efforts to capture the imagination of the public.*

Although I understand that I am talking under the auspices of the Democratic National Committee, I do not want to limit myself to politics. I do not want to feel that I am addressing an audience of Democrats, nor that I speak merely as a Democrat myself. The present condition of our national affairs is too serious to be viewed through partisan eyes for partisan purposes.

Fifteen years ago my public duty called me to an active part in a great national emergency—the World War. Success then was due to a leadership whose vision carried beyond the timorous and futile gesture of sending a tiny army of 150,000 trained soldiers and the regular Navy to the aid of our Allies.

The generalship of that moment conceived of a whole nation mobilized for war, economic, industrial, social and military resources gathered into a vast unit, capable of and actually in the process of throwing into the scales 10,000,000 men equipped with physical needs and sustained by the realization that behind them were the united efforts of 110,000,000 human beings. It was a great plan because it was built from bottom to top and not from top to bottom.

In my calm judgment, the nation faces today a more grave emergency than in 1917.

It is said that Napoleon lost the Battle of Waterloo because he forgot his infantry. He staked too much upon the more spectacular but less substantial cavalry.

The present Administration in Washington provides a close parallel. It has either forgotten or it does not want to remember the infantry of our economic army.

These unhappy times call for the building of plans that rest upon the forgotten, the unorganized but the indispensable units of economic power, for plans like those of 1917 that build from the bottom up and not from the top down, that put their faith once more in the forgotten man at the bottom of the economic pyramid.

Obviously, these few minutes tonight permit no opportunity to lay down the ten or a dozen closely related objectives of a plan to meet our present emergency, but I can draw a few essentials, a beginning, in fact, of a planned program.

It is the habit of the unthinking to turn in times like this to the illusions of economic magic. People suggest that a huge expenditure of public funds by the Federal Government and by State and local governments will completely solve the unemployment problem. But it is clear that even if we could raise many billions of dollars and find definitely useful public works to spend these billions on, even all that money would not give employment to the 7,000,000 or 10,000,000 people who are out of work.

Let us admit frankly that it would be only a stopgap. A real economic cure must go to the killing of bacteria in the system rather than to the treatment of external symptoms.

How much do the shallow thinkers realize, for example, that approximately one-half of our population, fifty or sixty million people, earn their living by farming or in small towns where existence immediately depends on farms. They have today lost their purchasing power. Why? They are receiving for farm products less than the cost to them of growing these farm products.

The result of this loss of purchasing power is that many other millions of people engaged in industry in the cities cannot sell industrial products to the farming half of the nation. This brings home to every city worker that his own employment is directly tied up with the farmer's dollar. No nation can long continue half bankrupt. Main Street, Broadway, the mills, the mines will close if half of the buyers are broke.

I cannot escape the conclusion that one of the essentials of a national program of restoration must be to restore purchasing power to the farming half of the country. Without this the wheels of railroads and of factories will not turn.

Closely associated with this first objective is the problem of keeping the home-owner and the farm-owner where he is, without being dispossessed through the foreclosure of his mortgage.

His relationship to the great banks of Chicago and New York is pretty remote. The two billion dollar fund which President Hoover and the Congress have put at the disposal of the big banks, the railroads and the corporations of the nation is not for him.

His is a relationship to his little local bank or local loan company. It is a sad fact that even though the local lender in many cases does not want to evict the farmer or home-owner by foreclosure proceedings, he is forced to do so in order to keep his bank or company solvent. Here should be an objective of government itself, to provide at least as much assistance to the little fellow as it is now giving to the large banks and corporations. That is another example of building from the bottom up.

One other objective closely related to the problem of selling American products is to provide a tariff policy based upon economic common sense rather than upon politics—hot air—pull.

This country during the past few years, culminating with the Hawley-Smoot Tariff of 1929, has compelled the world to build tariff fences so high that world trade is decreasing to the vanishing point. The value of goods internationally exchanged is today less than half of what it was three or four years ago.

Every man and woman who gives any thought to the subject knows that if our factories run even 80 per cent of capacity they will turn out more products than we as a nation can possibly use ourselves.

The answer is that if they are to run on 80 per cent of capacity we must sell some goods abroad. How can we do that if the outside nations cannot pay us in cash—and we know by sad experience that they cannot do that. The only way they can pay us is in their own goods or raw materials, but this foolish tariff of ours makes that impossible.

What we must do is this: To revise our tariff on the basis of a reciprocal exchange of goods, allowing other nations to buy and to pay for our goods by sending us such of their goods as will not seriously throw any of our industries out of balance, and, incidentally, making impossible in this country the continuance of pure monopolies which cause us to pay excessive prices for many of the necessities of life.

Such objectives as these three—restoring farmers' buying power, relief to the small banks and homeowners and a reconstructed tariff policy—these are only a part of ten or a dozen vital factors.

But they seem to be beyond the concern of a National Administration which can think in terms only of the top of the social and economic structure. They have sought temporary relief from the top down rather than permanent relief from the bottom up. They have totally failed to plan ahead in a comprehensive way. They have waited until something has cracked and then at the last moment have sought to prevent total collapse.

It is high time to get back to fundamentals. It is high time to admit with courage that we are in the midst of an emergency at least equal to that of war. Let us mobilize to meet it.

## ACCEPTANCE SPEECH

*Chicago. July 2, 1932*

*Nominated by the Democratic National Convention on the third ballot, Roosevelt flew out to Chicago to promise the delegates and the country a new deal.*

Chairman Walsh, my friends of the Democratic National Convention of 1932:

I appreciate your willingness after these six arduous days to remain here, for I know well the sleepless hours which you and I have had. I regret that I am late, but I have no control over the winds of Heaven and could only be thankful for my Navy training.

The appearance before a National Convention of its nominee for President, to be formally notified of his selection, is unprecedented and unusual, but these are unprecedented and unusual times. I have started out on the tasks that lie ahead by breaking the absurd traditions that the candidate should remain in professed ignorance of what has happened for weeks until he is formally notified of that event many weeks later.

My friends, may this be the symbol of my intention to be honest and to avoid all hypocrisy or sham, to avoid all silly shutting of the eyes to the truth in this campaign. You have nominated me and I know it, and I am here to thank you for the honor.

Let it also be symbolic that in so doing I broke traditions. Let it be from now on the task of our Party to break foolish traditions. We will break foolish traditions and leave it to the Republican leadership, far more skilled in that art, to break promises.

Let us now and here highly resolve to resume the country's interrupted march along the path of real progress, of real justice, or real equality for all of our citizens, great and small. Our indomitable leader in that interrupted march is no longer with us, but there still survives today his spirit. Many of his captains, thank God, are still with us, to give us wise counsel. Let us feel that in everything we do there still lives with us, if not the body, the great indomitable, unquenchable, progressive soul of our Commander-in-Chief, Woodrow Wilson. . . .

Wild radicalism has made few converts and the greatest tribute that I can pay to my countrymen is that in these days of crushing want there persists an orderly and hopeful spirit on the part of the millions of our people who have suffered so much. To fail to offer them a new chance is not only to betray their hopes but to misunderstand their patience.

To meet by reaction that danger of radicalism is to invite disaster. Reaction is no barrier to the radical. It is a challenge, a provocation. The way to meet that danger is to offer a workable program of reconstruction, and the Party to offer it is the party with clean hands.

This, and this only is a proper protection against blind reaction on the one hand and an improvised hit-or-miss, irresponsible opportunism on the other.

There are two ways of viewing the government's duty in matters affecting economic and social life. The first sees to it that a favored few are helped and hopes that some of their prosperity will leak through, sift through, to labor, to the farmer, to the small businessman. That theory belongs to the party of Toryism, and I had hoped that most of the Tories left this country in 1776.

But it is not and never will be the theory of the Democratic Party. This is no time for fear, for reaction or for timidity. And here and now I invite those nominal Republicans who find that their conscience cannot be squared with the groping and the failure of their party leaders to join hands with us; here and now, in equal measure, I warn those nominal Democrats who squint at the future with their faces turned toward the past, and who feel no responsibility to the demands of the new time, that they are out of step with their party.

Yes, the people of this country want a genuine choice this year, not a choice between two names for the same reactionary doctrine. Ours must be a Party of Liberal thought, of planned action, of enlightened international outlook, and of the greatest good to the greatest number of our citizens. . . .

Statesmanship and vision, my friends, require relief to all at the same time.

Just one word or two on taxes, the taxes that all of us pay toward the cost of government of all kinds.

Well, I know something of taxes. For three long years I have been going up and down this country preaching that government—federal and state and local—costs too much. I shall not stop that preaching. As an immediate program of action we must abolish useless offices. We must eliminate actual functions of government—functions, in fact, that are not definitely essential to the continuance of government. We must merge, we must consolidate subdivisions of government, and, like the private citizen, give up luxuries which we can no longer afford.

By our example at Washington itself, we shall have the opportunity of pointing the way of economy to local government, for let us remember well that out of every tax dollar in the average state in this nation, 40 cents enters the treasury in Washington, D. C., 10 or 12 cents only go to the state capitals, and 48 cents out of every dollar are consumed by the costs of local government in counties and cities and towns.

I propose to you, my friends, and through you, that government of all kinds, big and little, be made solvent and that the example be set by the President of the United States and his Cabinet.

And talking about setting a definite example, I congratulate this convention for having had the courage, fearlessly, to write into its declaration of principles what an overwhelming majority here assembled really thinks about the 18th Amendment. This convention wants repeal. Your candidate wants repeal. And I am confident that the United States of America wants repeal.

Two years ago the platform on which I ran for Governor the second time contained substantially the same provision. The overwhelming sentiment of the people of my State, as shown by the vote of that year, extends, I know, to the people of many of the other States. I say to you now that from this date on the 18th Amendment is doomed. When that happens, we as Democrats must and will, rightly and morally, enable the States to protect themselves against the importation of intoxicating liquor where such importation may violate their State laws. We must rightly and morally prevent the return of the saloon. . . .

What do the people of America want more than anything else? In my mind, two things: Work; work, with all the moral and spiritual values that go with work. And with work, a reasonable measure of security—security for themselves and for their wives and children. Work and security—these are more than words. They are more than facts. They are the spiritual values, the true goal toward which our efforts of reconstruction should lead. These are the values that this program is intended to gain; these are the values we have failed to achieve by the leadership we now have.

Our Republican leaders tell us economic laws—sacred, inviolable, unchangeable—that these laws cause panics which no one could prevent. But while they prate of economic laws, men and women are starving. We must lay hold of the fact that economic laws are not made by nature. They are made by human beings.

Yes, when—not if—when we get the chance, the Federal Government will assume bold leadership in distress relief. For years Washington has alternated between putting its head in the sand and saying there is no large number of destitute people in our midst who need food and clothing, and then saying the States should take care of them, if there are. Instead of planning two and a half years ago to do what they are now trying to do, they kept putting it off from day to day and week to week, and month to month, until the conscience of America demanded action.

I say that while primary responsibility for relief rests with localities now, as ever, yet the Federal Government has always had and still has a continuing responsibility for the broader public welfare. It will soon fulfill that responsibility. . . .

One word more: Out of every crisis, every tribulation, every disaster, mankind rises with some share of greater knowledge, of higher decency, of purer purpose. Today we shall have come through a period of loose thinking, descending morals, an era of selfishness, of individual men and women and of whole nations. Blame not governments alone for this. Blame ourselves in equal share. Let us be frank in acknowledgment of the truth that many amongst us have made obeisance to Mammon, that the profits of speculation, the easy road without toil, have lured us from the old barricades. To return to higher standards we must abandon the false prophets and seek new leaders of our own choosing.

Never before, never before in modern history have the essential differences between the two major American parties stood out in such striking contrast as they do today. Republican leaders not only have failed in material things, they have failed in National vision, because in disaster they have held out no hope, they have pointed out no path for the people below to climb back to places of security and of safety in our American life.

Throughout the nation, men and women, forgotten in the political philosophy of the government of the last years look to us here for guidance and for more equitable opportunity to share in the distribution of national wealth.

On the farms, in the large metropolitan areas, in the smaller cities and in the villages, millions of our citizens cherish the hope that their old standards of living and of thought have not gone forever. Those millions cannot and shall not hope in vain.

I pledge you—I pledge myself to a new deal for the American people. Let us all here assembled constitute ourselves prophets of a new order of competence and of courage. This is more than a political campaign; it is a call to arms. Give me your help, not to win votes alone, but to win in this crusade to restore America to its own people.

## COMMONWEALTH CLUB CAMPAIGN SPEECH

*San Francisco. September 23, 1932*

*This has been called the most important statement of political philosophy Roosevelt ever made.*

I count it a privilege to be invited to address the Commonwealth Club. It has stood in the life of this city and state, and it is perhaps accurate to add, the nation, as a group of citizen leaders interested in fundamental problems of government, and chiefly concerned with achievement of progress in government through non-partisan means. The privilege of addressing you, therefore, in the heat of a political campaign, is great. I want to respond to your courtesy in terms consistent with your policy.

I want to speak not of politics but of government. I want to speak not of parties, but of universal principles. They are not political, except in that larger sense in which a great American once expressed a definition of politics, that nothing in all of human life is foreign to the science of politics. . . .

The issue of government has always been whether individual men and women will have to serve some system of government or economics, or whether a system of government and economics exists to serve individual men and women. This question has persistently dominated the discussion of govern-

ment for many generations. On questions relating to these
things men have differed, and for time immemorial it is probable that honest men will continue to differ.

The final word belongs to no man; yet we can still believe
in change and in progress. Democracy, as a dear old friend of
mine in Indiana, Meredith Nicholson, has called it, is a quest,
a never-ending seeking for better things, and in the seeking
for these things and the striving for them, there are many
roads to follow. But, if we map the course of these roads, we
find that there are only two general directions.

When we look about us, we are likely to forget how hard
people have worked to win the privilege of government. The
growth of the national governments of Europe was a struggle
for the development of a centralized force in the nation,
strong enough to impose peace upon ruling barons. In many
instances the victory of the central government, the creation
of a strong central government, was a haven of refuge to the
individual. The people preferred the master far away to the
exploitation and cruelty of the smaller master near at hand.

But the creators of national government were perforce
ruthless men. They were often cruel in their methods, but they
did strive steadily toward something that society needed and
very much wanted, a strong central state, able to keep the
peace, to stamp out civil war, to put the unruly nobleman in
his place, and to permit the bulk of individuals to live safely.
The man of ruthless force had his place in developing a pioneer country, just as he did in fixing the power of the central
government in the development of nations. Society paid him
well for his services and its development. When the development among the nations of Europe, however, had been completed, ambition and ruthlessness, having served its term,
tended to overstep its mark.

There came a growing feeling that government was conducted for the benefit of a few who thrived unduly at the expense of all. The people sought a balancing—a limiting force.
There came gradually, through town councils, trade guilds,

national parliaments, by constitution and by popular participation and control, limitations on arbitrary power.

Another factor that tended to limit the power of those who ruled, was the rise of the ethical conception that a ruler bore a responsibility for the welfare of his subjects.

The American colonies were born in this struggle. The American Revolution was a turning point in it. After the revolution the struggle continued and shaped itself in the public life of the country. There were those who because they had seen the confusion which attended the years of war for American independence surrendered to the belief that popular government was essentially dangerous and essentially unworkable. They were honest people, my friends, and we cannot deny that their experience had warranted some measure of fear. The most brilliant, honest and able exponent of this point of view was Hamilton. He was too impatient of slow-moving methods. Fundamentally he believed that the safety of the republic lay in the autocratic strength of its government, that the destiny of individuals was to serve that government, and that fundamentally a great and strong group of central institutions, guided by a small group of able and public spirited citizens could best direct all government.

But Mr. Jefferson, in the summer of 1776, after drafting the Declaration of Independence turned his mind to the same problem and took a different view. He did not deceive himself with outward forms. Government to him was a means to an end, not an end in itself; it might be either a refuge and a help or a threat and a danger, depending on the circumstances. We find him carefully analyzing the society for which he was to organize a government. "We have no paupers. The great mass of our population is of laborers, our rich who cannot live without labor, either manual or professional, being few and of moderate wealth. Most of the laboring class possess property, cultivate their own lands, have families and from the demand for their labor, are enabled to exact from the rich and the competent such prices as enable them to feed abundantly, clothe above mere decency, to labor moderately and raise their families."

These people, he considered, had two sets of rights, those of "personal competency" and those involved in acquiring and possessing property. By "personal competency" he meant the right of free thinking, freedom of forming and expressing opinions, and freedom of personal living each man according to his own lights. To insure the first set of rights, a government must so order its functions as not to interfere with the individual. But even Jefferson realized that the exercise of the property rights might so interfere with the rights of the individual that the government, without whose assistance the property rights could not exist, must intervene, not to destroy individualism but to protect it.

You are familiar with the great political duel which followed; and how Hamilton, and his friends, building towards a dominant centralized power were at length defeated in the great election of 1800, by Mr. Jefferson's party. Out of that duel came the two parties, Republican and Democratic, as we know them today.

So began, in American political life, the new day, the day of the individual against the system, the day in which individualism was made the great watchword of American life. The happiest of economic conditions made that day long and splendid. On the Western frontier, land was substantially free. No one, who did not shirk the task of earning a living, was entirely without opportunity to do so. Depressions could, and did, come and go; but they could not alter the fundamental fact that most of the people lived partly by selling their labor and partly by extracting their livelihood from the soil, so that starvation and dislocation were practically impossible. At the very worst there was always the possibility of climbing into a covered wagon and moving west where the untilled prairies afforded a haven for men to whom the East did not provide a place. So great were our natural resources that we could offer this relief not only to our own people, but to the distressed of all the world; we could invite immigration from Europe, and welcome it with open arms. Traditionally, when a depression came a new section of land was opened in the West; and even our temporary misfortune served our manifest destiny.

It was in the middle of the 19th century that a new force was released and a new dream created. The force was what is called the industrial revolution, the advance of steam and machinery and the rise of the forerunners of the modern industrial plant. The dream was the dream of an economic machine, able to raise the standard of living for everyone; to bring luxury within the reach of the humblest; to annihilate distance by steam power and later by electricity, and to release everyone from the drudgery of the heaviest manual toil. It was to be expected that this would necessarily affect government. Heretofore, government had merely been called upon to produce conditions within which people could live happily, labor peacefully, and rest secure. Now it was called upon to aid in the consummation of this new dream. There was, however, a shadow over the dream. To be made real, it required use of the talents of men of tremendous will, and tremendous ambition, since by no other force could the problems of financing and engineering and new developments be brought to a consummation.

So manifest were the advantages of the machine age, however, that the United States fearlessly, cheerfully, and, I think, rightly, accepted the bitter with the sweet. It was thought that no price was too high to pay for the advantages which we could draw from a finished industrial system. The history of the last half century is accordingly in large measure a history of a group of financial Titans, whose methods were not scrutinized with too much care, and who were honored in proportion as they produced the results, irrespective of the means they used. The financiers who pushed the railroads to the Pacific were always ruthless, often wasteful, and frequently corrupt; but they did build railroads, and we have them today. It has been estimated that the American investor paid for the American railway system more than three times over in the process; but despite this fact the net advantage was to the United States. As long as we had free land; as long as population was growing by leaps and bounds; as long as our industrial plants were insufficient to supply our own needs, society chose to give the ambitious man free play and unlimited reward provided only that he produced the economic plant so much desired.

During this period of expansion, there was equal opportunity for all and the business of government was not to interfere but to assist in the development of industry. This was done at the request of business men themselves. The tariff was originally imposed for the purpose of "fostering our infant industry", a phrase I think the older among you will remember as a political issue not so long ago. The railroads were subsidized, sometimes by grants of money, oftener by grants of land; some of the most valuable oil lands in the United States were granted to assist the financing of the railroad which pushed through the Southwest. A nascent merchant marine was assisted by grants of money, or by mail subsidies, so that our steam shipping might ply the seven seas. Some of my friends tell me that they do not want the Government in business. With this I agree; but I wonder whether they realize the implications of the past. For while it has been American doctrine that the government must not go into business in competition with private enterprises, still it has been traditional particularly in Republican administrations for business urgently to ask the government to put at private disposal all kinds of government assistance. The same man who tells you that he does not want to see the government interfere in business— and he means it, and has plenty of good reasons for saying so —is the first to go to Washington and ask the government for a prohibitory tariff on his product. When things get just bad enough—as they did two years ago—he will go with equal speed to the United States government and ask for a loan; and the Reconstruction Finance Corporation is the outcome of it. Each group has sought protection from the government for its own special interests, without realizing that the function of government must be to favor no small group at the expense of its duty to protect the rights of personal freedom and of private property of all its citizens.

In retrospect we can now see that the turn of the tide came with the turn of the century. We were reaching our last frontier; there was no more free land and our industrial combinations had become great uncontrolled and irresponsible units of power within the state. Clear-sighted men saw with fear the danger that opportunity would no longer be equal; that the growing corporation, like the feudal baron of old, might threaten the economic freedom of individuals to earn a living. In that hour, our antitrust laws were born. The cry was raised against the great corporations. Theodore Roosevelt, the first great Republican progressive, fought a Presidential campaign on the issue of "trust busting" and talked freely about malefactors of great wealth. If the government had a policy it was rather to turn the clock back, to destroy the large combinations and to return to the time when every man owned his individual small business.

This was impossible; Theodore Roosevelt, abandoning the idea of "trust busting", was forced to work out a difference between "good" trusts and "bad" trusts. The Supreme Court set forth the famous "rule of reason" by which it seems to have meant that a concentration of industrial power was permissible if the method by which it got its power, and the use it made of that power, was reasonable.

Woodrow Wilson, elected in 1912, saw the situation more clearly. Where Jefferson had feared the encroachment of political power on the lives of individuals, Wilson knew that the new power was financial. He saw, in the highly centralized economic system, the despot of the twentieth century, on whom great masses of individuals relied for their safety and their livelihood, and whose irresponsibility and greed (if it were not controlled) would reduce them to starvation and penury. The concentration of financial power had not proceeded so far in 1912 as it has today; but it had grown far enough for Mr. Wilson to realize fully its implications. It is interesting, now, to read his speeches. What is called "radical" today (and I have reason to know whereof I speak) is mild compared to the campaign of Mr. Wilson. "No man can deny", he said, "that the lines of endeavor have more and more narrowed and stiffened; no man who knows anything about the development of industry in this country can have failed to observe that the larger kinds of credit are more and more difficult to obtain unless you obtain them upon terms of uniting your efforts with those who already control the industry of the country, and nobody can fail to observe that every man who tries to set himself up in competition with any process of manufacture which has taken place under the control of large combinations of capital will presently find himself either squeezed out or obliged to sell and allow himself to be absorbed." Had there been no World War—had Mr. Wilson been able to devote eight years to domestic instead of to international affairs—we might have had a wholly different situation at the present time. However, the then distant roar of European cannon, growing ever louder, forced him to abandon the study of this issue. The problem he saw so clearly is left with us as a legacy; and no one of us on either side of the political controversy can deny that it is a matter of grave concern to the government.

A glance at the situation today only too clearly indicates that equality of opportunity as we have known it no longer exists. Our industrial plant is built; the problem just now is whether under existing conditions it is not overbuilt. Our last frontier has long since been reached, and there is practically no more free land. More than half of our people do not live on the farms or on lands and cannot derive a living by cultivating their own property. There is no safety valve in the form of a Western prairie to which those thrown out of work by the Eastern economic machines can go for a new start. We are not able to invite the immigration from Europe to share our endless plenty. We are now providing a drab living for our own people.

Our system of constantly rising tariffs has at last reacted

against us to the point of closing our Canadian frontier on the north, our European markets on the east, many of our Latin American markets to the south, and a goodly proportion of our Pacific markets on the west, through the retaliatory tariffs of those countries. It has forced many of our great industrial institutions who exported their surplus production to such countries, to establish plants in such countries, within the tariff walls. This has resulted in the reduction of the operation of their American plants, and opportunity for employment.

Just as freedom to farm has ceased, so also the opportunity in business has narrowed. It still is true that men can start small enterprises, trusting to native shrewdness and ability to keep abreast of competitors; but area after area has been pre-empted altogether by the great corporations, and even in the fields which still have no great concerns, the small man starts under a handicap. The unfeeling statistics of the past three decades show that the independent business man is running a losing race. Perhaps he is forced to the wall; perhaps he cannot command credit; perhaps he is "squeezed out", in Mr. Wilson's words, by highly organized corporate competitors, as your corner grocery man can tell you. Recently a careful study was made of the concentration of business in the United States. It showed that our economic life was dominated by some six hundred odd corporations who controlled two-thirds of American industry. Ten million small business men divided the other third. More striking still, it appeared that if the process of concentration goes on at the same rate, at the end of another century we shall have all American industry controlled by a dozen corporations, and run by perhaps a hundred men. Put plainly, we are steering a steady course toward economic oligarchy, if we are not there already.

Clearly, all this calls for a re-appraisal of values. A mere builder of more industrial plants, a creator of more railroad systems, an organizer of more corporations, is as likely to be a danger as a help. The day of the great promoter or the financial Titan, to whom we granted anything if only he would build, or develop, is over. Our task now is not discovery or exploitation of natural resources, or necessarily producing more goods. It is the soberer, less dramatic business of administering resources and plants already in hand, of seeking to reestablish foreign markets for our surplus production, of meeting the problem of underconsumption, of adjusting production to consumption, of distributing wealth and products more equitably, of adapting existing economic organizations to the service of the people. The day of enlightened administration has come.

Just as in older times the central government was first a haven of refuge, and then a threat, so now in a closer economic system the central and ambitious financial unit is no longer a servant of national desire, but a danger. I would draw the parallel one step farther. We did not think because national government had become a threat in the 18th century that therefore we should abandon the principle of national government. Nor today should we abandon the principle of strong economic units called corporations, merely because their power is susceptible of easy abuse. In other times we dealt with the problem of an unduly ambitious central government by modifying it gradually into a constitutional democratic government. So today we are modifying and controlling our economic units.

As I see it, the task of government in its relation to business is to assist the development of an economic declaration of rights, an economic constitutional order. This is the common task of statesman and business man. It is the minimum requirement of a more permanently safe order of things. . . .

Every man has a right to life; and this means that he has also a right to make a comfortable living. He may by sloth or crime decline to exercise that right; but it may not be denied him. We have no actual famine or dearth; our industrial and agricultural mechanism can produce enough and to spare. Our government formal and informal, political and economic, owes to every one an avenue to possess himself of a portion of that plenty sufficient for his needs, through his own work.

Every man has a right to his own property; which means a

right to be assured, to the fullest extent attainable, in the safety of his savings. By no other means can men carry the burdens of those parts of life which, in the nature of things, afford no chance of labor; childhood, sickness, old age. In all thought of property, this right is paramount; all other property rights must yield to it. If, in accord with this principle, we must restrict the operations of the speculator, the manipulator, even the financier, I believe we must accept the restriction as needful, not to hamper individualism but to protect it.

These two requirements must be satisfied, in the main, by the individuals who claim and hold control of the great industrial and financial combinations which dominate so large a part of our industrial life. They have undertaken to be, not business men, but princes—princes of property. I am not prepared to say that the system which produces them is wrong. I am very clear that they must fearlessly and competently assume the responsibility which goes with the power. So many enlightened business men know this that the statement would be little more than a platitude, were it not for an added implication.

This implication is, briefly, that the responsible heads of finance and industry instead of acting each for himself, must work together to achieve the common end. They must, where necessary, sacrifice this or that private advantage; and in reciprocal self-denial must seek a general advantage. It is here that formal government—political government, if you choose, comes in. Whenever in the pursuit of this objective the lone wolf, the unethical competitor, the reckless promoter, the Ishmael or Insull whose hand is against every man's, declines to join in achieving an end recognized as being for the public welfare, and threatens to drag the industry back to a state of anarchy, the government may properly be asked to apply restraint. Likewise, should the group ever use its collective power contrary to the public welfare, the government must be swift to enter and protect the public interest.

The government should assume the function of economic regulation only as a last resort, to be tried only when pri-

vate initiative, inspired by high responsibility, with such assistance and balance as government can give, has finally
failed. As yet there has been no final failure, because there has
been no attempt; and I decline to assume that this nation is
unable to meet the situation.

The final term of the high contract was for liberty and the
pursuit of happiness. We have learnt a great deal of both in the
past century. We know that individual liberty and individual happiness mean nothing unless both are ordered in the
sense that one man's meat is not another man's poison. We
know that the old "rights of personal competency"—the right
to read, to think, to speak, to choose and live a mode of life,
must be respected at all hazards. We know that liberty to do
anything which deprives others of those elemental rights is outside the protection of any compact; and that government in
this regard is the maintenance of a balance, within which
every individual may have a place if he will take it; in which
every individual may find safety if he wishes it; in which every
individual may attain such power as his ability permits,
consistent with his assuming the accompanying responsibility. . . .

Faith in America, faith in our tradition of personal responsibility, faith in our institutions, faith in ourselves demands
that we recognize the new terms of the old social contact. We
shall fulfill them, as we fulfilled the obligation of the apparent
Utopia which Jefferson imagined for us in 1776, and which
Jefferson, Roosevelt and Wilson sought to bring to realization.
We must do so, lest a rising tide of misery engendered by our
common failure, engulf us all. But failure is not an American
habit; and in the strength of great hope we must all shoulder
our common load.

## LETTER TO HERBERT HOOVER

*Hyde Park. March 1, 1933*

*Elected by strong majorities, Roosevelt could not be inaugurated
for four months. President Hoover several times proposed co-*

*operation, but Roosevelt rightly believed that the outgoing President's purpose was to win commitments which would thwart the New Deal. The situation became dangerous late in the winter when a new series of panics closed many banks and states declared "bank holidays" to prevent utter disaster. Hoover believed that fear of unsound money policies under the new Administration was the cause of the trouble. Roosevelt believed that unsound private banking practices were the cause. Hoover urged Roosevelt to give assurances to the public, but Roosevelt's answer of February 20 was not sent until March 1. Senator Carter Glass of Virginia also feared an unsound money policy and refused Roosevelt's offer to appoint him Secretary of the Treasury. The banking crisis reached its climax on March 4, when practically all the banks of the nation closed. The new Administration then had a free hand to undertake fundamental measures of banking reform and management of the currency to stimulate general economic recovery.*

Dear Mr. President:—

I am dismayed to find that the enclosed letter, which I wrote in New York a week ago, did not go to you through an assumption by my secretary that it was only a draft of a letter.

Now I have yours of yesterday and can only tell you that I appreciate your fine spirit of cooperation, and that I am in constant touch with the situation through Mr. Woodin, who is conferring with [Secretary of the Treasury] Ogden [Mills] and with various people in New York. I am inclined to agree that a very early Special Session will be necessary—and by tonight or tomorrow I hope to settle on a definite time. I will let you know. You doubtless know of the proposal to give authority to the Treasury to deposit funds directly in *any* bank.

I get to Washington late tomorrow night and will look forward to seeing you on Friday.

Always sincerely,

*[Enclosure: February 20, 1933]*

Dear Mr. President:—

I am equally concerned with you in regard to the gravity of the present bank situation—but my thought is that it is so very deep-seated that the fire is bound to spread in spite of anything that is done by mere statement. The real trouble is that on present values very few financial institutions anywhere in the country are actually able to pay off their deposits in full, and the knowledge of this fact is widely held. Bankers with the narrower viewpoint have urged me to make a general statement, but even they seriously doubt if it would have a definite effect.

I had hoped to have Senator Glass' acceptance of the treasury post but he has definitely said "no" this afternoon. I am asking Mr. Woodin tomorrow and if he accepts I propose to announce it tomorrow, together with Senator Hull for the State Department. These announcements *may* have some effect on the banking situation, but frankly I doubt if anything short of a fairly general withdrawal of deposits can be prevented now.

In any event Mr. Woodin, if he accepts, will get into immediate touch with Mills and the bankers.

Very sincerely yours,

*Part*
*Three*

# The First New Deal
# End of the Honeymoon

MARCH 4, 1933 — JANUARY 1, 1935

## FIRST INAUGURAL ADDRESS

*Washington. March 4, 1933*

*This speech and the rapid-fire handling of the banking crisis that followed it rallied the spirit of the people.*

I am certain that my fellow Americans expect that on my induction into the Presidency I will address them with a candor and a decision which the present situation of our Nation impels. This is preeminently the time to speak the truth, the whole truth, frankly and boldly. Nor need we shrink from honestly facing conditions in our country today. This great Nation will endure as it has endured, will revive and will prosper. So, first of all, let me assert my firm belief that the only thing we have to fear is fear itself—nameless, unreasoning, unjustified terror which paralyzes needed efforts to convert retreat into advance. In every dark hour of our national life a leadership of frankness and vigor has met with that understanding and support of the people themselves which is essential to victory. I am convinced that you will again give that support to leadership in these critical days.

In such a spirit on my part and on yours we face our common difficulties. They concern, thank God, only material things. Values have shrunken to fantastic levels; taxes have risen; our ability to pay has fallen; government of all kinds is faced by serious curtailment of income; the means of exchange are frozen in the currents of trade; the withered leaves of industrial enterprise lie on every side; farmers find no markets for their produce; the savings of many years in thousands of families are gone.

More important, a host of unemployed citizens face the grim problem of existence, and an equally great number toil with little return. Only a foolish optimist can deny the dark realities of the moment.

Yet our distress comes from no failure of substance. We are stricken by no plague of locusts. Compared with the perils which our forefathers conquered because they believed and were not afraid, we have still much to be thankful for. Nature still offers her bounty and human efforts have multiplied it. Plenty is at our doorstep, but a generous use of it languishes in the very sight of the supply. Primarily this is because rulers of the exchange of mankind's goods have failed, through their own stubbornness and their own incompetence, have admitted their failure, and abdicated. Practices of the unscrupulous money changers stand indicted in the court of public opinion, rejected by the hearts and minds of men.

True they have tried, but their efforts have been cast in the pattern of an outworn tradition. Faced by failure of credit they have proposed only the lending of more money. Stripped of the lure of profit by which to induce our people to follow their false leadership, they have resorted to exhortations, pleading tearfully for restored confidence. They know only the rules of a generation of self-seekers. They have no vision, and when there is no vision the people perish.

The money changers have fled from their high seats in the temple of our civilization. We may now restore that temple to the ancient truths. The measure of the restoration lies in the extent to which we apply social values more noble than mere monetary profit.

Happiness lies not in the mere possession of money; it lies in the joy of achievement, in the thrill of creative effort. The joy and moral stimulation of work no longer must be forgotten in the mad chase of evanescent profits. These dark days will be worth all they cost us if they teach us that our true destiny is not to be ministered unto but to minister to ourselves and to our fellow men.

Recognition of the falsity of material wealth as the standard of success goes hand in hand with the abandonment of the false belief that public office and high political position are to be valued only by the standards of pride of place and personal profit; and there must be an end to a conduct in banking and in business which too often has given to a sacred trust the likeness of callous and selfish wrongdoing. Small wonder that confidence languishes, for it thrives only on honesty, on honor, on the sacredness of obligations, on faithful protection, on unselfish performance; without them it cannot live.

Restoration calls, however, not for changes in ethics alone. This Nation asks for action, and action now.

Our greatest primary task is to put people to work. This is no unsolvable problem if we face it wisely and courageously. It can be accomplished in part by direct recruiting by the Government itself, treating the task as we would treat the emergency of a war, but at the same time, through this employment, accomplishing greatly needed projects to stimulate and reorganize the use of our natural resources.

Hand in hand with this we must frankly recognize the overbalance of population in our industrial centers and, by engaging on a national scale in a redistribution, endeavor to provide a better use of the land for those best fitted for the land. The task can be helped by definite efforts to raise the values of agricultural products and with this the power to purchase the output of our cities. It can be helped by preventing realistically the tragedy of the growing loss through foreclosure of our small homes and our farms. It can be helped by insistence that the Federal, State, and local governments act forthwith on the demand that their cost be drastically reduced. It can be helped by the unifying of relief activities which today are often scattered, uneconomical, and unequal. It can be helped by national planning for and supervision of all forms of transportation and of communications and other utilities which have a definitely public character. There are many ways in which it can be helped, but it can never be helped merely by talking about it. We must act and act quickly.

Finally, in our progress toward a resumption of work we require two safeguards against a return of the evils of the old order; there must be a strict supervision of all banking and credits and investments; there must be an end to speculation with other people's money, and there must be provision for an adequate but sound currency.

These are the lines of attack. I shall presently urge upon a new Congress, in special session, detailed measures for their fulfillment, and I shall seek the immediate assistance of the several States.

Through this program of action we address ourselves to putting our own national house in order and making income balance outgo. Our international trade relations, though vastly important, are in point of time and necessity secondary to the establishment of a sound national economy. I favor as a practical policy the putting of first things first. I shall spare no effort to restore world trade by international economic readjustment, but the emergency at home cannot wait on that accomplishment.

The basic thought that guides these specific means of national recovery is not narrowly nationalistic. It is the insistence, as a first consideration, upon the interdependence of the various elements in and parts of the United States—a recognition of the old and permanently important manifestation of the American spirit of the pioneer. It is the way to recovery. It is the immediate way. It is the strongest assurance that the recovery will endure.

In the field of world policy I would dedicate this Nation to the policy of the good neighbor—the neighbor who resolutely respects himself and, because he does so, respects the rights of others—the neighbor who respects his obligations and respects the sanctity of his agreements in and with a world of neighbors.

If I read the temper of our people correctly, we now realize as we have never realized before our interdependence on each other; that we cannot merely take but we must give as well; that if we are to go forward, we must move as a trained and loyal army willing to sacrifice for the good of a common discipline, because without such discipline no progress is made, no leadership becomes effective. We are, I know, ready and willing to submit our lives and property to such discipline, because it makes possible a leadership which aims at a larger good. This I propose to offer, pledging that the larger purposes will bind upon us all as a sacred obligation with a unity of duty hitherto evoked only in time of armed strife.

With this pledge taken, I assume unhesitatingly the leadership of this great army of our people dedicated to a disciplined attack upon our common problems.

Action in this image and to this end is feasible under the form of government which we have inherited from our ancestors. Our Constitution is so simple and practical that it is possible always to meet extraordinary needs by changes in emphasis and arrangement without loss of essential form. That is why our constitutional system has proved itself the most superbly enduring political mechanism the modern world has produced. It has met every stress of vast expansion of territory, of foreign wars, of bitter internal strife, of world relations.

It is to be hoped that the normal balance of executive and legislative authority may be wholly adequate to meet the unprecedented task before us. But it may be that an unprecedented demand and need for undelayed action may call for temporary departure from that normal balance of public procedure.

I am prepared under my constitutional duty to recommend the measures that a stricken nation in the midst of a stricken world may require. These measures, or such other measures as the Congress may build out of its experience and wisdom, I shall seek, within my constitutional authority, to bring to speedy adoption.

But in the event that the Congress shall fail to take one of these two courses, and in the event that the national emergency is still critical, I shall not evade the clear course of duty that will then confront me. I shall ask the Congress for the one remaining instrument to meet the crisis—broad Executive power to wage a war against the emergency, as great as the power that would be given to me if we were in fact invaded by a foreign foe.

For the trust reposed in me I will return the courage and the devotion that befit the time. I can do no less.

We face the arduous days that lie before us in the warm courage of national unity; with the clear consciousness of seeking old and precious moral values; with the clean satisfaction that comes from the stern performance of duty by old and young alike. We aim at the assurance of a rounded and permanent national life.

We do not distrust the future of essential democracy. The people of the United States have not failed. In their need they have registered a mandate that they want direct, vigorous action. They have asked for discipline and direction under leadership. They have made me the present instrument of their wishes. In the spirit of the gift I take it.

In this dedication of a Nation we humbly ask the blessing of God. May He protect each and every one of us. May He guide me in the days to come.

## PRESS CONFERENCE #1

*The White House. March 8, 1933*

*His willingness to submit to spontaneous questioning gave the country an image of courage and candor. His ability to make news that dominated the front pages of the newspapers overcame the heavy editorial opposition his Administration ran into within a year or two. Under his humorous and masterly management, the press conference became a highly significant new instrument of Executive leadership.*

THE PRESIDENT: It is very good to see you all and my hope is that these conferences are going to be merely enlarged editions of the kind of very delightful family conferences I have been holding in Albany for the last four years.

I am told that what I am about to do will become impossible, but I am going to try it. We are not going to have any more written questions and of course while I cannot answer seventy-five or a hundred questions because I simply haven't got the physical time, I see no reason why I should not talk to you ladies and gentlemen off the record just the way I have been doing in Albany and the way I used to do it in the Navy Department down here. Quite a number of you, I am glad to see, date back to the days of the previous existence which I led in Washington.

(Interruption—"These two boys are off for Arizona." John and Franklin Roosevelt saying "good-bye".)

And so I think we will discontinue the practice of compelling the submitting of questions in writing before the conference in order to get an answer. There will be a great many questions, of course, that I won't answer, either because they are "if" questions—and I never answer them—and Brother Stephenson will tell you what an "if" question is—

MR. STEPHENSON: I ask forty of them a day.

THE PRESIDENT: And the others of course are the questions which for various reasons I don't want to discuss or I am not ready to discuss or I don't know anything about. There will be a great many questions you will ask about that I don't know enough about to answer.

Then, in regard to news announcements, Steve and I thought that it was best that street news for use out of here should be always without direct quotations. In other words, I don't want to be directly quoted, with the exception that direct quotations will be given out by Steve in writing. Of course that makes that perfectly clear.

Then there are two other matters we will talk about: The first is "background information", which means material which can be used by all of you on your own authority and responsibility and must not be attributed to the White House, because I don't want to have to revive the Ananias Club.

Then the second thing is the "off the record" information which means, of course, confidential information which is given only to those who attend the conference. Now there is one thing I want to say right now on which I think you will go along with me. I want to ask you not to repeat this "off the record" confidential information either to your own editors or associates who are not here because there is always the danger that while you people may not violate the rule, somebody may forget to say, "This is off the record and confidential", and the other party may use it in a story. That is to say, it is not to be used and not to be told to those fellows who happen not to come around to the conference. In other words, this is only for those present.

Now, as to news, I don't think there is any. (Laughter)

Steve reminds me that I have just signed the application for Associate Membership in the Press Club, which I am very happy to do.

Q: Will you go to Congress or send your message?

THE PRESIDENT: Sent it.

Q: When will it be available here for us?

THE PRESIDENT: Judging by the fact that I haven't started to write it, I should say at the very last minute possible. I shall let you have it as soon as I can. Of course it will be for release when transmitted. I doubt very much if you will get it very much more than half an hour before it is taken to the Capitol.

Q: Will it be brief?

THE PRESIDENT: The situation demands brevity.

Q: On the Hill they say you only recommend emergency stuff and that Congress will possibly adjourn next Monday or earlier and reconvene a short time after and take up permanent stuff as well as your complete program. Is that your idea of it?

THE PRESIDENT: I hope I can put it this way—and this comes under the second category—"background information" and "not off the record" because there is no reason why you should not use it in writing your stories. The general thought at the present time is that it is absolutely impossible by tomorrow to draft any complete or permanent legislation either on banking or on budget balancing or on anything else, because the situation, as you all know, is changing very much from day to day, so much so that if I were to ask for any specific and detailed legislation it might be that the details will have to be changed by a week from today and therefore it is necessary—I think you can make a pretty good guess—that I shall have to ask for fairly broad powers in regard to banking—such powers that would make it possible to meet the changing situation from day to day in different parts of the country. We cannot write a permanent banking act for the nation in three days. That is about the size of it.

Q: Do you favor national scrip or scrip issued by clearing houses?

THE PRESIDENT: Well, there again you are getting down to details and a very good illustration of why you cannot ask for too detailed legislation. About Monday, the day before yesterday, a very, very wide use of scrip seemed necessary and by last night it looked possible to avoid such a general use of scrip. But it does not mean that scrip will be eliminated by any means. Scrip may be used in many localities pending the working out of a sounder plan and more permanent plan to get additional currency into use. Now, I can't tell you any more about that, because we are still working on the details, but essentially it means an addition to the available currency.

Q: Could you comment on the report that no additional legislation is needed for the printing of additional currency; that a rider attached to the Home Loan Bank Bill provides for expansion to the extent of at least one and a half billion and that these Federal Reserve Bank notes are already being printed?

THE PRESIDENT: Frankly I don't know. I am inclined to think —and this answer is off the record because it is just a thought on my part—that separate legislation ought to be given on that instead of relying on some obscure clause in the Home Loan Bill. In other words, we want everything out on the table.

Q: You mentioned in your greetings to the Governors on Monday that you favored a unified banking system. Is that in your emergency plan?

THE PRESIDENT: That wasn't quite the way I put it to them. What I said to them was that it was necessary to treat the state and national banks the same way in this emergency so there would not be two different classes of banks in this country, and the other thing I said was to try to avoid forty-eight different plans of putting this into effect.

Q: Do I understand you are going to keep hold of this banking situation until permanent legislation is enacted?

THE PRESIDENT: Off the record answer, yes. . . .

Q: Shall we get ready to revive the term of "Controlled inflation?"

THE PRESIDENT: I wish somebody would invent a new term. I don't know what it is.

Q: May I ask if the long-time settlement of the banking situation is inter-meshed with the world economic conference?

THE PRESIDENT: I should say on that—background information—so far as banks go within the United States, no. So far as international exchange goes, yes. I think that is the easiest way of putting it. In other words, the opening of banks and the maintaining of banks once they are opened is not connected with the world economic conference.

Q: In your inaugural address, in which you only touched upon things, you said you are for sound and adequate—

THE PRESIDENT: I put it the other way around. I said "adequate but sound."

Q: Now that you have more time, can you define what that is?

THE PRESIDENT: No. In other words—and I should call this "off the record" information—you cannot define the thing too closely one way or the other. On Friday afternoon last we undoubtedly didn't have adequate currency. No question about that. There wasn't enough circulating money to go around.

Q: I believe that. (Laughter).

THE PRESIDENT: We hope that when the banks reopen a great deal of the currency that was withdrawn for one purpose or another will find its way back. We have got to provide an adequate currency. Last Friday we would have had to provide it in the form of scrip and probably some additional issues of Federal Bank notes. If things go along as we hope they will, the use of scrip can be very greatly curtailed and the amounts of new Federal Bank issues we hope can be also limited to a very great extent. In other words, what you are coming to now really is a managed currency, the adequateness of which will depend on the conditions of the moment. It may expand one week and it may contract another week. That part is all off the record.

Q: Can we use that part—managed?

THE PRESIDENT: No, I think not.

Q: That is a pretty good substitute for "controlled".

THE PRESIDENT: Go and ask [Secretary of the Treasury] Will Woodin about it.

Q: He's too busy.

Q: Now you came down to adequacy, but you haven't defined what you think is sound, or don't you want to define that now?

THE PRESIDENT: I don't want to define "sound" now. In other words, in its essence—this is entirely off the record—in its essence we must not put the Government any further in debt. Now, the real mark of delineation between sound and unsound is when the government starts to pay its bills by starting printing presses. That is about the size of it.

Q: Couldn't you take that out and give it to us. That's a very good thing at this time.

THE PRESIDENT: I don't think so. There may be some talk about it tomorrow.

Q: When you speak of a managed currency, do you speak of a temporary proposition or a permanent system?

THE PRESIDENT: It ought to be part of the permanent system —that is off the record—it ought to be part of the permanent system so we don't run into this thing again.

Q: Mr. President, you said there would be two or three other subjects considered at this special session of Congress?

THE PRESIDENT: There are going to be surprises. . . .

## LETTER TO SAMUEL I. ROSENMAN

*The White House. March 9, 1933*

*Judge Rosenman had acted as researcher and assistant to Governor Roosevelt in preparing speeches and messages. The Presi-*

*dent soon fell into the habit again of calling him for help. Unlike other members of the Brain Trust, Rosenman obtained very little publicity, but his association with Roosevelt was the longest of its kind.*

Dear Sammy:

I am waiting to hear what the Congress will do with my first bill. We worked until two o'clock this morning preparing it and it seemed queer to do this kind of work without you. After four years of such close association it is not easy to work with others.

I want you to know how grateful I am for the fine loyalty you have shown and for the unselfish service you gave me during the campaign. Even though you were not with me all the time I knew how hard you were working behind closed doors in smoke-filled rooms, and your contribution of Ray [Moley] and Rex [Tugwell] was probably the best that anyone made during the whole campaign.

I hardly need tell you that I want you to feel perfectly free to telephone or come to see me at any time. If I can be of help to you please let me know. I do hope that we will see you and Dorothy here in Washington often. Our contact has been too close to need constant correspondence or conversations. I just want you to know of my feeling toward you and my gratitude for all that you did.

As ever yours,

## LETTER TO ELEANOR ROOSEVELT

*The White House. March 17, 1933*

*On Saint Patrick's Day, 1905, President Theodore Roosevelt had reviewed the parade in New York City, given away his niece in marriage, and attracted away from the bride and groom all their guests at the reception. On their twenty-eighth anniversary, the groom found himself very busy.*

Dearest Babs:

After a fruitless week of thinking and lying awake to find whether you need or want undies, dresses, hats, shoes, sheets, towels, rouge, soup plates, candy, flowers, lamps, laxation pills, whisky, beer, etchings or caviar

I GIVE IT UP
!

And yet I know you lack some necessity of life—so go to it with my love and many happy returns of the day!

## MESSAGE TO CONGRESS PROPOSING THE TENNESSEE VALLEY AUTHORITY

*The White House. April 10, 1933*

*The banking crisis surmounted, Roosevelt bombarded Congress with proposals of the basic legislation of the First New Deal designed to achieve immediate recovery of prices, production and employment. But a few of his proposals transcended emergency needs and of these the TVA was probably the most far-reaching and successful.*

The continued idleness of a great national investment in the Tennessee Valley leads me to ask the Congress for legislation necessary to enlist this project in the service of the people.

It is clear that the Muscle Shoals development is but a small part of the potential public usefulness of the entire Tennessee River. Such use, if envisioned in its entirety, transcends mere power development: it enters the wide fields of flood control, soil erosion, afforestation, elimination from agricultural use of marginal lands, and distribution and diversification of industry. In short, this power development of war days leads logically to national planning for a complete river water shed involving many States and the future lives and welfare of millions. It touches and gives life to all forms of human concerns.

I, therefore, suggest to the Congress legislation to create a

Tennessee Valley Authority—a corporation clothed with the power of government but possessed of the flexibility and initiative of a private enterprise. It should be charged with the broadest duty of planning for the proper use, conservation and development of the natural resources of the Tennessee River drainage basin and its adjoining territory for the general social and economic welfare of the nation. This Authority should also be clothed with the necessary power to carry these plans into effect. Its duty should be the rehabilitation of the Muscle Shoals development and the coordination of it with the wider plan.

Many hard lessons have taught us the human waste that results from lack of planning. Here and there a few wise cities and counties have looked ahead and planned. But our nation has "just grown." It is time to extend planning to a wider field, in this instance comprehending in one great project many States directly concerned with the basin of one of our greatest rivers.

This in a true sense is a return to the spirit and vision of the pioneer. If we are successful here we can march on, step by step, in a like development of other great natural territorial units within our borders.

## PRESS CONFERENCE #11

*The White House. April 12, 1933*

*Struggling with the terms of industrial recovery legislation, the President exposed the thinking that eventually led to rejection of the National Industrial Recovery Act, not only by the Supreme Court because it gave the Executive too "wide latitude," but also by himself because it fostered monopoly—not by little sweater factories but by the leading corporations in the major branches of industry.*

Q: Will you give us the Administration's attitude toward the 30-hour bill?

THE PRESIDENT: I can tell you that as background. Miss Perkins and Secretary Roper and the Attorney General and I talked about it yesterday after the Cabinet meeting. I think we all felt that the bill must be given elasticity, without trying to tell the Congress the exact methods of elasticity. In other words, I told Miss Perkins that I thought it was better to tell the Congress that it should have a maximum number of hours of any particular number—whether 36, 42 or 44. I have not heard from her since she appeared before the committee.

Q: I think she did not appear yesterday; she is going up today.

Q: Has any decision been reached about prohibiting the importation of foreign goods made in factories that do not work thirty hours?

THE PRESIDENT: We did not mention it. I have not discussed it at all. That would be one of the phases to come up.

Q: It is satisfactory to you in principle, is it not, Mr. President?

THE PRESIDENT: It is pretty broad to say that. In other words, the question is whether, on the administration of the bill, the Administration is given a pretty wide latitude. It depends on the width of the latitude as to whether we approve it in principle or not. We do approve this in principle and I think we should. We are making two rather definite efforts. The first is to spread employment over a very large number of people as, for instance, in certain factories and certain industries where the work can be spread out over a larger number of people. The second principle is to prevent any one individual, man, woman or child, from working too many hours at a time in any twenty-four hours. Then there is a third principle involved which we have only discussed in a tentative way and that is whether the Government should try to spread work within a given industry over the whole industry and to prevent the concentration in the hands of any one or two units of the industry of all the work. Well, the simplest illustration is a story that was told me the other day. There was a certain little sweater factory in a little town—I won't even give you the location of it —where they normally employed only about 200 people. It was the only industry in town. The owners of the little sweater

factory and the employees had always been on exceedingly
good terms. It was difficult to sell enough sweaters to keep
them going because there were so many sweater factories. So,
the owners and the employees got together and talked the
situation over. They only had about six weeks' work in the
whole past year and all the other sweater factories in the
country had about the same kind of work—about six weeks out
of the year. Well, the result was the population in this little
town was practically starving to death. So they got together
and decided that the thing they wanted to do was to work,
even though it would be at much reduced pay. So they figured
out that if they could cut their wages 33 per cent they could
cut the cost of making these sweaters by the same amount
and in that way undersell every other sweater factory. So they
agreed to do that for a six months' period.

The selling agent went down to New York and in 24 hours,
on the new prices, based on a cut of 33 per cent, he sold
enough sweaters to keep that factory going for 6 months, 24
hours a day, 3 shifts. Now, of course that is bad business, in
all ways. In the first place, it cuts the scale of wages and the
scale of living. Of course, they get a good deal of cash into the
community because they have got three shifts working. But
the worst feature of it is that they undoubtedly, by taking
these orders, put two other sweater factories completely out of
business.

Now, that brings up the question as to whether we can work
out some kind of a plan that will distribute the volume of
consumption in a given industry over the whole industry. Instead of trying to concentrate production to meet that consumption into the hands of a small portion of the industry, we
want to spread it out.

Miss Perkins is going to talk to them about that feature of it.
There are a great many legal questions and a good many constitutional questions, and a good many questions as to whether
the Federal Government should embark on that. However, I
think it is fair to say that that might be called a step that looks
forward. It might be called the regulation of production or,

to put it better, the prevention of foolish over-production. It is a pretty important subject and I think about all we can say at the present time is that we are exploring it. . . .

## *"BOMBSHELL MESSAGE" TO THE LONDON ECONOMIC CONFERENCE*

*July 3, 1933*

*Preparations for the United States to join in measures of international economic cooperation had been made by President Hoover as well as by Roosevelt himself. But at the last moment he decided that domestic recovery of prices would be stimulated by further reduction of the gold value of the dollar, while France insisted that stabilization of currencies must precede agreements on tariffs and other problems. This Message therefore wrecked the Conference. In 1936, after considerable recovery of American prices and production had been achieved, Roosevelt agreed to currency stabilization with Great Britain and France.*

I would regard it as a catastrophe amounting to a world tragedy if the great Conference of Nations, called to bring about a more real and permanent financial stability and a greater prosperity to the masses of all nations, should, in advance of any serious effort to consider these broader problems, allow itself to be diverted by the proposal of a purely artificial and temporary experiment affecting the monetary exchange of a few nations only. Such action, such diversion, shows a singular lack of proportion and a failure to remember the larger purposes for which the Economic Conference was called together.

I do not relish the thought that insistence on such action should be made an excuse for the continuance of the basic economic errors that underlie so much of the present world wide depression.

The world will not long be lulled by the specious fallacy of achieving a temporary and probably an artificial stability in foreign exchange on the part of a few large countries only.

The sound internal economic system of a nation is a greater factor in its well being than the price of its currency in changing terms of the currencies of other nations. . . .

The Conference was called to better and perhaps to cure fundamental economic ills. It must not be diverted from that effort.

## RADIO ADDRESS ON THE RECOVERY PROGRAM

*The White House. July 24, 1933*

*The President relied on "fireside chats" to explain and win support for his policies. This one clarified the mass of new laws enacted since March 4, and launched the "Blue Eagle" campaign for compliance with the National Industrial Recovery Act.*

After the adjournment of the historical special session of the Congress five weeks ago I purposely refrained from addressing you for two very good reasons.

First, I think that we all wanted the opportunity of a little quiet thought to examine and assimilate in a mental picture the crowding events of the hundred days which had been devoted to the starting of the wheels of the New Deal.

Secondly, I wanted a few weeks in which to set up the new administrative organization and to see the first fruits of our careful planning.

I think it will interest you if I set forth the fundamentals of this planning for national recovery; and this I am very certain will make it abundantly clear to you that all of the proposals and all of the legislation since the fourth day of March have not been just a collection of haphazard schemes but rather the orderly component parts of a connected and logical whole.

Long before Inauguration Day I became convinced that individual effort and local effort and even disjointed Federal effort had failed and of necessity would fail and, therefore, that a rounded leadership by the Federal Government had become a necessity both of theory and of fact. Such leadership, however, had its beginning in preserving and strengthening the credit of the United States Government, because without that no leadership was a possibility. For years the Government had not lived within its income. The immediate task was to bring our regular expenses within our revenues. That has been done.

It may seem inconsistent for a government to cut down its regular expenses and at the same time to borrow and to spend billions for an emergency. But it is not inconsistent because a large portion of the emergency money has been paid out in the form of sound loans which will be repaid to the Treasury over a period of years; and to cover the rest of the emergency money we have imposed taxes to pay the interest and the installments on that part of the debt.

So you will see that we have kept our credit good. We have built a granite foundation in a period of confusion. That foundation of the Federal credit stands there broad and sure. It is the base of the whole recovery plan.

Then came the part of the problem that concerned the credit of the individual citizens themselves. You and I know of the banking crisis and of the great danger to the savings of our people. On March sixth every national bank was closed. One month later 90 per cent of the deposits in the national banks had been made available to the depositors. Today only about 5 per cent of the deposits in national banks are still tied up. The condition relating to state banks, while not quite so good on a percentage basis, is showing a steady reduction in the total of frozen deposits—a result much better than we had expected three months ago.

The problem of the credit of the individual was made more difficult because of another fact. The dollar was a different dollar from the one with which the average debt had been incurred. For this reason large numbers of people were actually losing possession of and title to their farms and homes. All of you know the financial steps which have been taken to correct this inequality. In addition the Home Loan Act, the Farm Loan Act and the Bankruptcy Act were passed.

It was a vital necessity to restore purchasing power by reducing the debt and interest charges upon our people, but while we were helping people to save their credit it was at the same time absolutely essential to do something about the physical needs of hundreds of thousands who were in dire straits at that very moment. Municipal and State aid were being stretched to the limit. We appropriated half a billion dollars to supplement their efforts and in addition, as you know, we have put 300,000 young men into practical and useful work in our forests and to prevent flood and soil erosion. The wages they earn are going in greater part to the support of the nearly one million people who constitute their families.

In this same classification we can properly place the great public works program running to a total of over three billion dollars—to be used for highways and ships and flood prevention and inland navigation and thousands of self-sustaining state and municipal improvements. Two points should be made clear in the allotting and administration of these projects —first, we are using the utmost care to choose labor creating quick-acting, useful projects, avoiding the smell of the pork barrel; and secondly, we are hoping that at least half of the money will come back to the government from projects which will pay for themselves over a period of years.

Thus far I have spoken primarily of the foundation stones— the measures that were necessary to re-establish credit and to head people in the opposite direction by preventing distress and providing as much work as possible through governmental agencies. Now I come to the links which will build us a more lasting prosperity. I have said that we cannot attain that in a nation half boom and half broke. If all of our people have work and fair wages and fair profits, they can buy the products of their neighbors and business is good. But if you take away the wages and the profits of half of them, business is only half as good. It doesn't help much if the fortunate half is very prosperous—the best way is for everybody to be reasonably prosperous.

For many years the two great barriers to a normal prosperity

have been low farm prices and the creeping paralysis of unemployment. These factors have cut the purchasing power of
the country in half. I promised action. Congress did its part
when it passed the farm and the industrial recovery acts. Today we are putting these two acts to work and they will work
if people understand their plain objectives.

First, the Farm Act: It is based on the fact that the purchasing power of nearly half our population depends on adequate prices for farm products. We have been producing more
of some crops than we consume or can sell in a depressed
world market. The cure is not to produce so much. Without
our help the farmers cannot get together and cut production,
and the Farm Bill gives them a method of bringing their production down to a reasonable level and of obtaining reasonable prices for their crops. I have clearly stated that this
method is in a sense experimental, but so far as we have gone
we have reason to believe that it will produce good results.

It is obvious that if we can greatly increase the purchasing
power of the tens of millions of our people who make a living
from farming and the distribution of farm crops, we will
greatly increase the consumption of those goods which are
turned out by industry.

That brings me to the final step—bringing back industry
along sound lines.

Last Autumn, on several occasions, I expressed my faith that
we can make possible by democratic self-discipline in industry
general increases in wages and shortening of hours sufficient
to enable industry to pay its own workers enough to let those
workers buy and use the things that their labor produces. This
can be done only if we permit and encourage cooperative
action in industry because it is obvious that without united
action a few selfish men in each competitive group will pay
starvation wages and insist on long hours of work. Others in
that group must either follow suit or close up shop. We have
seen the result of action of that kind in the continuing descent
into the economic Hell of the past four years.

There is a clear way to reverse that process: If all employers in each competitive group agree to pay their workers the same wages—reasonable wages—and require the same hours—reasonable hours—then higher wages and shorter hours will hurt no employer. Moreover, such action is better for the employer than unemployment and low wages, because it makes more buyers for his product. That is the simple idea which is the very heart of the Industrial Recovery Act.

On the basis of this simple principle of everybody doing things together, we are starting out on this nation-wide attack on unemployment. It will succeed if our people understand it —in the big industries, in the little shops, in the great cities and in the small villages. There is nothing complicated about it and there is nothing particularly new in the principle. It goes back to the basic idea of society and of the nation itself that people acting in a group can accomplish things which no individual acting alone could even hope to bring about.

Here is an example. In the Cotton Textile Code and in other agreements already signed, child labor has been abolished. That makes me personally happier than any other one thing with which I have been connected since I came to Washington. In the textile industry—an industry which came to me spontaneously and with a splendid cooperation as soon as the recovery act was signed,—child labor was an old evil. But no employer acting alone was able to wipe it out. If one employer tried it, or if one state tried it, the costs of operation rose so high that it was impossible to compete with the employers or states which had failed to act. The moment the Recovery Act was passed, this monstrous thing which neither opinion nor law could reach through years of effort went out in a flash. As a British editorial put it, we did more under a Code in one day than they in England had been able to do under the common law in eighty-five years of effort. I use this incident, my friends, not to boast of what has already been done but to point the way to you for even greater cooperative efforts this Summer and Autumn.

We are not going through another Winter like the last. I doubt if ever any people so bravely and cheerfully endured a season half so bitter. We cannot ask America to continue to face such needless hardships. It is time for courageous action, and the Recovery Bill gives us the means to conquer unemployment with exactly the same weapon that we have used to strike down Child Labor.

The proposition is simply this:

If all employers will act together to shorten hours and raise wages we can put people back to work. No employer will suffer, because the relative level of competitive cost will advance by the same amount for all. But if any considerable group should lag or shirk, this great opportunity will pass us by and we will go into another desperate Winter. This must not happen.

We have sent out to all employers an agreement which is the result of weeks of consultation. This agreement checks against the voluntary codes of nearly all the large industries which have already been submitted. This blanket agreement carries the unanimous approval of the three boards which I have appointed to advise in this, boards representing the great leaders in labor, in industry, and in social service. The agreement has already brought a flood of approval from every State, and from so wide a cross-section of the common calling of industry that I know it is fair for all. It is a plan—deliberate, reasonable and just—intended to put into effect at once the most important of the broad principles which are being established, industry by industry, through codes. Naturally, it takes a good deal of organizing and a great many hearings and many months, to get these codes perfected and signed, and we cannot wait for all of them to go through. The blanket agreements, however, which I am sending to every employer will start the wheels turning now, and not six months from now.

There are, of course, men, a few of them who might thwart this great common purpose by seeking selfish advantage. There are adequate penalties in the law, but I am now asking the cooperation that comes from opinion and from conscience. These are the only instruments we shall use in this great summer offensive against unemployment. But we shall use them to the limit to protect the willing from the laggard and to make the plan succeed.

In war, in the gloom of night attack, soldiers wear a bright badge on their shoulders to be sure that comrades do not fire on comrades. On that principle, those who cooperate in this program must know each other at a glance. That is why we have provided a badge of honor for this purpose, a simple design with a legend, "We do our part," and I ask that all those who join with me shall display that badge prominently. It is essential to our purpose.

Already all the great, basic industries have come forward willingly with proposed codes, and in these codes they accept the principles leading to mass reemployment. But, important as is this heartening demonstration, the richest field for results is among the small employers, those whose contribution will give new work for from one to ten people. These smaller employers are indeed a vital part of the backbone of the country, and the success of our plans lies largely in their hands.

Already the telegrams and letters are pouring into the White House—messages from employers who ask that their names be placed on this special Roll of Honor. They represent great corporations and companies, and partnerships and individuals. I ask that even before the dates set in the agreements which we have sent out, the employers of the country who have not already done so—the big fellows and the little fellows—shall at once write or telegraph to me personally at the White House, expressing their intention of going through with the plan. And it is my purpose to keep posted in the postoffice of every town, a Roll of Honor of all those who join with me.

I want to take this occasion to say to the twenty-four governors who are now in conference in San Francisco, that nothing thus far has helped in strengthening this great movement more than their resolutions adopted at the very outset of their meeting, giving this plan their instant and unanimous approval, and pledging to support it in their states.

To the men and women whose lives have been darkened by

the fact or the fear of unemployment, I am justified in saying a word of encouragement because the codes and the agreements already approved, or about to be passed upon, prove that the plan does raise wages, and that it does put people back to work. You can look on every employer who adopts the plan as one who is doing his part, and those employers deserve well of everyone who works for a living. It will be clear to you, as it is to me, that while the shirking employer may undersell his competitor, the saving he thus makes is made at the expense of his country's welfare.

While we are making this great common effort there should be no discord and dispute. This is no time to cavil or to question the standard set by this universal agreement. It is time for patience and understanding and cooperation. The workers of this country have rights under this law which cannot be taken from them, and nobody will be permitted to whittle them away but, on the other hand, no aggression is now necessary to attain those rights. The whole country will be united to get them for you. The principle that applies to the employers applies to the workers as well, and I ask you workers to cooperate in the same spirit.

When Andrew Jackson, "Old Hickory," died, someone asked, "Will he go to Heaven," and the answer was, "He will if he wants to." If I am asked whether the American people will pull themselves out of this depression, I answer, "They will if they want to." The essence of the plan is a universal limitation of hours of work per week for any individual by common consent, and a universal payment of wages above a minimum, also by comment consent. I cannot guarantee the success of this nation-wide plan, but the people of this country can guarantee its success. I have no faith in "cure-alls" but I believe that we can greatly influence economic forces. I have no sympathy with the professional economists who insist that things must run their course and that human agencies can have no influence on economic ills. One reason is that I happen to know that professional economists have changed their definition of economic laws every five or ten years for a very long time, but

I do have faith, and retain faith, in the strength of common purpose, and in the strength of unified action taken by the American people.

That is why I am describing to you the simple purposes and the solid foundations upon which our program of recovery is built. That is why I am asking the employers of the Nation to sign this common covenant with me—to sign it in the name of patriotism and humanity. That is why I am asking the workers to go along with us in a spirit of understanding and of helpfulness.

## PRESS CONFERENCE #38

*Hyde Park. August 2, 1933*
*While the first influx of New Deal administrators suffered in the Washington heat, the President indulged the reporters' sense of humor.*

Q: We understand you are going to be invited out to Vassar Friday afternoon.

THE PRESIDENT: This is wholly off the record. What I want to do is to go out to Vassar and go to the School of Euthenics. Did I ever tell you the story of the School of Euthenics? This is one thousand per cent off the record. When I was elected to the Board about 1924 and went to my first meeting in the Commodore Hotel in New York, there was present the Board of Trustees consisting of perhaps eight or ten eminent gentlemen and women from very prominent families. President McCracken presided at the Board of Trustees. He got up and announced various gifts that the College had had, and among others he announced the gift of the new Euthenics Building. I need not tell you the name of the donor other than to say that he was well known to us all and very beloved by all of us. Whereupon, being very innocent, I said, "Mr. President, would you mind telling me what the purpose of this building is or, I should say, what are euthenics? I never heard the word in my life." Well, McCracken got up and he waved at a lady sitting beside me. She was a very wonderful looking lady, she looked like a million dollars and had on half a million dollars worth of jewelry. So the lady looks at me and puts a lorgnette to her eyes and says, "Perhaps if Mr. Roosevelt were familiar with his Greek, he would realize that the word, 'euthenics', comes from 'eu', meaning 'well' and the word 'thenics', meaning 'the sense of living'. In other words, it means 'the sense of good living.'" And she sat down.

Well, I was properly and completely squelched. Then one of my fellow trustees alongside of me leaned over and said, "What she means is 'home economics'." (Laughter)

The building was given by a very marvelous lady who was, I think, connected with the Cadillac Motor Company out at Detroit. Well, I went down to see the building in its first summer of operation. I drove into the grounds and there, on the grass plot, I saw, oh, there must have been twenty long-haired men and short-haired women in a circle on the grass. In the middle of the circle were two unfortunate children, one about one year old and the other about two years old, and the motions of the children were being watched to see what they meant. So, if you want a real thrill, go down and watch the Class in Euthenics. (Laughter)

Q: That is something else to do in Poughkeepsie.

Q: You know, Mr. President, Ed Roddan has been trying to get up over the wall, but now he will have an opportunity to go through the gates. (Laughter) . . .

## LETTER TO JAMES A. FARLEY

*The White House. August 17, 1933*

*The President, an ardent stamp collector, particularly enjoyed dabbling in the province of his Postmaster General. Sometimes he helped design new stamps.*

Dear Jim:

Thank you for the N.R.A. postage stamp and cover. The honest farmer, who looks like me; the honest business man, who looks like Grover T. Whalen; and the honest blacksmith, who looks like Lionel Barrymore, are magnificent. But Oh Heavens what a girl! She is wearing a No. 11 shoe, also a bustle, and if recovery is dependent on women like that I am agin recovery.

In spite of the above, it is a grand stamp, gotten out in record time, and will do worlds of good. Congratulations!

Sincerely,

## PRESS CONFERENCE #54 ✓

*The White House. September 21, 1933*

*Poverty in the midst of plenty was the most painful paradox of the depression.*

THE PRESIDENT: I have got quite an important thing here that I thought you would like to see. . . . (*Reading*)

"The President today announced a program to help correct one of the most flagrant maladjustments of American economic well-being. Through his action much of the oversupply of important foodstuffs will be placed in the hands of the destitute unemployed who are living on the short shift of public unemployment relief."

In other words, there are lots of places, like West Virginia, where they give a definite amount to a father and a mother and five children to last for a week and it just cannot be done. That is the standard in some municipalities, so this is in addition to that. (*Reading*)

"Following conferences with Secretary of Agriculture Henry A. Wallace, George N. Peek, Agricultural Adjustment Administrator, and Harry L. Hopkins, Federal Emergency Relief Administrator, the President announced that the Agricultural Adjustment Administration is preparing to make further purchases of surpluses for distribution by the Federal Emergency Relief Administration to the unemployed in the various States.

"The announcement followed the recent allocation by Mr.

Hopkins of 100,000,000 pounds of cured pork which had been processed recently from millions of hogs purchased from surpluses by the Agricultural Adjustment Administration. The meat will go to the various State relief administrations for distribution to the unemployed on their relief rolls.

"Additional products under consideration for similar handling include, among others, beef, dairy and poultry products, and products of cotton and cotton seed.

"There are approximately 3,500,000 families now on relief rolls throughout the country. It is known that even with recent improvements in relief administration resulting in higher standards of relief, the amounts of food and clothing given the destitute are still inadequate. On the other hand, in large part, because these millions of potential consumers are not able to purchase a normal amount of commodities, huge surpluses of basic food products are glutting the markets and making their production unprofitable to farmers.

"By using funds of the Agricultural Adjustment Administration, supplemented by those of the Federal Emergency Relief Administration, and the nation-wide network of State and local relief administrations for distribution, a real effort to bridge the gap between supplies and consumption will be made. In this way two major objectives of the Recovery Program will be promoted—feeding and clothing the unemployed more adequately and hastening the agricultural recovery.

"It was emphasized that the commodities given the unemployed will be in addition to amounts they are now receiving, wherever they are now inadequate, for the purpose of giving them reasonable standards of sustenance. They will add to and not replace items of relief already provided.

"In removing the surpluses from the market, carefully applied safeguards will forestall any disturbance of the regular channels of production, processing, and distribution.

"The President said he considered the program arranged between the Agricultural Adjustment Administration and the Federal Emergency Relief Administration one of the most direct blows at the economic paradox which has choked farms with an abundance of farm products while many of the unemployed have gone hungry. He has directed the departments concerned to expedite in every possible way their combined attack on the food-surplus and hunger problems."

The two go right together.

"While this joint effort is being made to increase domestic consumption of surplus farm products, the Agricultural Adjustment Administration will intensify its program of preventing accumulation of farm surpluses so great that they cannot be consumed, but result only in ruinous prices to farmers, destroying purchasing power and aggravating rural and urban distress."

. . . You see, it is a double-barreled thing. It improves relief tremendously. Especially, we will try to improve it where the relief is now inadequate, such as in many of the coal mining areas, and where it is not even adequate in a great many places to sustain life. Then the second thing, of course, is that it is going to help materially in reducing the large surpluses, overhanging things. . . .

You see, here is another thing: The supply of clothing, this says, has been actually inadequate in a great many places in relief work. As a matter of fact, they have not had any supply of clothing. For instance, there is a story, off the record. You know Miss Hickok [Miss Lorena A. Hickok]? She went down, for Hopkins' department, I think it was somewhere around Southeastern Kentucky. She got into one of those mining towns and came around a corner of an alley and started to walk up the alley. There was a group of miners sitting in front of the shacks, and they pulled down their caps over their faces. As soon as she caught sight of that she walked up and said, "What is the matter? What are you pulling your caps down for?" They said, "Oh, it is all right." "Why pull your caps down?" They said, "It is a sort of custom to pull caps down because so many of the women have not enough clothes to cover them."

Now, we are going to buy a lot of cotton and have it processed and provide clothes—I mean, have it manufactured into cotton cloth. Now, that means organizing local—that means organizing groups to sew it together into clothing. . . .

## LETTER TO EDWARD M. HOUSE

*Warm Springs. November 21, 1933*

*The President had great confidence in the wisdom of this famous adviser and diplomatic agent of President Wilson. O. W. M. Sprague of the Treasury Department was a former adviser of the Bank of England. On this day he resigned in protest against Roosevelt's policy of buying gold at increasing dollar prices in order to stimulate a rise in commodity prices. The "meeting" suggested by Sprague was held at Carnegie Hall, New York, to protest the same policy. On November 25, Al Smith announced, "I am for gold dollars as against baloney dollars." The honeymoon of the new Administration was ending.*

My dear Friend:

Dan [Roper] showed me your letter, and the next day I sent for the Sprague person. To tell you the honest truth I had had no intention of hurting Sprague's feelings by not sending for him, but equally honestly I did not send for him because of the very simple reason that I had entirely forgotten his existence for at least a month!

On several occasions after his return from London, I had long talks with him and tried to get from him some concrete proposal or suggestion which would help us to lift the price level and therefore the debt burden under which the Country, especially the West and South, was staggering. He gave me absolutely no constructive thought—only the same old suggestions about open market purchases and stabilization of the dollar with the pound. Everyone who is not blind knows that the open market purchases have practically no immediate effect and only a very doubtful long-range effect; also that every time stabilization on the old level of about $4.50 was mentioned, cotton, wheat, corn and everything else started to go down. A continuation of the fall of the price level which ran from the middle of September to the middle of October would have brought the whole Recovery Program toppling about our ears.

Sprague is a nuisance. He carries no real weight except with the Bank of England crowd and some of our New York City bankers, and I regard his suggestion of a meeting as absolutely disloyal. In any event, I kept him from formally delivering a silly letter to me, had Woodin talk with him and subsequently Morgenthau, Jr. Sprague has said that if he resigned, Government bonds would go down five points!

Now let me tell you something cheerful. This Southland has a smile on its face. Ten cent cotton has stopped foreclosures, saved banks and started people definitely on the upgrade. That means all the way from Virginia to Texas. Sears-Roebuck sales in Georgia are 110 per cent above 1932.

Another angle: Hugh Johnson has just telephoned me to be sure to read the latest Dun & Bradstreet Report. He says every section of the country is showing definite gain.

I had a nice talk with Jack Morgan the other day and he seemed more worried about Tugwell's speech than about anything else, especially when Tugwell said, "From now on property rights and financial rights will be subordinated to human rights." J.P.M. did not seem much troubled over the gold purchasing, and confessed that he had been completely misled in regard to the Federal expenditures.

The real truth of the matter is, as you and I know, that a financial element in the larger centers has owned the Government ever since the days of Andrew Jackson—and I am not wholly excepting the Administration of W. W. The country is going through a repetition of Jackson's fight with the Bank of the United States—only on a far bigger and broader basis.

I am having a grand rest and am catching up on much needed sleep. Take care of yourself and do write me soon.

Always sincerely,

## LETTER TO GEORGE A. OLSON

*December 12, 1933*

*The ability of the President and Mrs. Roosevelt to convince people of their genuine interest brought forth floods of letters like this one from George A. Olson of Ridgeland, Wisconsin, November 10, 1933:*

*Dear Madam:—First please excuse this quality paper & pencil but this is best I had. I have heard you & President Roosevelt over the Radio as well as some of your writings and it has appealed to me. Though I dont agree with our Presidents way of handling the farm problems I have lots of respect for him. Though I am on strike, holding my milk Potatoes, live stock and etc for better price. Potatoes was selling at 70 cents per cwt. I have been holding a few beef cows hoping for better price If I sold now I'd get about $7.00 to $10.00 a head. and Uncle Sam buying canned beef for consumption in civilian conservation camps. That's a tradgety to me. These cows of mine would of been worth from $100, to $120 apiece a few year ago. I am trying to hold my farm and get food for my children but it is hard this year. Money is scarce and hard to get. and everything has gone up. last year I bought 49 lbs sack of Pillsbury flour for $1.10 now it is $1.95. I bought an overall Jacket for my six year old boy & It cost 89 cents. Uncle Sam in 1926 adjusted our Foreign debts on the following bases scaled them down 57% gave them 62 year to pay it in, and charged them 1.625 per cent interest annually and 1.64 per cent to be applied annually. England paying a fraction of this. but the Farmer must pay in full at big interest I am sending you a couple of clippings of interest. I suppose this letter will be considered a crank letter and be throwed into waist basket and still it may not. I have one request read this letter to the President and these clippings Please. Respectfully George A. Olson.*

*Mrs. Roosevelt sent the letter to the President with this note: "I hardly know what we could say to this farmer. It is important to say the right thing as he is one of those on strike. His letter is moderate in tone."*

My dear Mr. Olson:

Mrs. Roosevelt has shown me your letter, and I want you to know that I am glad you wrote to her and to me. You are absolutely right that many things which the farmers raise have not by any means reached a proper level or one which will put the farmer back to a reasonable parity of purchasing power with other people.

As you know, we are trying out a good many different methods for the building up of prices and values. We have succeeded in part, as is shown by the much better prices for wheat, corn and cotton than existed a year ago or last spring. I raise cattle myself down in Georgia and I know what 5 or 5½ cents a pound means. When the Agricultural Adjustment Act was passed last spring we wanted cattle classed as one of the basic agricultural commodities, but the Senate struck it out, and therefore we have not had the legal machinery to try to improve the cattle situation.

All I can ask you to do is to believe that we are honestly trying to do our best, and that we think we are slowly but surely improving conditions.

Very sincerely yours,

## PRESS CONFERENCE #125

*The White House. May 25, 1934*

*Early in 1934, the National Recovery Administration ran into heavy criticism as an instrument of monopoly. Prices and production were rising but employment and wages were not keeping pace. Employers avoided the intent of NIRA, Section 7A, by organizing company unions to "represent" their employees. Independent unions, often pushed by rank-and-file groups, turned to militant strike tactics. Senator Wagner and others wanted to put teeth into Section 7A. The President slowly moved from faith in the NIRA idea of cooperation between business and labor under business leadership towards sympathy with organized labor.*

Q: Mr. President, anything you care to say about the strike situation?

THE PRESIDENT: I don't think so. I think I had better not. It is awfully difficult to say anything without going into details and differentiations. I think it is probably better I should not. We are all working on it, as you know.

Q: You still need legislation of the type of the Wagner bill dealing with this?

THE PRESIDENT: It would be very helpful. There is no question about it but it would be very helpful because it would clarify administrative procedure and at the same time would create methods that were perfectly clear under the law. In the individual strike cases people would know on both sides exactly the procedure, who they come under and to whom they go and what authority there is in any given case.

Q: Is it fair to assume, then, that you want this legislation this Session?

THE PRESIDENT: I would like to have it very much. I think it would be helpful. I think you had better put this off the record.

Q: What you are saying now?

THE PRESIDENT: Yes, what I am saying now. It would be perfectly all right to say I am in favor of this legislation and hope it will go through but, off the record, you all know that in any period of this kind you are bound to have, with a return of prosperity and a return of reemployment and an increase in values, more strikes. I look for a great many strikes in the course of this Summer, a good many more. It is a normal and logical thing. I think I have said this before at a strike conference. They are brought about by a great many causes. For instance, keeping this again entirely off the record, in this Toledo case, the strike originated with only 400 employees in one factory but there are a lot of other factors involved. They had pretty serious political trouble where a lot of graft and misgovernment, etc., was shown in the city. The result was that the population as a whole got sore. It wasn't just these 400 men.

Yesterday, when this crowd of between 5,000 and 10,000 people started, they were, as a body, sore at certain definite people. As they got along, throwing stones, they would throw stones at one particular factory or shop and then they would go along past several other factories or shops they were not sore at and then they would pick out the next fellow at whom they were sore.

Charlie Taft telephoned to Miss Perkins about two hours ago and made the point that it is not an indiscriminatory strike, it is a strike against people they are sore at and it is not just the 400 strikers, it is a very large element of the population.

So each case really has to be taken up on the merits of that particular, individual case. There is no general statement that can be made relating to it. Miss Perkins used a parallel which, of course, has got to be entirely off the record. She said in conference today that it is not a general revolutionary feeling but a feeling against certain old-line politicians and a feeling against certain industrialists. It is a pretty discriminating opposition. It is based on reason of some kind.

In the Toledo situation, of course, the one thing that all of us ought to appreciate and write about is that there are methods of settlement and that the attitude of employers in many cases has been so autocratic. Take, for instance, the man in one of the papers this morning who said that he would consider that he was demeaning himself if he sat in the same room with William Green. Now that kind of autocratic attitude on the part of a steel company official does not make for working things out. On the other hand, there are people on the other end of the camp, the labor end, who are just as autocratic. . . .

## LETTER TO ELEANOR ROOSEVELT

*Aboard* U.S.S. Houston. *July 5, 1934*

*The President took the occasion of a vacation cruise to announce the end of the United States protectorate over the Republic of Haiti.*

Dearest Babs:

The Lord only knows when this will catch up with my Will o' the Wisp wife, but at least I am proceeding according to schedule, and it is a grand trip thus far. Yesterday we had a good day's fishing, stopping for 9 hours in the S.E. Bahamas, and F[ranklin, Jr.] and J[ohn] and I all got fish. . . .

Today's ceremony at Cap Haitien was most colorful and interesting. A gayly decorated barge, specially built up to let us go on it from a gangplank conveyed us to a specially built landing where stood President Vincent and his whole cabinet, with the Garde d'Haiti drawn up behind and a huge crowd of cheering populace lining the quays and the roofs. Vincent and I drove through many streets and a good many of the buildings date back to Spanish and French days—then to the Club where there was a reception, a speech and toast by Vincent and a speech and toast by me—part in French, but when I got to the serious part I shifted to English!

When we first anchored F. and J. went right ashore and drove to the Palace of Christopher Sans Souci and saw the "Citadel" from the foot of the mountains. They rejoined me at the Club and we all returned to the Houston and received Vincent and his cabinet for a 15 minute return call. Many guns and much ceremony all day but I hope it will do good to Haiti and that they won't start revolting as soon as we withdraw the last marines on Aug. 15th. Perhaps the Haitians will recognize the vast amount of good things we have done for them in these 18 years. The *people* do, but the ruling mulatto class doesn't, I fear. . . .

Ever so much love and do take very good care of yourself.

Your devoted,

## PRESS CONFERENCE #137

*The White House. August 24, 1934*

*Growing opposition to the New Deal led Al Smith and a group of conservative Democrats to join leading businessmen in organizing the American Liberty League.*

Q: Anything you can say on the formation of the American Liberty League? Anything to say about it? . . .

THE PRESIDENT: . . . I suppose you can use this for background, the thing to note about an organization of this kind—of course there are a great many of them, with all kinds of names—you will find in history organizations of this kind that are fraternal and semi-religious, and everything else. Personally, my own feeling is this: that when you come down to the definition of American principles you want to go the whole hog; you want to go all the way, instead of stopping short. An organization that only advocates two or three out of the Ten Commandments, may be a perfectly good organization in the sense that you couldn't object to the two or three out of the Ten Commandments, but that it would have certain shortcomings in having failed to advocate the other seven or eight Commandments. To put it again in a Biblical way, it has been said that there are two great Commandments—one is to love God, and the other to love your neighbor. A gentleman with a rather ribald sense of humor suggested that the two particular tenets of this new organization say you shall love God and then forget your neighbor, and he also raised the question as to whether the other name for their God was not "property." Now as a matter of fact these two things are worth reading. One is that the organization will designate officials that will teach the necessity of respect for the rights of persons and property as fundamental to every successful form of government, and will teach that government to encourage enterprise.

Going back again, there isn't much said about your neighbor, and if you analyze certain things in the Declaration of Independence which helped opportunity—life, liberty and the pursuit of happiness—there are quite a number of other things that the average, and more than average human, gets out of government besides these two things. There is no mention made here in these two things about the concern of the community, in other words the Government, to try to make it possible for people who are willing to work, to find work to do. For people who want to keep themselves from starvation, keep a roof over their heads, lead decent lives, have proper educational standards, those are the concerns of government, besides these two points, and another thing which isn't mentioned, and that is the protection of the life and the liberty of the individual against elements in the community that seek to enrich or advance themselves at the expense of their fellow-citizens. They have just as much right to protection by government as anybody else. I don't believe that any further comment is necessary after this, what would you call it—a homily? Except that in the *Times* this morning—I lay in bed and laughed for ten minutes—if you will turn to the financial page of the *Times,* "Topics In Wall Street"; that has a short paragraph—one that appealed to me. Darned good too, most of them, because they give you a real highlight on what's going on, and there was one paragraph that started off like this—I forget the exact phraseology—"The speculative fraternity in Wall Street regards the new American Liberty League as a direct answer from Heaven to their prayer."

Q: Do you subscribe to the view of Secretary Ickes that this will draw lines pretty sharply between liberals and reactionaries?

THE PRESIDENT: I don't want to say anything about it. . . .

# ANNUAL MESSAGE TO CONGRESS

*January 4, 1935*

*This Message announced a turn in the President's domestic policy. Besides some agricultural improvement, only industrial production, prices and profits showed substantial gains to date. Henceforth labor, the unemployed, and less advantaged groups of farmers were to be the chief beneficiaries of legislation and planning, while the privileges of business and the wealthy were to be reduced. Roosevelt's decision to launch this new "security program," rather than invalidation by the Supreme Court of early New Deal laws (all of which, except the pro-business features of NIRA, were re-enacted and found constitutional), produced a Second New Deal.*

Mr. President, Mr. Speaker, Members of the Senate and of the House of Representatives:

. . . We have undertaken a new order of things: yet we progress to it under the framework and in the spirit and intent of the American Constitution. We have proceeded throughout the nation a measurable distance on the road towards this new order. Materially, I can report to you substantial benefits to our agricultural population, increased industrial activity, and profits to our merchants. Of equal moment, there is evident a restoration of that spirit of confidence and faith which marks the American character. Let him who, for speculative profit or partisan purpose, without just warrant would seek to disturb or dispel this assurance, take heed before he assumes responsibility for any act which slows our onward steps. . . .

Let us, for a moment, strip from our simple purpose the confusion that results from a multiplicity of detail and from millions of written and spoken words.

We find our population suffering from old inequalities, little changed by past sporadic remedies. In spite of our efforts and in spite of our talk, we have not weeded out the over-privileged and we have not effectively lifted up the under-privileged. Both of these manifestations of injustice have retarded happiness. No wise man has any intention of destroying what is known as the profit motive: because by the profit motive we mean the right by work to earn a decent livelihood for ourselves and for our families.

We have, however, a clear mandate from the people, that Americans must foreswear that conception of the acquisition of wealth which, through excessive profits, creates undue private power over private affairs and, to our misfortune, over public affairs as well. In building toward this end we do not destroy ambition nor do we seek to divide our wealth into equal shares on stated occasions. We continue to recognize the greater ability of some to earn more than others. But we do assert that the ambition of the individual to obtain for him and his a proper security, a reasonable leisure, and a decent living throughout life, is an ambition to be preferred to the appetite for great wealth and great power.

I recall to your attention my Message to the Congress last June in which I said—"among our objectives I place the security of the men, women and children of the nation first." That remains our first and continuing task; and in a very real sense every major legislative enactment of this Congress should be a component part of it.

In defining immediate factors which enter into our quest, I have spoken to the Congress and the people of three great divisions:

1. The security of a livelihood through the better use of the national resources of the land in which we live.
2. The security against the major hazards and vicissitudes of life.
3. The security of decent homes.

I am now ready to submit to the Congress a broad program designed ultimately to establish all three of these factors of security—a program which because of many lost years will take many future years to fulfill.

A study of our national resources, more comprehensive than

any previously made, shows the vast amount of necessary and practicable work which needs to be done for the development and preservation of our natural wealth for the enjoyment and advantage of our people in generations to come. The sound use of land and water is far more comprehensive than the mere planting of trees, building of dams, distributing of electricity or retirement of sub-marginal land. It recognizes that stranded populations, either in the country or the city, cannot have security under the conditions that now surround them.

To this end we are ready to begin to meet this problem—the intelligent care of population throughout our nation, in accordance with an intelligent distribution of the means of livelihood for that population. A definite program for putting people to work, of which I shall speak in a moment, is a component part of this greater program of security of livelihood through the better use of our national resources.

Closely related to the broad problem of livelihood is that of security against the major hazards of life. Here also a comprehensive survey of what has been attempted or accomplished in many nations and in many States proves to me that the time has come for action by the National Government. I shall send to you, in a few days, definite recommendations based on these studies. These recommendations will cover the broad subjects of unemployment insurance and old age insurance, of benefits for children, for mothers, for the handicapped, for maternity care and for other aspects of dependency and illness where a beginning can now be made.

The third factor—better homes for our people—has also been the subject of experimentation and study. Here, too, the first practical steps can be made through the proposals which I shall suggest in relation to giving work to the unemployed.

Whatever we plan and whatever we do should be in the light of these three clear objectives of security. We cannot afford to lose valuable time in haphazard public policies which cannot find a place in the broad outlines of these major purposes. In that spirit I come to an immediate issue made for us by hard and inescapable circumstance—the task of putting people to work. In the spring of 1933 the issue of destitution seemed to stand apart; today, in the light of our experience and our new national policy, we find we can put people to work in ways which conform to, initiate and carry forward the broad principles of that policy.

The first objectives of emergency legislation of 1933 were, to relieve destitution, to make it possible for industry to operate in a more rational and orderly fashion, and to put behind industrial recovery the impulse of large expenditures in government undertakings. The purpose of the National Industrial Recovery Act to provide work for more people succeeded in a substantial manner within the first few months of its life, and the Act has continued to maintain employment gains and greatly improved working conditions in industry.

The program of public works provided for in the Recovery Act launched the Federal government into a task for which there was little time to make preparation and little American experience to follow. Great employment has been given and is being given by these works.

More than two billions of dollars have also been expended in direct relief to the destitute. Local agencies of necessity determined the recipients of this form of relief. With inevitable exceptions the funds were spent by them with reasonable efficiency and as a result actual want of food and clothing in the great majority of cases has been overcome.

But the stark fact before us is that great numbers still remain unemployed.

A large proportion of these unemployed and their dependents have been forced on the relief rolls. The burden on the Federal Government has grown with great rapidity. We have here a human as well as an economic problem. When humane considerations are concerned, Americans give them precedence. The lessons of history, confirmed by the evidence immediately before me show conclusively that continued dependence upon relief induces a spiritual and moral disintegration fundamentally destructive to the national fibre. To dole out relief in this way is to administer a narcotic, a subtle destroyer of the human spirit. It is inimical to the dictates of sound policy, it is in violation of the traditions of America. Work must be found for able bodied but destitute workers.

The Federal government must and shall quit this business of relief.

I am not willing that the vitality of our people be further sapped by the giving of cash, of market baskets, of a few hours of weekly work cutting grass, raking leaves or picking up papers in the public parks. We must preserve not only the bodies of the unemployed from destitution but also their self-respect, their self-reliance and courage and determination. This decision brings me to the problem of what the government should do with approximately five million unemployed now on the relief rolls.

About one million and a half of these belong to the group which in the past was dependent upon local welfare efforts. Most of them are unable for one reason or another to maintain themselves independently—for the most part, through no fault of their own. Such people, in the days before the great depression, were cared for by local efforts—by states, by counties, by towns, by cities, by churches and by private welfare agencies. It is my thought that in the future they must be cared for as they were before. I stand ready through my own personal efforts, and through the public influence of the office that I hold, to help these local agencies to get the means necessary to assume this burden.

The security legislation which I shall propose to the Congress will, I am confident, be of assistance to local effort in the care of this type of cases. Local responsibility can and will be resumed, for, after all, common sense tells us that the wealth necessary for this task existed and still exists in the local community, and the dictates of sound administration require that this responsibility be in the first instance a local one.

There are however an additional three and one half million employable people who are on relief. With them the problem is different and the responsibility is different. This group was the victim of a nationwide depression caused by conditions which were not local but national. The Federal government is the only governmental agency with sufficient power and credit to meet this situation. We have assumed this task and we shall not shrink from it in the future. It is a duty dictated by every intelligent consideration of national policy to ask you to make it possible for the United States to give employment to all of these three and one half million employable people now on relief, pending their absorption in a rising tide of private employment.

It is my thought that with the exception of certain of the normal public building operations of the government, all emergency public works shall be united in a single new and greatly enlarged plan.

With the establishment of this new system we can supersede the Federal Emergency Relief Administration with a coordinated authority which will be charged with the orderly liquidation of our present relief activities and the substitution of a national chart for the giving of work. . . .

Ever since the adjournment of the 73rd Congress, the Administration has been studying from every angle the possibility and the practicability of new forms of employment. As a result of these studies I have arrived at certain very definite convictions as to the amount of money that will be necessary for the sort of public projects that I have described. I shall submit these figures in my budget message. I assure you now they will be within the sound credit of the government.

The work itself will cover a wide field including clearance of slums, which for adequate reasons cannot be undertaken by private capital; in rural housing of several kinds, where, again, private capital is unable to function; in rural electrification; in the reforestation of the great watersheds of the nation; in an intensified program to prevent soil erosion and to reclaim blighted areas; in improving existing road systems and in constructing national highways designed to handle modern traffic; in the elimination of grade crossings; in the extension and enlargement of the successful work of the Civilian Conservation Corps; in non-Federal work, mostly self-liquidating and highly useful to local divisions of Government; and on many other projects which the nation needs and cannot afford to neglect. . . .

I cannot with candor tell you that general international relationships outside the borders of the United States are improved. On the surface of things many old jealousies are resurrected, old passions aroused; new strivings for armament and power, in more than one land, rear their ugly heads. I hope that calm counsel and constructive leadership will provide the steadying influence and the time necessary for the coming of new and more practical forms of representative government throughout the world wherein privilege and power will occupy a lesser place and world welfare a greater.

I believe, however, that our own peaceful and neighborly attitude towards other nations is coming to be understood and appreciated. The maintenance of international peace is a matter in which we are deeply and unselfishly concerned. Evidence of our persistent and undeniable desire to prevent armed conflict has recently been more than once afforded. . . .

The ledger of the past year shows many more gains than losses. Let us not forget that, in addition to saving millions from utter destitution, child labor has been for the moment outlawed, thousands of homes saved to their owners and most important of all, the morale of the nation has been restored. Viewing the year 1934 as a whole, you and I can agree that we have a generous measure of reasons for giving thanks.

It is not empty optimism that moves me to a strong hope in the coming year. We can, if we will, make 1935 a genuine period of good feeling, sustained by a sense of purposeful progress. Beyond the material recovery, I sense a spiritual recovery as well. The people of America are turning as never before to those permanent values that are not limited to the physical objectives of life. There are growing signs of this on every hand. In the face of these spiritual impulses we are sensible of the Divine Providence to which Nations turn now, as always, for guidance and fostering care.

# LETTER TO GOVERNOR EUGENE TALMADGE OF GEORGIA

(n.p.) *February 13, 1935*

*Talmadge was one of the most vociferous white-supremacy Southerners of the era. He had written to the President enclosing a complaint by a Mr. Andrews of Smithville, Georgia, that he was unable to obtain farm labor for forty or fifty cents a day because wages on work relief projects were higher than that. After writing the following answer, the President decided not to send it but referred the matter to Harry Hopkins, head of the Works Progress Administration, for reply. Hopkins sent Talmadge a letter stressing that the wage standards the Governor approved put people on the relief rolls in Georgia "underfed, sick, and ragged, and their children out of school for lack of food, clothes and school books."*

My dear Governor Talmadge:—

I am interested in your letter of February eleventh with its enclosure.

I take it, from your sending the letter of the gentleman from Smithville to me, that you approve paying farm labor forty to fifty cents per day. Your correspondent does not mention the hours of work per day, but I assume that the forty or fifty cents is paid for working at least ten and possibly twelve hours. If one of these farm laborers were employed three hundred days a year, which means six days a week excluding Sundays and holidays, he would make, at forty cents a day, one hundred and twenty dollars a year; or if he were paid fifty cents a day he would make one hundred and fifty dollars for his work. In view of the fact, however, that this type of employment is generally seasonal, I take it that the man described would actually have to live on from sixty to seventy-five dollars a year.

Somehow I cannot get it into my head that wages on such a scale make possible a reasonable American standard of living.

Very sincerely yours,

# LETTER TO COLONEL EDWARD M. HOUSE

*The White House. April 10, 1935*

*In the face of the concurrent rise of isolationist sentiment in Congress and of the Hitler menace abroad, the President sought means within his power to cooperate with any movement of the peaceful nations for a united front against aggression.*

Dear Colonel:

. . . I do wish I had someone to fulfill for me the splendid missions which you carried out in Europe before we got into the war—but there is only one *you* and I know of no other. I am, of course, greatly disturbed by events on the other side—perhaps more than I should be. I have thought over two or three different methods by which the weight of America could be thrown into the scale of peace and of stopping the armament race. I reject each in turn for the principal reason that I fear any suggestion on our part would meet with the same kind of chilly, half-contemptuous reception on the other side as an appeal would have met in July or August, 1914.

I wish you would give some thought, however, to the following, which is based solely on the event of some form of joint military and naval action against Germany. It seems to me that if France, Italy, England and the "Little Entente" decide on positive action they would be far wiser not to invade Germany but rather to establish a complete blockade of Germany. This would involve blockading the Polish, Czecho-Slovak, Austrian, Swiss, French, Belgian, Dutch and Danish borders. The ports of Germany would be taken care of by British Naval operations. Such a blockade would raise for us the question of its effectiveness. If we found it was an effective blockade, as a matter of fact, recognition of the blockade by us would obviously follow. This, after all, is not a boycott nor an economic sanction, but in effect it is the same thing. A boycott or sanction could not be recognized by us without Congressional action but a blockade would fall under the Executive's power after establishment of the fact. I advance this thought because rumor has come to me that something along this line may be discussed at Stresa. . . .

Affectionately,

# SPECIAL MESSAGE TO CONGRESS ON INHERITANCE AND INCOME TAXES

*June 19, 1935*

*This proposal was regarded by some as punitive. But Congress passed the Wealth Tax Act largely to forestall extreme demands by such ominous movements as the Share-the-Wealth Clubs ("Every Man a King"—a federal-guaranteed minimum annual income of $5,000 for every family head) of Senator Huey P. Long, the virtual dictator of Louisiana.*

. . . The movement towards progressive taxation of wealth and of income has accompanied the growing diversification and interrelation of effort which marks our industrial society. Wealth in the modern world does not come merely from individual effort; it comes from a combination of individual effort and of the manifold uses to which the community puts that effort. The individual does not create the product of his industry with his own hands; he utilizes the many processes and forces of mass production to meet the demands of a national and international market.

Therefore, in spite of the great importance in our national life of the efforts and ingenuity of unusual individuals, the people in the mass have inevitably helped to make large fortunes possible. Without mass cooperation great accumulations of wealth would be impossible save by unhealthy speculation. As Andrew Carnegie put it, "Where wealth accrues honorably, the people are always silent partners." Whether it be wealth achieved through the cooperation of the entire community or riches gained by speculation—in either case the ownership of such wealth or riches represents a great public interest and a great ability to pay.

My first proposal, in line with this broad policy, has to do with inheritances and gifts. The transmission from generation to generation of vast fortunes by will, inheritance, or gift is not consistent with the ideals and sentiments of the American people.

The desire to provide security for one's self and one's family is natural and wholesome, but it is adequately served by a reasonable inheritance. Great accumulations of wealth cannot be justified on the basis of personal and family security. In the last analysis such accumulations amount to the perpetuation of great and undesirable concentration of control in a relatively few individuals over the employment and welfare of many, many others.

Such inherited economic power is as inconsistent with the ideals of this generation as inherited political power was inconsistent with the ideals of the generation which established our government.

Creative enterprise is not stimulated by vast inheritances. They bless neither those who bequeath nor those who receive. As long ago as 1907, in a message to Congress, President Theodore Roosevelt urged this wise social policy:

"A heavy progressive tax upon a very large fortune is in no way such a tax upon thrift or industry as a like tax would be on a small fortune. No advantage comes either to the country as a whole or to the individuals inheriting the money by permitting the transmission in their entirety of the enormous fortunes which would be affected by such a tax; and as an incident to its function of revenue raising, such a tax would help to preserve a measurable equality of opportunity for the people of the generations growing to manhood."

A tax upon inherited economic power is a tax upon static wealth, not upon that dynamic wealth which makes for the healthy diffusion of economic good.

Those who argue for the benefits secured to society by great fortunes invested in great businesses should note that such a tax does not affect the essential benefits that remain after the death of the creator of such a business. The mechanism of production that he created remains. The benefits of corporate

organization remain. The advantage of pooling many investments in one enterprise remains. Governmental privileges such
as patents remain. All that is gone is the initiative, energy and
genius of the creator—and death has taken these away.

I recommend, therefore, that in addition to the present
estate taxes, there should be levied an inheritance, succession,
and legacy tax in respect to all very large amounts received
by any one legatee or beneficiary; and to prevent, so far as
possible, evasions of this tax, I recommend the imposition of
gift taxes suited to this end. . . .

The disturbing effects upon our national life that come
from great inheritances of wealth and power can in the future
be reduced, not only through the method I have just described,
but through a definite increase in the taxes now levied upon
very great individual net incomes.

To illustrate: The application of the principle of a graduated tax now stops at $1,000,000 of annual income. In other
words, while the rate for a man with a $6,000 income is double
the rate for one with a $4,000 income, a man having a
$5,000,000 annual income pays at the same rate as one whose
income is $1,000,000.

Social unrest and a deepening sense of unfairness are dangers to our national life which we must minimize by rigorous
methods. People know that vast personal incomes come not
only through the effort or ability or luck of those who receive
them, but also because of the opportunities for advantage
which government itself contributes. Therefore, the duty rests
upon the government to restrict such incomes by very high
taxes. . . .

We have established the principle of graduated taxation in
respect to personal incomes, gifts and estates. We should apply the same principle to corporations. Today the smallest
corporation pays the same rate on its net profits as the corporation which is a thousand times its size.

I, therefore, recommend the substitution of a corporation
income tax graduated according to the size of corporation income in place of the present uniform corporation income tax

of 13 3/4 per cent. The rate for smaller corporations might well be reduced to 10 3/4 per cent, and the rates graduated upward to a rate of 16 3/4 per cent on net income in the case of the largest corporations. . . .

## STATEMENT UPON SIGNING THE NATIONAL LABOR RELATIONS ACT

*July 5, 1935*

*This law (the Wagner Act) re-enacted and put teeth into the guarantee of the right of collective bargaining for labor which had been invalidated by the Supreme Court with the rest of NIRA. The Court found the new law constitutional in 1937. It is one of the most important laws in American history and a keystone of the Second New Deal. Under it workers in the mass production industries were successfully organized into independent unions.*

This Act defines, as a part of our substantive law, the right of self-organization of employees in industry for the purpose of collective bargaining, and provides methods by which the Government can safeguard that legal right. It establishes a National Labor Relations Board to hear and determine cases in which it is charged that this legal right is abridged or denied, and to hold fair elections to ascertain who are the chosen representatives of employees.

A better relationship between labor and management is the high purpose of this Act. By assuring the employees the right of collective bargaining it fosters the development of the employment contract on a sound and equitable basis. By providing an orderly procedure for determining who is entitled to represent the employees, it aims to remove one of the chief causes of wasteful economic strife. By preventing practices which tend to destroy the independence of labor, it seeks, for every worker within its scope, that freedom of choice and action which is justly his.

The National Labor Relations Board will be an independent quasi-judicial body. It should be clearly understood that it will not act as mediator or conciliator in labor disputes. The function of mediation remains, under this Act, the duty of the Secretary of Labor and of the Conciliation Service of the Department of Labor. It is important that the judicial function and the mediation function should not be confused. Compromise, the essence of mediation, has no place in the interpretation and enforcement of the law.

This Act, defining rights, the enforcement of which is recognized by the Congress to be necessary as both an act of common justice and economic advance, must not be misinterpreted. It may eventually eliminate one major cause of labor disputes, but it will not stop all labor disputes. It does not cover all industry and labor, but is applicable only when violation of the legal right of independent self-organization would burden or obstruct interstate commerce. Accepted by management, labor and the public with a sense of sober responsibility and of willing cooperation, however, it should serve as an important step toward the achievement of just and peaceful labor relations in industry.

## LETTER TO J. N. DARLING

*The White House. July 29, 1935*

*The cartoonist "Ding" opposed the New Deal, but made an exception in favor of ducks.*

Dear Jay:

As I was saying to the Acting Director of the Budget the other day—"this fellow Darling is the only man in history who got an appropriation through Congress, past the Budget and signed by the President without anybody realizing that the Treasury had been raided."

You hold an all-time record. In addition to the six million dollars ($6,000,000) you got, the Federal Courts say that the United States Government has a perfect constitutional right to condemn millions of acres for the welfare, health and happiness of ducks, geese, sandpipers, owls and wrens, but has no constitutional right to condemn a few old tenements in the slums for the health and happiness of the little boys and girls who will be our citizens of the next generation!

Nevertheless, more power to your arm! Go ahead with the six million dollars ($6,000,000) and talk with me about a month hence in regard to additional lands, *if* I have any more money left.

As ever yours,

## STATEMENT UPON SIGNING THE SOCIAL SECURITY ACT

*August 14, 1935*

*Some of the many private and governmental groups whose studies had gone into the writing of this great law witnessed the President's signature.*

Today a hope of many years standing is in large part fulfilled. The civilization of the past hundred years, with its startling industrial changes, has tended more and more to make life insecure. Young people have come to wonder what would be their lot when they came to old age. The man with a job has wondered how long the job would last.

This social security measure gives at least some protection to thirty million of our citizens who will reap direct benefits through unemployment compensation, through old age pensions and through increased services for the protection of children and the prevention of ill health.

We can never insure one hundred per cent of the population against one hundred per cent of the hazards and vicissitudes of life but we have tried to frame a law which will give some measure of protection to the average citizen and to his family against the loss of a job and against poverty-ridden old age.

This law, too, represents a corner stone in a structure which is being built but is by no means complete—a structure intended to lessen the force of possible future depressions, to act as a protection to future Administrations of the Government against the necessity of going deeply into debt to furnish relief to the needy—a law to flatten out the peaks and valleys of deflation and of inflation—in other words, a law that will take care of human needs and at the same time provide for the United States an economic structure of vastly greater soundness.

I congratulate all of you ladies and gentlemen, all of you in the Congress, in the executive departments and all of you who come from private life, and I thank you for your splendid efforts in behalf of this sound, needy and patriotic legislation.

If the Senate and the House of Representatives in this long and arduous session had done nothing more than pass this Bill, the session would be regarded as historic for all time.

## STATEMENT UPON SIGNING THE NEUTRALITY ACT

*August 31, 1935*

*Contrary to the President's desire for authority to impose an arms embargo on aggressor nations while permitting sale of arms to their victims, Congress passed a bill requiring an arms embargo on aggressors and victims alike. He signed the bill, and approved some sections of it, but made a significant objection to the arms embargo.*

. . . It is the policy of this government to avoid being drawn into wars between other nations, but it is a fact that no Congress and no executive can foresee all possible future situations. History is filled with unforeseeable situations that call for some flexibility of action. It is conceivable that situations may arise in which the wholly inflexible provisions of Section I of this Act might have exactly the opposite effect from that which was intended. In other words, the inflexible provisions might drag us into war instead of keeping us out. . . .

## LETTER TO HENRY A. WALLACE

*Warm Springs. November 24, 1935*

*Secretary of Agriculture Wallace had sent the President some interesting historical material.*

Dear Henry:

I am delighted to have the excerpts in regard to the Ever Normal Granary in B.C. China, and also the Chinese New Deal of the Eleventh Century A.D. It is excellent proof that there is nothing really new under the sun. However, I am consoled by the thought that the Ever Normal Granary plan was carried on, though somewhat sporadically, for nearly two thousand years and that the New Deal of Wang An-shih lasted ten years before the profiteers ran the old man out of town! . . .

As ever yours,

## STATEMENT UPON SIGNING THE SOIL CONSERVATION AND DOMESTIC ALLOTMENT ACT

*March 1, 1936*

*This law rescued the President's main farm program from the failure of the Agricultural Adjustment Act to meet the test of the Supreme Court.*

In signing the Soil Conservation and Domestic Allotment Act, I feel that I am approving a measure which helps to safeguard vital public interests, not only for today, but for generations to come.

This legislation represents an attempt to develop, out of the far-reaching and partly emergency efforts under the Agricultural Adjustment Act, a long-time program for American agriculture.

The new law has three major objectives which are inseparably and of necessity linked with the national welfare. The first of these aims is conservation of the soil itself through wise and proper land use. The second purpose is the reestablishment and maintenance of farm income at fair levels so that the great gains made by agriculture in the past three years can be preserved and national recovery can continue. The third major objective is the protection of consumers by assuring adequate supplies of food and fiber now and in the future.

The Federal Government, with an annual expenditure far less than the actual yearly wastage of fertility by erosion in the past will make grants of money to farmers, conditioned upon actual evidence of good land use. Thus, in carrying out the soil conservation plan, there will be provided a positive incentive to and protection for those who voluntarily shift from soil-depleting surplus crops, such as cotton, corn, wheat and tobacco, into erosion-preventing and soil-building crops, such as grasses and legumes, of which there is no surplus. This will help to bring about and maintain a healthy supply and demand situation from farm commodities, and will have a beneficial effect on farm prices and farm income. . . .

The history of every nation is eventually written in the way in which it cares for its soil. The United States, as evidenced by the progressive public opinion and vigorous demand which resulted in the enactment of this law, is now emerging from its youthful stage of heedless exploitation and is beginning to realize the supreme importance of treating the soil well.

I do not regard this farm act as a panacea or as a final plan. Rather I consider it a new basis to build and improve upon, as experience discloses its points of weakness and of strength. Aiming at justice for agriculture and self-interest for the nation, the plan seeks to salvage and conserve the greatest values in human life and resources with which this nation is endowed.

## ADDRESS OF ACCEPTANCE OF THE NOMINATION FOR A SECOND TERM

*Philadelphia. June 27, 1936*

*By this time few conservatives remained among Roosevelt's supporters. He launched his campaign for a second term by attacking his chief opponents as "economic royalists."*

Senator Robinson, Members of the Democratic Convention, my friends:

Here and in every community throughout the land we are met at a time of great moment to the future of the Nation. It is an occasion to be dedicated to the simple and sincere expression of an attitude towards problems, the determination of which will profoundly affect America. . . .

But I cannot, with candor, tell you that all is well with the world. Clouds of suspicion, tides of ill will and intolerance gather darkly in many places. In our own land we enjoy indeed a fullness of life greater than that of most nations. But the rush of modern civilization itself has raised for us new difficulties, new problems which must be solved if we are to preserve to the United States the political and economic freedom for which Washington and Jefferson planned and fought.

Philadelphia is a good city in which to write American history. This is fitting ground on which to reaffirm the faith of our fathers; to pledge ourselves to restore to the people a wider freedom—to give to 1936 as the founders gave to 1776 —an American way of life.

That very word freedom, in itself and of necessity, suggests freedom from some restraining power. In 1776 we sought freedom from the tyranny of a political autocracy—from the eighteenth century royalists who held special privileges from the crown. It was to perpetuate their privilege that they governed without the consent of the governed; that they denied the right of free assembly and free speech; that they restricted the worship of God; that they put the average man's property and the average man's life in pawn to the mercenaries of dynastic power—that they regimented the people.

And so it was to win freedom from the tyranny of political autocracy that the American Revolution was fought. That victory gave the business of governing into the hands of the average man, who won the right with his neighbors to make and order his own destiny through his own Government. Political tyranny was wiped out at Philadelphia on July 4, 1776.

But, since that struggle, man's inventive genius released new forces in our land which re-ordered the lives of our people. The age of machinery, of railroads, of steam and electricity; the telegraph and the radio; mass production, mass distribution—all of these combined to bring forward a new civilization and with it a problem for those who sought to remain free.

For out of this modern civilization economic royalists carved new dynasties. New Kingdoms were built upon concentration of control over material things. Through new uses of corporations, banks and securities, new machinery of industry and agriculture, of labor and capital—all undreamed of by the fathers—the whole structure of modern life was impressed into this royal service.

There was no place among this royalty for our many thousands of small business men and merchants who sought to make a worthy use of the American system of initiative and profit. They were no more free than the worker or the farmer. Even honest and progressive-minded men of wealth, aware of their obligation to their generation, could never know just where they fitted into this dynastic scheme of things.

And so it was natural and perfectly human that the privileged princes of these new economic dynasties, thirsting for power, reached out for control over government itself. They created a new despotism and wrapped it in the robes of legal sanction. In its service new mercenaries sought to regiment the people, their labor, their property. And as a result the average man once more confronts the problem that faced the Minute Man of seventy-six.

The hours men and women worked, the wages they received, the conditions of their labor—these had passed beyond the control of the people, and were imposed by this new industrial dictatorship. The savings of the average family, the capital of the small business man, the investments set aside for old age—other people's money—these were tools which the new economic royalty used to dig itself in.

Those who tilled the soil no longer reaped the rewards which were their right. The small measure of their gains was decreed by men in distant cities.

Throughout the Nation, opportunity was limited by monopoly. Individual initiative was crushed in the cogs of a great machine. The field open for free business was more and more restricted. Private enterprise, indeed, became too private. It became privileged enterprise, not free entrprise.

An old English judge said once upon a time: "Necessitous men are not free men." Liberty requires opportunity to make a living—a living decent according to the standard of the time, a living which gives man not only enough to live by, but something to live for.

For too many of us the political equality we once had won was meaningless in the face of economic inequality. A small group had concentrated into their own hands an almost complete control over other people's property, other people's money, other people's labor—other people's lives. For too many of us life was no longer free; liberty no longer real; men could no longer follow the pursuit of happiness.

Against economic tyranny such as this, the American citizen could only appeal to the organized power of government. We will remember that the collapse of 1929 showed up the despotism for what it was. The election of 1932 was the people's mandate to end it. Under that mandate it is being ended.

The royalists I have spoken of—the royalists of the economic order have conceded that political freedom was the business of the government, but they have maintained that economic slavery was nobody's business. They granted that the government could protect the citizen in his right to vote but they denied that the goverment could do anything to protect the citizen in his right to work and his right to live.

Today we stand committed to the proposition that freedom is no half and half affair. If the average citizen is guaranteed equal opportunity in the polling place, he must have equal opportunity in the market place.

These economic royalists complain that we seek to overthrow the institutions of America. What they really complain of is that we seek to take away their power. Our allegiance to American institutions requires the overthrow of this kind of power. In vain they seek to hide behind the Flag and the Constitution. In their blindness they forget what the Flag and the Constitution stand for. Now, as always, for over a century and a half, the Flag, the Constitution, stand against a dictatorship by mob rule and the over-privileged alike, and the Flag and the Constitution stand for democracy, not tyranny; for freedom, but not subjection. . . .

It is a sobering thing, my friends, to be a servant of this great cause. We try in our daily work to remember that the cause belongs not to us but to the people. The standard is not in the hands of you and me alone. It is carried by America. We seek, all of us I hope, we seek daily to profit from experience, to learn to do better as our task proceeds.

Governments can err—Presidents do make mistakes, but the immortal Dante tells us that divine justice weighs the sins of the cold-blooded and the sins of the warm-hearted in different scales.

Better the occasional faults of a government that lives in a spirit of charity than the consistent omissions of a government frozen in the ice of its own indifference.

There is a mysterious cycle in human events. To some generations much is given. Of other generations much is expected. This generation of Americans has a rendezvous with destiny.

In this world of ours in other lands, there are some people, who, in times past, have lived and fought for freedom, and seem to have grown too weary to carry on the fight. They have sold their heritage of freedom for the illusion of a living. They have yielded their democracy.

I believe in my heart that only our success can stir their ancient hope. They begin to know that here in America we are waging a great and successful war. It is not alone a war against want and destitution and economic demoralization. It is more than that, it is a war for the survival of democracy. We are fighting, fighting to save a great and precious form of government for ourselves and for the world.

And so I accept the commission you have tendered me. I join with you. I am enlisted for the duration of the war.

## LETTER TO WILLIAM E. DODD

*Hyde Park. August 5, 1936*

*The eminent historian William E. Dodd was Ambassador to Germany. Nothing came of the suggestion in the last paragraph, but it illustrates the President's search for a way to cooperate with the nations for peace even while isolationism was in the ascendant.*

My dear Dodd:

Many thanks for your note. I am sorry, indeed, that I have not had the chance of seeing you again before you sail.

The election this year has, in a sense, a German parallel. If the Republicans should win or make enormous gains, it would prove that an 85 per cent control of the Press and a very definite campaign of misinformation can be effective here just as it was in the early days of the Hitler rise to power. Democracy is verily on trial. I am inclined to say something a little later on about the great need for freedom of the press in this country, i.e., freedom to confine itself to actual facts in its news columns and freedom to express editorially any old opinion it wants to.

Drop me a line soon after your return. I should like to have your slant, in the utmost confidence, as to what would happen if Hitler were personally and secretly asked by me to outline the limit of German foreign objectives during, let us say a ten year period, and to state whether or not he would have any sympathy with a general limitation of armaments' proposal. You cannot, of course, ask any questions regarding this in such a way as to let any inference be drawn that we were even thinking of such a thing. I should merely like to get your own opinion on the probability of his attitude under certain conditions.

My warm regards,
As ever yours,

## ADDRESS AT THE TERCENTENARY CELEBRATION OF HARVARD UNIVERSITY

*Cambridge. September 18, 1936*

*The President enjoyed taking a respite from the campaign to point out the propensity of Harvard to celebrate its anniversaries when Democrats were Presidents of the United States.*

President Conant, distinguished guests, my fellow alumni:

I am here today in a joint and several capacity. First, as the President of the United States. Second, as Chairman of the United States Harvard Tercentenary Commission. . . . Finally, I am here as a son of Harvard who gladly returns to this spot where men have sought truth for three hundred years.

Our roots are deep in the past. And it is pleasant to remember today that this meeting is being held in pursuance of an adjournment expressly taken one hundred years ago on motion of Josiah Quincy.

At that time many of the Alumni of Harvard were sorely troubled concerning the state of the Nation. Andrew Jackson was President. On the two hundred and fiftieth anniversary of the founding of Harvard College, Alumni again were sorely troubled. Grover Cleveland was President. Now, on the three hundredth anniversary, I am President. (Laughter, applause) To go back a little further, in the words of Euripides:

> "There be many shapes of mystery.
> And many things God makes to be,
> Past hope or fear.
> And the end men looked for cometh not,
> And a path is there where no man sought.
> So hath it fallen here."

And in spite of fears Harvard and the Nation of which it is a part have marched steadily to new and successful achievements, changing their formations and their strategy to meet new conditions; but marching always under the old banner of freedom.

In the olden days of New England, it was Increase Mather who told the students of Harvard that they were "pledged to the word of no particular master", that they should "above all find a friend in truth."

That became the creed of Harvard. Behind the tumult and the shouting it is still the creed of Harvard.

In this day of modern witch-burning, when freedom of thought has been exiled from many lands which were once its home, it is the part of Harvard and America to stand for the freedom of the human mind and to carry the torch of truth. . . .

## CAMPAIGN SPEECH

*Chicago. October 14, 1936*

*Roosevelt had now sharpened his oratorical style to its ultimate pitch. He had become the master of dramatized facts and ideas, of slashing attacks against his opponents paced by laughter, and of warm sympathy for human beings, all realized in very plain prose.*

Mr. Chairman, Governor Horner, Mayor Kelly, my friends of the great State of Illinois:

I seem to have been here before.

Four years ago I dropped into this city from the airways—an old friend come in a new way—to accept in this hall the nomination for the Presidency of the United States. I came to a Chicago fighting with its back to the wall—factories closed, markets silent, banks shaky, ships and trains empty. Today those factories sing the song of industry—markets hum with bustling movement, banks are secure; ships and trains are running full. Once again it is a Chicago that smiles. And with Chicago a whole nation that had not been cheerful for years is full of cheer once more.

On this trip I have talked to farmers, I have talked to miners, I have talked to industrial workers—and in all that I have seen and heard one fact has been clear as crystal—that they are part and parcel of a rounded whole, and that none of them can succeed in their chosen occupations if those in the other occupations fall or fail in their prosperity. I have driven that point home.

And tonight, in this center of business of America, I give the same message to the business men of America—to those who make and sell the processed goods the Nation uses and to the men and women who work for them.

To them I say:

Do you have a deposit in the bank? It is safer today than it has ever been in our history. It is guaranteed. Last October first marked the end of the first full year in 55 years without a single failure of a national bank in the United States. Isn't that on the credit side of the government's account with you?

Are you an investor? Your stocks and bonds are up to a five and six year high level.

Are you a merchant? Your markets have the precious life-blood of purchasing power. Your customers on the farms have better incomes and smaller debts. Your customers in the cities have more jobs, surer jobs, better jobs. Didn't your government have something to do with this?

Are you in industry? Industrial earnings, industrial profits are the highest in four, six, or even seven years! Bankruptcies are at a new low. Your government takes some credit for that.

Are you in railroads? Freight loadings are steadily going up and so are passenger receipts because, for one reason, your government made the railroads cut rates and make money.

Are you a middleman in the great stream of farm products? The meat and grain that move through your yards and elevators have a steadier supply, a steadier demand and steadier prices than you have known for years. And your government is trying to keep it that way.

Now, my friends, some people say that all this recovery has just happened. But in a complicated modern world recoveries from depressions do not just happen. The years from 1929 to 1933 when we waited for recovery just to happen, proves the point.

But in 1933, after March 4th, we did not wait—we acted. Behind the growing recovery of today is a story of deliberate government acceptance of responsibility to save business—to save the American system of private enterprise and economic democracy—a record unequalled by any modern government in history. . . .

Because we cherished our system of private property and free enterprise and were determined to preserve it as the foundation of our traditional American system, we recalled the warning of Thomas Jefferson that "widespread poverty and concentrated wealth cannot long endure side by side in a democracy."

And so our job was to preserve the American ideal of economic as well as political democracy, against the abuse of concentration of economic power that had been insidiously growing up among us in the last fifty years, particularly during the twelve years of preceding Administrations. Free economic enterprise was being weeded out at an alarming pace.

During those years of false prosperity one business after another, one small corporation after another, their resources depleted, had failed or had fallen into the lap of a bigger competitor.

A dangerous thing was happening. More than half of the

corporate wealth of the country had come under the control of less than two hundred big corporations. That is not all. These huge corporations in some cases did not even try to compete with each other. They themselves were tied together by interlocking directors, interlocking bankers and interlocking lawyers.

This concentration of wealth and power has been built upon other people's money, other people's business, other people's labor. Under this concentration independent business was allowed to exist only by sufferance. It has been a menace to the social system as well as the economic system which we call American Democracy.

As a matter of practical fact, there is no excuse for it in the cold terms of industrial efficiency.

There is no excuse for it from the point of view of the average investor.

There is no excuse for it from the point of view of the independent business man.

I believe, I have always believed, and I always will believe in private enterprise as the backbone of economic well-being in the United States.

But I know, and you know, and every independent business man who has had to struggle against the competition of monopolies knows, that this concentration of economic power in all-embracing corporations does not represent private enterprise as we Americans cherish it and propose to foster it. On the contrary, it represents private enterprise which has become a kind of private government and is a power unto itself—a regimentation of other people's money and other people's lives.

Back in Kansas I spoke about bogey-men and fairy tales which the real Republican leaders, many of whom are part of this concentrated power, are using to spread fear among the American people.

You good people have heard about these fairy tales and bogey-men too. You have heard about how antagonistic to business this Administration is supposed to be. You have heard all about the dangers which the business of America is supposed to be facing if this Administration continues.

My friends, the answer to that is the record of what we have done. It was this Administration which saved the system of private profit and free enterprise after it had been dragged to the brink of ruin by these same leaders who now try to scare you.

Look at the advance in private business in the last three and a half years; and read there what we think about private business.

Today for the first time in seven years the banker, the store-keeper, the small factory owner, the industrialist, can all sit back and enjoy the company of their own ledgers. They are in the black. That is where we want them to be; that is where our policies aim that they shall be; that is where we intend them to be in the days to come.

Some of these people really forget how sick they were. But I know how sick they were. I have their fever charts. I know how the knees of all of our rugged individualists were trembling four years ago and how their hearts fluttered. They came to Washington in great numbers. Washington did not look like a dangerous bureaucracy to them then. No, it looked like an emergency hospital. And all of these distinguished patients wanted two things—a quick hypodermic to end the pain and they wanted a course of treatment to cure the disease. They wanted them in a hurry, and we gave them both. And now, my frends, most of the patients seem to be doing very nicely. Some of them are even well enough to throw their crutches at the doctor.

I believe in individualism. I believe in it in the arts, the sciences and professions. I believe in it in business. I believe in individualism in all these things—up to the point where the individualist starts to operate at the expense of society. And the overwhelming majority of American business men do not believe in it beyond that point. We have all suffered in the past from individualism run wild—society has suffered and business has suffered.

And so, believing in the solvency of business, the solvency of farmers and the solvency of workers, I believe also in the solvency of Government. Your Government is solvent.

The net Federal debt today is lower in proportion to the income of the Nation and in proportion to the wealth of the Nation than it was on March 4, 1933. ("Right", applause.)

And in the future it will become lower still because with the rising tide of national income and national wealth, the very causes of our emergency spending are starting to disappear, Government expenditures are coming down and Government income is going up. And so, my friends, the opportunities for private enterprise will continue to expand.

The people of America have no quarrel with business. They insist only that the power of concentrated wealth shall not be abused.

We have come through a hard struggle to preserve democracy in America. Where other nations in other parts of the world have lost that fight, we have won it.

The businessmen of America and all other citizens have joined in a firm resolve to hold the fruits of that victory—to cling to the old ideals, to cling to the old fundamentals upon which America has grown great. (Prolonged applause)

## CAMPAIGN SPEECH

*Wilmington, Delaware. October 29, 1936*

*In the home town of the Du Ponts, leaders of the Liberty League, he spoke very quietly, using a Republican President's words for his authority, on the subject of liberty.*

Save for my own home State of New York, this meeting in Wilmington marks the close of my campaign for the Presidency.

It seems appropriate that on this occasion I should make no political speech because I can better describe the kind of liberty which our Administration has sought and continues to seek by reading to you the simple words of a great President who believed in the kind of liberty that we believe in—the great President who preserved the American Union.

Those words are from the speech made by President Abraham Lincoln at the Sanitary Fair in Baltimore in 1864. And I ask that you good people give heed to these words for, although they are three-quarters of a century old, yet I think you will find that they apply to 1936. Abraham Lincoln said this:

"The world has never had a good definition of the word liberty, and the American people, just now, are much in want of one. We all declare for liberty; but in using the same word we do not all mean the same thing. With some the word liberty may mean for each man to do as he pleases with himself, and the product of his labor; while with others the same word may mean for some men to do as they please with other men, and the product of other men's labor. Here are two, not only different, but incompatible things, called by the same name, liberty. And it follows that each of the things is, by the respective parties, called by two different and incompatible names—liberty and tyranny."

And then Abraham Lincoln used this homely example. He said:

"The shepherd drives the wolf from the sheep's throat, for which the sheep thanks the shepherd as his liberator, while the wolf denounces him for the same act, as the destroyer of liberty. . . . Plainly, the sheep and the wolf are not agreed upon a definition of the word liberty; and precisely the same difference prevails today among us human creatures . . . and all professing to love liberty. Hence we behold the process by which thousands are daily passing from under the yoke of bondage hailed by some as the advance of liberty, and bewailed by others as the destruction of all liberty."

And, in closing, Lincoln said this:

"Recently, as it seems, the people . . . have been doing something to define liberty, and thanks to them that, in what they have done, the wolf's dictionary has been repudiated."

My friends, today, in 1936, the people have been doing something to define liberty. And the wolf's dictionary has again been repudiated.

What Abraham Lincoln said three-quarters of a century ago applies today as it did then. The people, men and women, of the City of Wilmington and the State of Delaware will, I think, appreciate their significance in the same measure as men and women in every part of the United States.

And that is why, my friends, on Tuesday evening next I expect to get a message from the State of Delaware telling me that all is well.

## CAMPAIGN SPEECH

*Madison Square Garden, New York City. October 31, 1936*

*The pallid performance of the Republican candidate, Governor Alf Landon of Kansas, led to desperate measures during the last days. Former President Hoover made speeches. Employers inserted political messages in pay envelopes. The* Literary Digest *poll predicted Republican victory. Roosevelt fought all the harder. He was particularly sensitive to the Republican charge that he had not specified his objectives if he were re-elected. It was true that he avoided answering the question of what he would do about adverse decisions of the Supreme Court.*

Senator Wagner, Governor Lehman, ladies and gentlemen:

. . . Only desperate men with their backs to the wall would descend so far below the level of decent citizenship as to foster the current pay-envelope campaign against America's working people. (Boos) Only reckless men, heedless of consequences, would risk the disruption of the hope for a new peace between worker and employer by returning to the tactics of the labor spy. (Boos)

Here is an amazing paradox! The very employers and politicians and newspapers who talk most loudly of class antagonism and the destruction of the American system now undermine that system by this attempt to coerce the votes of the wage earners of this country. It is the 1936 version of the old threat to close down the factory or the office if a particular candidate does not win. It is an old strategy of tyrants to delude their victims into fighting their battles for them.

Every message in a pay envelope, even if it is the truth, is a command to vote according to the will of the employer. But this propaganda is worse—it is deceit.

They tell the worker that his wage will be reduced by a contribution to some vague form of old-age insurance. But they carefully conceal from him the fact that for every dollar of premium he pays for that insurance, the employer pays another dollar. That omission is deceit.

They carefully conceal from him the fact that under the federal law, he receives another insurance policy to help him if he loses his job, and that the premium of that policy is paid 100% by the employer and not one cent by the worker. But they do not tell him that the insurance policy that is bought for him is far more favorable to him than any policy that any private insurance company could possibly afford to issue. And that omission is deceit.

They imply to him that he pays all the cost of both forms of insurance. They carefully conceal from him the fact that for every dollar put up by him his employer puts up three dollars —three for one. And that omission is deceit.

But they are guilty of more than deceit. When they imply that the reserves thus created against both these policies will be stolen by some future Congress—diverted to some wholly foreign purpose, they attack the integrity and honor of American Government itself. Those who suggest that, are already aliens to the spirit of American democracy. Let them emigrate and try their lot under some foreign flag in which they have more confidence. (Applause)

The fraudulent nature of this attempt is well shown by the record of votes on the passage of the Social Security Act. In addition to an overwhelming majority of Democrats in both Houses, seventy-seven Republican Representatives voted for it and only eighteen against it and fifteen Republican Senators voted for it and only five against it. Where does this last-minute drive of the Republican leadership leave these Republican Representatives and Senators who helped to enact the law?

I am sure that the vast majority of law-abiding business men who are not parties to this propaganda fully appreciate the extent of the threat to honest business contained in this coercion.

I have expressed indignation at this form of campaigning and I am confident that the overwhelming majority of employers, workers and the general public share that indignation and will show it at the polls on Tuesday next.

But, aside from this phase of it, I prefer to remember this campaign not as bitter but only as hard-fought. There should be no bitterness or hate where the sole thought is the welfare of the United States of America. No man can occupy the office of President without realizing that he is President of all the people.

It is because I have sought to think in terms of the whole Nation that I am confident that today, just as four years ago, the people want more than promises.

And our vision for the future contains more than promises.

This is our answer to those who, silent about their own plans, ask us to state our objectives.

Of course we will continue to seek to improve working conditions for the workers of America—to reduce hours that are over-long, to increase wages that spell starvation, to end the labor of children, and to wipe out sweatshops. Of course we will continue every effort to end monopoly in business, to support collective bargaining, to stop unfair competition, and to abolish dishonorable trade practices. And for all these we have only just begun to fight. (Applause)

Of course we will continue to work for cheaper electricity in the homes and on the farms of America, for better and cheaper transportation, for low interest rates, for sounder home financing, for better banking, for the regulation of security issues, for reciprocal trade among nations, for the wiping out of slums.

For all these we have only just begun to fight. (Applause)

Of course we will continue our efforts in behalf of the farmers of America. With their continued cooperation we will do all in our power to end the piling up of huge surpluses which spelled ruinous prices for their crops. We will persist in successful action for better land use, for reforestation, for the conservation of water all the way from its source to the sea, for drought control and flood control, for better marketing facilities for farm commodities, for a reduction of farm tenancy, for encouragement of farm cooperatives, for crop insurance and for a stable food supply for the Nation. For all these too we have only just begun to fight. (Applause)

Of course we will provide useful work for the needy unemployed because we prefer useful work to the pauperism of a dole. (Applause)

Here and now I want to make myself clear about those who disparage their fellow citizens on the relief rolls. They say that those on relief are not merely jobless—they say they are worthless. Their solution for the relief problem is to end relief —to purge the rolls by starvation. To use the language of the stock broker, our needy unemployed would be cared for when, as, and if some fairy godmother should happen to come on the scene.

But you and I will continue to refuse to accept that estimate of our unemployed fellow Americans. Your Government is still on the same side of the street with the Good Samaritan and not with those who pass by on the other side. (Applause)

To go on—what of our objectives?

Of course we will continue our efforts for young men and women so that they may obtain an education and an opportunity to put it to use. Of course, we will continue our help for the crippled, for the blind, for the mothers—our insurance for the unemployed—our security for the aged. Of course we will continue to protect the consumer against unnecessary price spreads, against the costs that are added by monopoly and speculation. We will continue our successful efforts to increase his purchasing power and to keep it constant.

And for these things, too, and for a multitude of things like them we have only just begun to fight. . . .

## SPEECH TO THE GRIDIRON CLUB

*Washington. December 21, 1936*

*He carried the election by the greatest landslide vote in American party history. At the next traditional, unreported evening of fun with the Washington correspondents, he followed their satirical sketches of himself with a few barbs of his own.*

Su Excelencia, Presidente Gableman, Senores y socios del Club Gridiron:

Durante mi reciente viaje de buena voluntad a Sud America, yo hice el gran descubrimiento que la poderosa influencia de su Club no ha llegado a hacerse sentir en el hemisferio del Sur. Nuestros amigos en las republicas hermanas tienen la desventaja de leer solamente puras noticias. No tienen la costumbre Norte Americana de interpretar las noticias. Tal vez en el porvenir Ustedes podrian ofrecer sus servicios.

This comment, Gentlemen, deserves your serious consideration, especially on an occasion like this which brings us together just before Christmas with larger grace and a more pervading spirit of good will than—shall we say—at the Spring dinner when the Congress is in session.

I am delighted that a fellow guest tonight is Governor Landon of Kansas. I felt it an honor to have him as an opponent. This morning we had a delightful talk about all kinds of things—international affairs, domestic problems and sport—fishing and shooting and the big outdoors. And may I say to him that his sense of sportsmanship is not confined to fishing and hunting, and that I appreciate his sportsmanship in the larger field.

As usual I have enjoyed every minute of our entertainment tonight. A number of us perhaps have found the various skits more factual than the writings of their journalistic authors during the recent campaign.

Between June and November I became an even more omnivorous reader of papers than in the past. I use the word "papers" because in common with a hundred million or more fellow Americans I have come to discriminate between the word "paper" and the word "newspaper."

In a great serial which ran for several months in the papers, one of the characters bore the name of Franklin D. Roosevelt. Whether this character was to be a hero or a villain I could not at first make out. But as that magnificent work of imagination developed, I decided that this character Roosevelt was a villain. He combined the worst features of Ivan the Terrible, Machiavelli, Judas Iscariot, Henry VIII, Charlotte Corday and Jesse James. He was engaged in a plot to wreck the American Constitution, to poison the Supreme Court, to demolish capitalism, to destroy old age security, to get us into war, and to assassinate all the men in the United States who had red hair or as newspaper publishers claimed the rank of Colonel—in short, to blot from the face of the earth the United States as we have known it.

I began to believe it myself. Didn't I read it in the columns of our great papers? These papers had been awarded prizes for their artistic make-up and sometimes even for their enterprise in ferreting out facts. Moreover, if the slightest doubt remained in the reader's mind, the most penetrating, permeating editorial intellect assured him that it was so.

Yes, I began to believe it myself. One morning, about the middle of October, I became curious about this man Roosevelt and I went to a beautiful, old mirror of the early Federal period and took a careful look at him in the glass. He smiled. I remembered that one of the most damning indictments that had been brought against him was that self-same smile. I smiled back. And after a careful examination I decided that all that this villain looked like to me was a man who wanted to be re-elected President of the United States.

He was re-elected and the great 1936 campaign serial turned out to have a most surprising ending. On the morning of November fourth the editors decided that this villain was, after all, a reasonable person. He was deluged with editorial advice —suave advice, friendly advice, advice based on the apparent assumption that this man was really a reincarnation of a cross between Little Eva and Simple Simon.

May I recommend this habit of standing in front of a mirror? It is a good habit. It restores perspective. It brings out all the blemishes one ought to know about.

It is a much better habit than some others that recently have been practised. Before the mirror you can talk to the man you see there but the same voice comes back. And that perhaps is better than trying the art of ventriloquism.

There was one other aspect of the campaign which was personally deflating to me—the newspaper poll. When I first entered politics there were no polls—we had only the prognostication of the political Chairmen. Sometimes they were as right as Jim Farley and sometimes they were as wrong as John Hamilton. And by the way, here is a simple problem in mental arithmetic. If John Hamilton gets $25,000 a year for carrying Maine and Vermont, what should Jim Farley's salary be?

Our campaigns in the past developed the practice of straw votes and recently what we call Digest Polls. I read the oscillations of voting percentages with bated breath. I do not know how Governor Landon felt but I wondered throughout those long weeks whether I was not some sort of stock traded in on the Stock Exchange—off a quarter, up a half, down two. I passed through a bewildering series of highs, lows and net changes until I could hardly write my name without putting a plus or minus sign before it. And what did it prove in the end? It proved that with all of our journalistic genius for prognostication, a sure fire method of dignosing, deciphering and anticipating American public opinion still remains to be discovered.

Yet as far as the American Press is concerned, no one could

admire it more than I. Its freedom, its technical facilities, its network of communications, its speed, its alertness and the plentitude of its coverage are unequaled in the world.

Yet some people—mostly people with indigestion or bad consciences—speak of the danger of the regimentation of our Press. Let us analyze. Suppose the Government of the United States were a dictatorship. Suppose the Government required newspapers to purchase and print some of the canned editorial features dealing with national affairs that now fill our Press! The outcries of editors present here tonight would be heard round the world! Gentlemen, it needs no Government dictatorship to regiment the American Press. Any regimenting of the American Press which is present today or looms in the offing comes from the regimenting of it by the Press itself.

But the Gridiron Club is not regimented, and it brings to us all the saving graces of humor and perspective. It is good for me to be here. It is good, I think, for the Chief Justice to be here. It is good for Governor Landon to be here. It is good for Republicans and Democrats and Socialists and Communists to sit at these tables and laugh at themselves and at each other. The Gridiron Club offers twice a year the largest of mirrors for us all to look at ourselves in. As we think of those sections of the world in which fear, hatred and bitter political rivalries have great peoples within their grasp, who of us cannot feel a spirit of humble gratitude to Providence that our national destinies are emerging from the strains of recent times with our American tradition of tolerance and perspective unimpaired?

"Court Packing" Fight
Primaries "Purge" Campaign
Fight to Repeal Arms Embargo

JANUARY 1, 1937 — SEPTEMBER 1, 1939

# SPECIAL MESSAGE TO CONGRESS
# ON FARM SECURITY

*February 16, 1937*

*Earlier farm programs had been found in practice to benefit chiefly the largest farmers and the farm corporations, and in some cases actually to injure tenants, sharecroppers and farm laborers. The President now proposed measures to benefit these groups. Congress subsequently established the Farm Security Administration, but it became a focus of rising Congressional opposition to the New Deal, and appropriations for it were sharply curtailed despite the excellent record of repayment to the Government of loans which enabled tenants to become farm owners.*

I transmit herewith for the information of the Congress the report of the Special Committee on Farm Tenancy.

The facts presented in this report reveal a grave problem of great magnitude and complexity. The American dream of the family-size farm, owned by the family which operates it, has become more and more remote. The agricultural ladder, on which an energetic young man might ascend from hired man to tenant to independent owner, is no longer serving its purpose.

Half a century ago one of every four farmers was a tenant. Today, two of every five are tenants, and on some of our best farm lands seven of every ten farmers are tenants. All told, they operate land and buildings valued at eleven billion dollars.

For the past ten years, the number of new tenants every year has been about forty thousand. Many tenants change farms every two or three years, and apparently one out of three changes farms every year. The agricultural ladder, for these American citizens, has become a treadmill.

At the same time, owners of family-size farms have been slipping down. Thousands of farmers commonly considered owners are as insecure as tenants. The farm owner-operator's equity in his property is, on the average, 42 percent, and in some of our best farming sections is as little as one-fifth.

When fully half the total farm population of the United States no longer can feel secure, when millions of our people have lost their roots in the soil, action to provide security is imperative, and will be generally approved. . . .

The Special Committee on Farm Tenancy emphasizes the necessity for action of at least four types: First, action to open the doors of ownership to tenants who now have the requisite ability and experience, but who can become owners only with the assistance of liberal credit, on long terms, and technical advise; second, modest loans, with the necessary guidance and education to prevent small owners from slipping into tenancy, and to help the masses of tenants, croppers and farm laborers at the very bottom of the agricultural ladder increase their standards of living, achieve greater security, and begin the upward climb toward land ownership; third, the retirement by public agencies of land proved to be unsuited for farming, and assistance to the families living thereon in finding homes on good land; fourth, cooperation with state and local agencies of government to improve the general leasing system. These activities which bear such close relation to each other should furnish a sound basis for the beginning of a program for improving the present intolerable condition of the lowest income farm families. . . .

# FIRESIDE CHAT ON THE "COURT PACKING" BILL

*March 9, 1937*

*This was Roosevelt's strongest bid for public support to influence wavering Senators and Representatives in favor of his Judiciary Reorganization Bill. It failed. The fight ran far into the summer and split the huge Democratic majorities in both Houses. Too many Americans distrusted anything that seemed to mean Exec-*

*utive tampering with the independence of the Judiciary. But the Supreme Court itself, before Roosevelt had opportunity to appoint a single Justice, began to find in favor of New Deal measures, most dramatically in cases involving the National Labor Relations Act and the Social Security Act. Roosevelt afterwards declared that although he had lost a battle (for the Bill), he had won the war (for the constitutionality of the New Deal). He had also suffered his first major defeat in Congress.*

My friends, last Thursday I described in detail certain economic problems which everyone admits now face the Nation. For the many messages which have come to me after that speech, and which it is physically impossible to answer individually, I take this means of saying "Thank you."

Tonight, sitting at my desk in the White House, I make my first radio report to the people in my second term of office.

I am reminded of that evening in March, four years ago, when I made my first radio report to you. We were then in the midst of the great banking crisis.

Soon after, with the authority of the Congress, we asked the Nation to turn over all of its privately held gold, dollar for dollar, to the Government of the United States.

Today's recovery proves how right that policy was.

But when, almost two years later, it came before the Supreme Court, its constitutionality was upheld only by a five-to-four vote. The change of one vote would have thrown all the affairs of this great Nation back into hopeless chaos. In effect, four Justices ruled that the right under a private contract to exact a pound of flesh was more sacred than the main objectives of the Constitution to establish an enduring Nation.

In 1933 you and I knew that we must never let our economic system get completely out of joint again—that we could not afford to take the risk of another great depression.

We also became convinced that the only way to avoid a repetition of those dark days was to have a government with power to prevent and to cure the abuses and the inequalities which had thrown that system out of joint.

We then began a program of remedying those abuses and inequalities—to give balance and stability to our economic system—to make it bomb-proof against the causes of 1929.

Today we are only part-way through that program—and recovery is speeding up to a point where the dangers of 1929 are again becoming possible, not this week or month perhaps, but within a year or two.

National laws are needed to complete that program. Individual or local or state effort alone cannot protect us in 1937 any better than ten years ago.

It will take time—and plenty of time—to work out our remedies administratively even after legislation is passed. To complete our program of protection in time, therefore, we cannot delay one moment in making certain that our National Government has power to carry through.

Four years ago action did not come until the eleventh hour. It was almost too late.

If we learned anything from the depression we will not allow ourselves to run around in new circles of futile discussion and debate, always postponing the day of decision.

The American people have learned from the depression. For in the last three national elections an overwhelming majority of them voted a mandate that the Congress and the President begin the task of providing that protection—not after long years of debate, but now.

The Courts, however, have cast doubts on the ability of the elected Congress to protect us against catastrophe by meeting squarely our modern social and economic conditions.

We are at a crisis, a crisis in our ability to proceed with that protection. It is a quiet crisis. There are no lines of depositors outside closed banks. But to the far-sighted it is far-reaching in its possibilities of injury to America.

I want to talk with you very simply tonight about the need for present action in this crisis—the need to meet the unanswered challenge of one-third of a Nation ill-nourished, ill-clad, ill-housed.

Last Thursday I described the American form of Government as a three-horse team provided by the Constitution to the American people so that their field might be plowed. The three horses are, of course, the Congress, the Executive and the Courts. Two of the horses, the Congress and the Executive, are pulling in unison today; the third is not. Those who have intimated that the President of the United States is trying to drive that team, overlook the simple fact that the President, as Chief Executive, is himself one of the three horses.

It is the American people themselves who are in the driver's seat. It is the American people themselves who want the furrow plowed.

It is the American people themselves who expect the third horse to pull in unison with the other two.

I hope that you have re-read the Constitution of the United States in these past few weeks. Like the Bible, it ought to be read again and again.

It is an easy document to understand when you remember that it was called into being because the Articles of Confederation under which the original thirteen States tried to operate after the Revolution showed the need of a National Government with power enough to handle national problems. In its Preamble, the Constitution states that it was intended to form a more perfect Union and promote the general welfare; and the powers given to the Congress to carry out those purposes can best be described by saying that they were all the powers needed to meet each and every problem which then had a national character and which could not be met by merely local action.

But the framers went further. Having in mind that in succeeding generations many other problems then undreamed of would become national problems, they gave to the Congress the ample broad powers "to levy taxes . . . and provide for the common defense and general welfare of the United States."

That, my friends, is what I honestly believe to have been the clear and underlying purpose of the patriots who wrote a Federal Constitution to create a National Government with national power, intended as they said, "to form a more perfect union . . . for ourselves and our posterity."

For nearly twenty years there was no conflict between the Congress and the Court. Then, in 1803, Congress passed a statute which the Court said violated an express provision of the Constitution. The Court claimed the power to declare it unconstitutional and did so declare it. But a little later the Court itself admitted that it was an extraordinary power to exercise and through Mr. Justice Washington laid down this limitation upon it. He said: "It is but a decent respect due to the wisdom, the integrity and the patriotism of the Legislative body, by which any law is passed, to presume in favor of its validity until its violation of the Constitution is proved beyond all reasonable doubt."

But since the rise of the modern movement for social and economic progress through legislation, the Court has more and more often and more and more boldly asserted a power to veto laws passed by the Congress and by State Legislatures in complete disregard of this original limitation, which I have just read.

In the last four years the sound rule of giving statutes the benefit of all reasonable doubt has been cast aside. The Court has been acting not as a judicial body, but as a policy-making body.

When the Congress has sought to stabilize national agriculture, to improve the conditions of labor, to safeguard business against unfair competition, to protect our national resources, and in many other ways to serve our clearly national needs, the majority of the Court has been assuming the power to pass on the wisdom of these Acts of the Congress—and to approve or disapprove the public policy written into these laws.

That is not only my accusation. It is the accusation of most distinguished Justices of the present Supreme Court. I have not the time to quote to you all the language used by dissenting Justices in many of these cases. But in the case holding the Railroad Retirement Act unconstitutional, for instance, Chief Justice Hughes said in a dissenting opinion that the majority opinion was "a departure from sound principles," and placed "an unwarranted limitation upon the commerce clause." And three other Justices agreed with him.

In the case holding the Triple A unconstitutional, Justice Stone said of the majority opinion that it was a "tortured construction of the Constitution." And two other Justices agreed with him.

In the case holding the New York Minimum Wage Law unconstitutional, Justice Stone said that the majority were actually reading into the Constitution their own "personal economic predilections," and that if the legislative power is not left free to choose the methods of solving the problems of poverty, subsistence and health of large numbers in the community, then "government is to be rendered impotent." And two other Justices agreed with him.

In the face of these dissenting opinions, there is no basis for the claim made by some members of the Court that something in the Constitution has compelled them regretfully to thwart the will of the people.

In the face of such dissenting opinions, it is perfectly clear that, as Chief Justice Hughes has said: "We are under a Constitution but the Constitution is what the Judges say it is."

The Court, in addition to the proper use of its judicial functions, has improperly set itself up as a third House of the Congress—a super-legislature, as one of the Justices has called it—reading into the Constitution words and implications which are not there, and which were never intended to be there.

We have, therefore, reached the point as a Nation where we must take action to save the Constitution from the Court and the Court from itself. We must find a way to take an appeal from the Supreme Court to the Constitution itself. We want a Supreme Court which will do justice under the Constitution —not over it. In our Courts we want a government of laws and not of men.

I want—as all Americans want—an independent judiciary as proposed by the framers of the Constitution. That means a

Supreme Court that will enforce the Constitution as written—
that will refuse to amend the Constitution by the arbitrary
exercise of judicial power—amendment, in other words, by
judicial say-so. It does not mean a judiciary so independent
that it can deny the existence of facts which are universally
recognized.

How then could we proceed to perform the mandate given
us? It was said in last year's Democratic platform, and here
are the words, "If these problems cannot be effectively solved
within the Constitution, we shall seek such clarifying amendment as will assure the power to enact those laws, adequately
to regulate commerce, protect public health and safety, and
safeguard economic security." In other words, we said we
would seek an amendment only if every other possible means
by legislation were to fail.

When I commenced to review the situation with the problem squarely before me, I came by a process of elimination to
the conclusion that short of amendments the only method
which was clearly constitutional, and would at the same time
carry out other much needed reforms, was to infuse new
blood into all our Courts. We must have men worthy and
equipped to carry out impartial justice. But, at the same time,
we must have Judges who will bring to the Courts a present-
day sense of the Constitution—Judges who will retain in the
Courts the judicial functions of a court, and reject the legislative powers which the Courts have today assumed.

It is well for us to remember that in forty-five out of the
forty-eight States of the Union Judges are chosen not for life
but for a period of years. In many states Judges must retire
at the age of seventy. Congress has provided financial security
by offering life pensions at full pay for Federal Judges on all
Courts who are willing to retire at seventy. In the case of
Supreme Court Justices that pension is $20,000. a year. But
all Federal Judges, once appointed, can, if they choose, hold
office for life, no matter how old they may get to be.

What is my proposal? It is simply this: Whenever a Judge or
Justice of any Federal Court has reached the age of seventy

and does not avail himself of the opportunity to retire on a pension, a new member shall be appointed by the President then in office, with the approval, as required by the Constitution, of the Senate of the United States.

That plan has two chief purposes. By bringing into the Judicial system a steady and continuing stream of new and younger blood, I hope, first, to make the administration of all Federal justice, from the bottom to the top, speedier and, therefore, less costly; secondly, to bring to the decision of social and economic problems younger men who have had personal experience and contact with modern facts and circumstances under which average men have to live and work. This plan will save our national Constitution from hardening of the judicial arteries.

The number of Judges to be appointed would depend wholly on the decision of present Judges now over seventy, or those who would subsequently reach the age of seventy.

If, for instance, any one of the six Justices of the Supreme Court now over the age of seventy should retire as provided under the plan, no additional place would be created. Consequently, although there never can be more than fifteen, there may be only fourteen, or thirteen, or twelve. And there may be only nine.

There is nothing novel or radical about this idea. It seeks to maintain the Federal bench in full vigor. It has been discussed and approved by many persons of high authority ever since a similar proposal passed the House of Representatives in 1869.

Why was the age fixed at seventy? Because the laws of many states, and the practice of the Civil Service, the regulations of the Army and Navy, and the rules of many of our universities and of almost every great private business enterprise, commonly fix the retirement age at seventy years or less.

The statute would apply to all the Courts in the Federal system. There is general approval so far as the lower Federal courts are concerned. The plan has met opposition only so far as the Supreme Court of the United States itself is concerned.

But, my friends, if such a plan is good for the lower courts it certainly ought to be equally good for the highest Court from which there is no appeal.

Those opposing this plan have sought to arouse prejudice and fear by crying that I am seeking to "pack" the Supreme Court and that a baneful precedent will be established.

What do they mean by the words "packing the Supreme Court"?

Let me answer this question with a bluntness that will end all honest misunderstanding of my purposes.

If by that phrase "packing the Court" it is charged that I wish to place on the bench spineless puppets who would disregard the law and would decide specific cases as I wished them to be decided, I make this answer—that no President fit for his office would appoint, and no Senate of honorable men fit for their office would confirm, that kind of appointees to the Supreme Court.

But if by that phrase the charge is made that I would appoint and the Senate would confirm Justices worthy to sit beside present members of the Court who understand modern conditions—that I will appoint Justices who will not undertake to override the judgment of the Congress on legislative policy—that I will appoint Justices who will act as Justices and not as legislators—if the appointment of such Justices can be called "packing the Court," then I say that I, and with me the vast majority of the American people, favor doing just that thing—now.

Is it a dangerous precedent for the Congress to change the number of the Justices? The Congress has always had, and will have, that power. The number of Justices has been changed several times before—in the Administrations of John Adams and Thomas Jefferson—both of them signers of the Declaration of Independence—in the Administrations of Andrew Jackson, Abraham Lincoln and Ulysses S. Grant.

I suggest only the addition of Justices to the bench in accordance with a clearly defined principle relating to a clearly defined age limit. Fundamentally, if in the future, America cannot trust the Congress it elects to refrain from abuse of our Constitutional usages, democracy will have failed far beyond the importance to democracy of any kind of precedent concerning the Judiciary.

We think it so much in the public interest to maintain a vigorous judiciary that we encourage the retirement of elderly Judges by offering them a life pension at full salary. Why then should we leave the fulfillment of this public policy to chance or make it dependent upon the desire or prejudice of any individual Justice?

It is the clear intention of our public policy to provide for a constant flow of new and younger blood into the Judiciary. Normally every President appoints a large number of District and Circuit Judges and a few members of the Supreme Court. Until my first term practically every President of the United States in our history had appointed at least one member of the Supreme Court. President Taft appointed five members and named a Chief Justice—President Wilson three—President Harding four including a Chief Justice—President Coolidge one—President Hoover three including a Chief Justice.

Such a succession of appointments should have provided a Court well-balanced as to age. But chance and the disinclination of individuals to leave the Supreme bench have now given us a Court in which five Justices will be over seventy-five years of age before next June and one over seventy. Thus a sound public policy has been defeated.

So, I now propose that we establish by law an assurance against any such ill-balanced Court in the future. I propose that hereafter, when a Judge reaches the age of seventy, a new and younger Judge shall be added to the Court automatically. In this way I propose to enforce a sound public policy by law instead of leaving the composition of our Federal Courts, including the highest, to be determined by chance or the personal decision of individuals.

If such a law as I propose is regarded as establishing a new precedent—is it not a most desirable precedent?

Like all lawyers, like all Americans, I regret the necessity of this controversy. But the welfare of the United States, and indeed of the Constitution itself, is what we all must think about first. Our difficulty with the Court today rises not from the Court as an institution but from human beings within it. But we cannot yield our constitutional destiny to the personal judgment of a few men who, being fearful of the future, would deny us the necessary means of dealing with the present.

This plan of mine is no attack on the Court; it seeks to restore the Court to its rightful and historic place in our system of Constitutional Government and to have it resume its high task of building anew on the Constitution "a system of living law." The Court itself can best undo what the Court has done. . . .

## LETTER TO H. G. WELLS

*The White House. March 29, 1937*

*The famous British author was advocating a World Encyclopaedia as the only lasting way of alleviating the world's troubles.*

My dear Wells:

I have been an unconscionable time in thanking you for your good note of the end of the year but, as you know, I have been going through all kinds of troubles with the Supreme Court—the like of which you have not got in England.

I liked your lecture before the Royal Institution with its suggestion of a World Encyclopaedia. Good luck to you in it —but I must tell you frankly that you are more good to the world in writing books, which hundreds of thousands of people read and discuss, then in catering to the intelligentsia— there are so few of them.

Give us some more books that will teach people who can read but have never thought, more about the past and more about the possibilities of the future. Thus you will greatly sustain social democracy.

When are you coming over here again? Do come to see me.

Always sincerely,

## PRESS CONFERENCE #367

*The White House. May 18, 1937*

*Hatred of Roosevelt had become a way of life in some circles.*

THE PRESIDENT: How has everybody been behaving in Washington? We had a grand time on the trip. . . . There are a lot of people coming in today.

MR. YOUNG: They are just curious today.

MR. DONALDSON: All in.

THE PRESIDENT: There isn't very much news but before we talk about news, I am going to ask you for a very few minutes to resolve ourselves into a Committee of the Whole. Off the record, wholly off the record, I just wanted to tell you a story that I think you ought to know because it does affect the Press of the country. I think you will all agree on that when you hear what I am going to read. As you know, I have always encouraged and am entirely in favor of absolute freedom for all news writers. That should be and will continue to be the general rule in Washington. That applies to all news services, for that matter.

There has come out, though, in the past couple of weeks two things from one news service that in a sense does affect the Press of the country as a whole.

The McClure Syndicate, as you probably know—I don't know if you have all seen it—they send out to about 270 papers every week these (indicating) white sheets for publication which constitutes the column in these papers. Of course it is absolutely legitimate that they should collect this news at the White House or from Congress or anybody else. At the same time, with these white sheets for publication, there goes out a pink sheet as information for the editor, marked as being not for publication and is sent to the editor in confidence. Of course you and I know that that is not a news service in the strict sense of the word, but it goes out with the news service and you pay for the whole service at the same time.

Now, there are two things in here that I think you people ought to know about. As I say, this is off the record and just in the family. This pink slip (indicating) dated May 14-15, has the following:

"Unchecked. A New York specialist high in the medical field is authority for the following, which is given in the strictest confidence to editors:

" 'Towards the end of last month Mr. Roosevelt was found in a coma at his desk. Medical examination disclosed the neck rash which is typical of certain disturbing symptoms. Immediate treatment of the most skilled kind was indicated, with complete privacy and detachment from official duties. Hence the trip to southern waters, with no newspaper men on board and a naval convoy which cannot be penetrated.

" 'The unusual activities of Vice President Garner are believed to be in connection with the current situation and its possible developments.'

"Checking has been impossible."

That is number one.

Number 2. This is from the McClure Newspaper Syndicate of May 12-13:

"At a recent private dinner in New York an official of the American Cyanamid expressed in extreme form the bitterness towards the administration which is typical of the personal reactions of many right-wing leaders in business and finance.

"The gentleman in question asserted in so many words that 'the paranoiac in the White House' is destroying the nation, that a couple of well-placed bullets would be the best thing for the country, and that he for one would buy a bottle of champagne as quick as he could get it to celebrate such news."

That is all I wanted to tell you because, after all, all I think I have to do is to repeat that I have been in favor, as you all know, of any legitimate news reporting or news service, no matter what its origin may be and no matter whether for friendly papers or hostile papers—it makes no difference. . . .

Q: That is not newspaper reporting.

THE PRESIDENT: That is just it, it is not newspaper reporting.

Q: Have you taken the matter up with the syndicate?

THE PRESIDENT: No, certainly not.

Q: Isn't that second one actionable under law?

THE PRESIDENT: You know, that does not make any difference at all. The President of the United States does not sue for libel and the Department of Justice does not proceed libelly.

Q: Is it due to the syndicate itself. It might be a fraud? (Laughter)

MR. EARLY: It was checked with Mr. Waldo and Mr. Waldo promised to retract the pink slip with reference to the coma and the President's compulsion to make the trip south if the White House would issue an official denial. Of course the White House would not do it.

Q: How much of this is off the record?

THE PRESIDENT: It is all off the record; all strictly in the family and nothing else, because I thought you people were entitled to know some of the things that go on that none of us approve of. Neither you, nor I, nor the public, nor I believe the great majority of editors would approve of it.

So, that is all right; the Committee will now recess. . . .


## SPECIAL MESSAGE ON FAIR LABOR STANDARDS

*May 24, 1937*

*Now that the Supreme Court was more sympathetic to progressive legislation, Roosevelt pressed Congress to re-enact and put teeth into those parts of NIRA, Section 7A, which had provided national standards of wages and hours and prohibited child la-*

*bor. In 1938 he signed the Fair Labor Standards Act. It pro-*
*vided protection for that majority of American workingmen who*
*belonged to no union and were therefore not directly benefited*
*by the National Labor Relations Act. It was the last important*
*New Deal law Congress would pass.*

The time has arrived for us to take further action to extend the frontiers of social progress. Such further action initiated by the legislative branch of the government, administered by the executive, and sustained by the judicial, is within the common sense framework and purpose of our Constitution and receives beyond doubt the approval of our electorate.

The overwhelming majority of our population earns its daily bread either in agriculture or in industry. One third of our population, the overwhelming majority of which is in agriculture or industry, is ill-nourished, ill-clad and ill-housed.

The overwhelming majority of this Nation has little patience with that small minority which vociferates today that prosperity has returned, that wages are good, that crop prices are high and that government should take a holiday. . . .

Today, you and I are pledged to take further steps to reduce the lag in the purchasing power of industrial workers and to strengthen and stabilize the markets for the farmers' products. The two go hand in hand. Each depends for its effectiveness upon the other. Both working simultaneously will open new outlets for productive capital. Our Nation so richly endowed with natural resources and with a capable and industrious population should be able to devise ways and means of insuring to all our able-bodied working men and women a fair day's pay for a fair day's work. A self-supporting and self-respecting democracy can plead no justification for the existence of child labor, no economic reason for chiseling workers' wages or stretching workers' hours.

Enlightened business is learning that competition ought not to cause bad social consequences which inevitably react upon the profits of business itself. All but the hopelessly reactionary will agree that to conserve our primary resources of man power, government must have some control over maximum hours, minimum wages, the evil of child labor and the exploitation of unorganized labor.

Nearly twenty years ago in his dissenting opinion in *Hammer v. Dagenhart*, Mr. Justice Holmes expressed his views as to the power of the Congress to prohibit the shipment in interstate or foreign commerce of the product of the labor of children in factories below what Congress then deemed to be civilized social standards. Surely the experience of the last twenty years has only served to reinforce the wisdom and the rightness of his views. And, surely if he was right about the power of the Congress over the work of children in factories, it is equally right that the Congress has the power over decent wages and hours in those same factories.

"I had thought that the propriety of the exercise of a power admitted to exist in some cases was for the consideration of Congress alone and that this Court had always disavowed the right to intrude its judgment upon questions of policy or morals. It is not for this Court to pronounce when prohibition is necessary to regulation if it ever may be necessary—to say that it is permissible as against strong drink but not as against the product of ruined lives. . . ."

But although Mr. Justice Holmes spoke for a *minority* of the Supreme Court he spoke for a *majority* of the American people.

One of the primary purposes of the formation of our federal union was to do away with the trade barriers between the states. To the Congress and not to the states was given the power to regulate commerce among the several states. Congress cannot interfere in local affairs but when goods pass through the channels of commerce from one state to another they become subject to the power of the Congress, and the Congress may exercise that power to recognize and protect the fundamental interests of free labor.

And so to protect the fundamental interests of free labor and a free people we propose that only goods which have been produced under conditions which meet the minimum standards of free labor shall be admitted to interstate commerce. Goods produced under conditions which do not meet

rudimentary standards of decency should be regarded as con-
traband and ought not to be allowed to pollute the channels
of interstate trade. . . .

Our problem is to work out in practice those labor standards
which will permit the maximum but prudent employment
of our human resources to bring within the reach of the
average man and woman a maximum of goods and of services
conducive to the fulfillment of the promise of American life.

Legislation can, I hope, be passed at this session of the
Congress further to help those who toil in factory and on farm.
We have promised it. We cannot stand still.


# "QUARANTINE THE AGGRESSORS" SPEECH

*Chicago. October 5, 1937*

*The spread of war—Mussolini's invasion of Abyssinia in 1935,
Franco's rebellion with Mussolini's and Hitler's aid against the
Spanish Republic in 1936, and in July, 1937, Japan's attack on
China—led Roosevelt to go to the isolationist Middle West to
see whether he could win support for an American policy that
would help to unite the peaceful nations in a stand against the
aggressors. He failed.*

Mayor Kelly, Governor Horner, my friends in Chicago:

. . . It is because the people of the United States must, for
the sake of their own future, give thought to the rest of the
world, that I, as the responsible executive head of the Nation,
have chosen this great inland city and this gala occasion to
speak to you on a subject of definite national importance.

The political situation in the world, which of late has been
growing progressively worse, is such as to cause grave concern
and anxiety to all the peoples and nations who wish to live in
peace and amity with their neighbors.

Some fifteen years ago the hopes of mankind for a continuing era of international peace were raised to great heights
when more than sixty nations solemnly pledged themselves
not to resort to arms in furtherance of their national aims

and policies. The high aspirations expressed in the Briand-Kellogg Peace Pact and the hopes for peace thus raised have of late given way to a haunting fear of calamity. The present reign of terror and international lawlessness began a few years ago.

It began through unjustified interference in the internal affairs of other nations or the invasion of alien territory in violation of treaties. It has now reached a stage where the very foundations of civilization are seriously threatened. The landmarks, the traditions which have marked the progress of civilization toward a condition of law and order and justice are being wiped away.

Without a declaration of war and without warning or justification of any kind civilians, including vast numbers of women and children, are being ruthlessly murdered with bombs from the air. In times of so-called peace ships are being attacked and sunk by submarines without cause or notice. Nations are fomenting and taking sides in civil warfare in nations that have never done them any harm. Nations claiming freedom for themselves deny it to others.

Innocent peoples, innocent nations are being cruelly sacrificed to a greed for power and supremacy which is devoid of all sense of justice and humane consideration.

To paraphrase a recent author "perhaps we foresee a time when men, exultant in the technique of homicide, will rage so hotly over the world that every precious thing will be in danger, every book, every picture, every harmony, every treasure garnered through two milleniums, the small, the delicate, the defenseless—all will be lost or wrecked or utterly destroyed."

If those things come to pass in other parts of the world, let no one imagine that America will escape, that America may expect mercy, that this Western Hemisphere will not be attacked and that it will continue tranquially and peacefully to carry on the ethics and the arts of civilization.

No, if those days come "there will be no safety by arms, no help from authority, no answer in science. The storm will rage till every flower of culture is trampled and all human beings are leveled in a vast chaos."

If those days are not to come to pass—if we are to have a world in which we can breathe freely and live in amity without fear—then the peace-loving nations must make a concerted effort to uphold laws and principles on which alone peace can rest secure.

The peace-loving nations must make a concerted effort in opposition to those violations of treaties and those ignorings of humane instincts which today are creating a state of international anarchy, international instability from which there is no escape through mere isolation or neutrality.

Those who cherish their freedom and recognize and respect the equal rights of their neighbors to be free and live in peace, must work together for the triumph of law and moral principles in order that peace, justice and confidence may prevail throughout the world. There must be a return to a belief in the pledged word, in the value of a signed treaty. There must be recognition of the fact that national morality is as vital as private morality.

A bishop wrote to me the other day: "It seems to me that something greatly needs to be said in behalf of ordinary humanity against the present practice of carrying the horrors of war to helpless civilians, especially women and children. It may be that such a protest may be regarded by many, who claim to be realists, as futile, but may it not be that the heart of mankind is so filled with horror at the present needless suffering that that force could be mobilized in sufficient volume to lessen such cruelty in the days ahead. Even though it may take twenty years, which God forbid, for civilization to make effective its corporate protest against this barbarism, surely strong voices may hasten the day."

There is a solidarity, an interdependence about the modern world, both technically and morally, which makes it impossible for any nation completely to isolate itself from political and economic upheavals in the rest of the world, especially when such upheavals appear to be spreading and not declining. There can be no stability or peace either within nations or between nations except under laws and moral standards adhered to by all. International anarchy destroys every foundation for peace. It jeopardizes either the immediate or the future security of every nation, large or small. And it is, therefore, a matter of vital interest and concern to the people of the United States that the sanctity of international treaties and the maintenance of international morality be restored.

The overwhelming majority of all the peoples and nations of the world today want to live in peace. They seek the removal of barriers against trade. They want to exert themselves in industry, in agriculture, in business, that they may increase their wealth through the production of wealth-producing goods rather than striving to produce military planes and bombs and machine guns and cannon for the destruction of human lives and useful property.

In those nations of the world which seem to be piling armament on armament for purposes of aggression, and those other nations which fear acts of aggression against them and their security, a very high proportion of their national income is being spent directly for armaments. It runs from thirty to as high as fifty per cent in most of those cases.

We are fortunate. The proportion that we spend in the United States is far less—eleven or twelve per cent.

How happy we are that the circumstances of the moment permit us to put our money into bridges and boulevards, dams and reforestation, the conservation of our soil and many other kinds of useful works rather than into huge standing armies and vast supplies of implements of war.

Nevertheless, my friends, I am compelled and you are compelled to look ahead. The peace, the freedom, the security of ninety per cent of the population of the world is being jeopardized by the remaining ten per cent who are threatening a breakdown of all international order and law. Surely the ninety per cent who want to live in peace under law and in accordance with moral standards that have received almost uni-

versal acceptance through the centuries, can and must find
some way to make their will prevail.

Yes, the situation is definitely of universal concern. The
questions involved relate not merely to violations of specific
provisions of particular treaties; they are questions of war and
peace, of international law and especially of principles of humanity. It is true that they involve definite violations of
agreements, and especially of the Covenant of the League of
Nations, the Briand-Kellogg Pact and the Nine Power Treaty.
And we have signed both of the last two. But they involve
also problems of world economy, world security and world
humanity.

It is true that the moral consciousness of the world must
recognize the importance of removing injustices and well-
founded grievances; but at the same time it must be aroused
to the cardinal necessity of honoring sanctity of treaties, of
respecting the rights and liberties of others and of putting an
end to acts of international aggression.

It seems to be unfortunately true that the epidemic of world
lawlessness is spreading.

And mark this well! When an epidemic of physical disease
starts to spread, the community approves and joins in a
quarantine of the patients in order to protect the health of
the community against the spread of the disease.

It is my determination to pursue a policy of peace. It is my
determination to adopt every practicable measure to avoid
involvement in war. It ought to be inconceivable that in this
modern era, and in the face of experience, any nation could
be so foolish and ruthless as to run the risk of plunging the
whole world into war by invading and violating in contraven-
tion of solemn treaties, the territory of other nations that have
done them no real harm and which are too weak to protect
themselves adequately. Yet the peace of the world and the
welfare and security of every nation, including our own, is
today being threatened by that very thing.

No nation which refuses to exercise forbearance and to

respect the freedom and rights of others can long remain strong and retain the confidence and respect of other nations. No nation ever loses its dignity or its good standing by conciliating its differences, and by exercising great patience, patience with, and consideration for, the rights of other nations.

War is a contagion, whether it be declared or undeclared. It can engulf states and peoples remote from the original scene of hostilities. Yes, we are determined to keep out of war, yet we cannot insure ourselves against the disastrous effects of war and the dangers of involvement. We are adopting such measures as will minimize our risk of involvement but we cannot have complete protection in a world of disorder in which confidence and security have broken down.

If civilization is to survive the principles of the Prince of Peace must be restored. Shattered trust between nations must be revived.

Most important of all, the will for peace on the part of peace-loving nations must express itself to the end that nations that may be tempted to violate their agreements and the rights of others will desist from such a cause. There must be positive endeavors to preserve peace.

America hates war. America hopes for peace. Therefore, America actively engages in the search for peace.

## LETTER TO RHODA HINKLEY

*The White House. December 16, 1937*

*Warding off the influence of an anti-Administration radio commentator on a Dutchess County friend, Roosevelt tried to explain why he had no confidence in isolationism. But he knew that he had lost the struggle for public opinion, and he did not revive the quarantine idea publicly for another year until he saw the Second World War imminent.*

Dear Rhoda:

You shot so many questions at me that it would take me half an hour to answer them verbally. The simplest way of putting it to you is that Boake Carter's statements, as a general proposition, are half of them untrue and the other half misstated. The particular ones you wrote me about fall into both categories.

The point is that not only this Administration but this Nation want peace—but at the same time they do not want the kind of peace which means definite danger to us at home in the days to come.

I happen to know a very nice Chinese family which lives quite far in the interior. For years they have said that China wanted peace at any price and that they felt no possible harm could come to them back from the seacoast. The other day most of the family was wiped out by some Japanese bombing planes which wrecked their community and killed one thousand people. I got a message from one of the survivors which read "we are no longer for peace at any price."

I hope to see you one of these days soon.

My best wishes for a happy Christmas.

Very sincerely yours,

## LETTER TO JOHN MAYNARD KEYNES

(n.p.) *March 3, 1938*

*The influence of Keynesian economic theory upon the policies of the Roosevelt Administration was evidently quite great. But it worked through assistants and advisers of the President rather than directly, despite such efforts by Keynes as a letter of February 1, 1938, containing an acute analysis of the cause and cure of the current American economic recession, and a suggestion that the recession was in part psychological in origin and the President's fault: "Business men have a different set of delusions from politicians; and need, therefore, different handling. They are, however, much milder than politicians, at the same time allured and terrified by the glare of publicity, easily persuaded to be 'patriots', perplexed, bemused, indeed terrified, yet only too anxious to take a cheerful view, vain perhaps but very unsure of themselves, pathetically responsive to a kind word. You could do anything you liked with them, if you would treat them (even*

*the big ones), not as wolves and tigers, but as domestic animals
by nature, even though they have been badly brought up and
not trained as you would wish. It is a mistake to think that they
are more immoral than politicians. If you work them into the
surly, obstinate, terrified mood, of which domestic animals,
wrongly handled, are so capable, the nation's burdens will not
get carried to market; and in the end public opinion will veer
their way. Perhaps you will rejoin that I have got quite a wrong
idea of what all the backchat amounts to. Nevertheless I record
accurately how it strikes observers here. Forgive the candour of
these remarks. They come from an enthusiastic well-wisher of
you and your policies. . . ." The President sent the following
perfunctory reply, the carbon copy of which in the Roosevelt
Library is marked, "Draft prepared by the Secretary of the
Treasury."*

Dear Mr. Keynes:

I am in receipt of your letter of February first, which I
enjoyed reading. It was very pleasant and encouraging to
know that you are in agreement with so much of the Administration's economic program. This confirmation coming from so
eminent an economist is indeed welcome.

Your analysis of the present business situation is very interesting. The emphasis you put upon the need for stimulating
housing construction is well placed, and I hope that our
efforts will be successful in removing the barriers to the
revival of this industry.

The course of democracy and world peace is of deep concern to me. Domestic prosperity, you will agree, is one of the
most effective contributions the United States can make to
their maintenance. You will likewise appreciate, I am sure,
that prosperity in the United States will be more potent in
attaining the ends we are all interested in if other democracies
strive persistently for similar objectives.

I remember your previous visit very well and I hope we may
have the opportunity to meet again.

Very sincerely yours,

# PRESS CONFERENCE #447

*The White House. April 1, 1938*

*The sharpest test of the Good Neighbor Policy came in Mexico, where the radical-nationalist Cardenas government expropriated American-owned lands and, in a great act of self-determination in 1938, vast American and British oil properties. Some Americans urged the Government to intervene in Mexico by force; the oil companies demanded that the Government exact payment not only for their investments in Mexico but a far larger sum for unexploited subsoil rights. The Administration resisted both demands. It subsequently received the support of the Cardenas Government in the organization of Hemispheric political solidarity.*

Q: Anything you can tell us in regard to the developments in Mexico?

THE PRESIDENT: No, except that somebody—that the discussion seemed to be coming along in a very satisfactory way.

Q: I think that either off the record or for background what we need is a seminar course in America history on the obligations of this country under the construction of the Monroe Doctrine, I mean as far as foreign investments there are concerned.

THE PRESIDENT: That does not involve the Monroe Doctrine in any shape, manner or form. Just for background, the primary question in Mexico is this: There have been two things that have happened over the last—a good many years, which do affect American citizens. The first is the small fellow, the small American, who has gone down there to ranch and farm, etc., and has put everything he has had into his ranch or farm. Under the Mexican policy of distribution of land ownership, quite a number of those poor Americans have been stripped, and their property has been taken, or a part of their property has been taken, and so far, they have not been able to realize on a settlement. Those people, the Mexican Government assures us, are going to be taken care of. They are the real hardship cases.

Then you come to another type of American investment, the Americans who went to Mexico, like William Randolph Hearst, and bought a state legislature, bribed officials and acquired title—this is all background—acquired title to hundreds of thousands of acres of land for practically nothing except the cost of the bribe, or they paid three cents on the acre for it, things like that, and then claimed all kinds of damages in a sum far in excess of the amount of money that he had actually put in. We have not got much sympathy with trying to collect that excessive sum for him.

The same thing in a different way, without any bribery—leave out that element—in the case of oil companies. It comes down to the same proposition of the holding company in this country. Oil companies have gone down there and they have invested money. Now, the Mexican Government would expropriate their property; they are condemning it. We feel that these oil companies should get payment from the Mexican Government for the actual sum invested in the oil lands and in the drilling operations and the pumping and the refining, and so forth and so on, less depreciation, so that they would come out with a whole skin.

That is the policy of the Government, we have always wanted to do that, and the Mexican Government has sent a note from President Cardenas, which got to Washington this morning, and which they will give out in Washington, which seems to be a very satisfactory thing. That is why I say that the situation is, on the whole, developing all right.

Those companies ought not to have prospective profits given to them. If I have a piece of land at Warm Springs that is worth $5,000., and the Government, or the State of Georgia wants to take it over, I ought to get $5,000. out of it. I ought not to be able to say, "In a few years this is going to be worth $20,000., so you have got to pay me $20,000. . . ."

# SPEECH IN DEMOCRATIC PRIMARY
# ELECTION CAMPAIGN

*Barnesville, Georgia. August 11, 1938*

*Conservative Democrats in Congress, chiefly Southerners, were combining with Republicans to defeat Administration policies. In the Congressional primaries of 1938, the President urged that the Republican Party become the exclusive home of conservatives and the Democratic the exclusive home of liberals. With one exception in New York, the "purge" campaign failed. On this occasion his target sat on the platform with him.*

Governor Rivers, Senator George, Senator Russell, and my neighbors of Georgia:

. . . Fourteen years ago a democratic Yankee, a comparatively young man, came to a neighboring county in the State of Georgia, came in search of a pool of warm water wherein he might swim his way back to health, and he found it. The place—Warm Springs—was at that time a rather dilapidated small summer resort. But his new neighbors there extended to him the hand of genuine hospitality, welcomed him to their firesides and made him feel so much at home that he built himself a house, bought himself a farm and has been coming back ever since. Yes, he proposes to keep to that good custom. I intend coming back very often.

In those days, there was only one discordant note in that first stay of mine at Warm Springs: When the first of the month bill came in for electric light in my little cottage I found that the charge was eighteen cents a kilowatt hour—about four times as much as I was paying in another community, Hyde Park, New York. And that light bill started my long study of proper public utility charges for electric current, started in my mind the whole subject of getting electricity into farm homes throughout the United States.

And so, my friends, it can be said with a good deal of truth that a little cottage at Warm Springs, Georgia, was the birthplace of the Rural Electrification Administration. Six years ago, in 1932, there was much talk about the more wide-spread and the cheaper use of electricity, but it is only since March 4, 1933, that your Government has reduced that talk to practical results. Yes, electricity is a modern necessity of life, not a luxury. That necessity ought to be found in every village, in every home and on every farm in every part of the wide United States. The dedication of this Rural Electrification Administration project in Georgia today is a symbol of the progress we are making—and, my friends, we are not going to stop.

As you know, when I want to go somewhere I generally try to choose the most direct route but I slipped up this time. I wanted to come to Georgia, but I had to come via California, the Galapagós Islands, the Equator, the Panama Canal and Pensacola. But, before I left on that trip about a month ago, I invited a group of distinguished, broad-minded Southerners to meet in Washington to discuss the economic conditions, the problems of the South. And, when they met I said this to them:

"My intimate interest in all that concerns the South is, I believe, known to all of you; but this interest is far more than a sentimental attachment born of a considerable residence in your section and of close personal friendship for so many of your people. It proceeds even more from my feeling of responsibility toward the whole Nation. It is my conviction that the South presents right now, in 1938, the Nation's No. 1 economic problem—the Nation's problem, not merely the South's. For we have an economic unbalance in the Nation as a whole, due to this very condition in the South itself.

"It is an unbalance that can and must be righted, righted for the sake of the South and of the Nation."

The day before yesterday when I landed in Florida I received the report and the recommendations based on the advice of this distinguished commission. This report and the recommendations will be made public in the course of the next day or two and I hope you will read it.

It is well said that this report "presents in only a small degree the manifold assets and advantages possessed by the

South" because the report is concerned primarily not with boasting about what the South has but in telling what the South needs. It is a short report divided into fifteen short sections and it covers in a broad way subjects of vital importance, such as economic resources, soil, water, population, private and public income, education, health, housing, labor, ownership and use of land, credit, use of natural resources, industry and purchasing power. . . .

You are familiar enough with the processes of Government to know that the Chief Executive cannot take action on national or regional problems unless they have been first translated into Acts of Congress passed by the Senate and the House of Representatives of the United States.

Such action by the Congress, it is equally clear, must be vigorously supported by the Senators and Representatives whose constituents are directly concerned with Southern economics and Southern economic needs. Senators and Congressmen who are not wholeheartedly in sympathy with these needs cannot be expected to give them vigorous support.

Translating that into more intimate terms, it means that if the people of the State of Georgia want definite action in the Congress of the United States, they must send to that Congress Senators and Representatives who are willing to stand up and fight—fight night and day for Federal statutes drawn to meet actual needs—not something that serves merely to gloss over the evils of the moment, gloss them over for the time being, but laws with teeth in them that will go to the root of the problem; which remove the inequities, raise the standards and, over a period of years, give constant improvement to the conditions of human life in this State.

You, the people of Georgia, in the coming Senatorial primary, for example, have a perfect right to choose any candidate you wish. I do not seek to impair that right and I am not going to impair that right of the people of this State,—but because Georgia has been good enough to call me her adopted son and because for many long years I have regarded this State as my "other state," I feel no hesitation in telling you what I would do if I could vote here next month. And, my friends, I am strengthened in that decision to give you my personal opinion of the coming Senatorial primary by the fact that during the past few weeks I have had many requests from distinguished citizens of Georgia—from people high and low—from the Chief Justice of the highest court of Georgia and many others.

And let me preface my statement by saying that I have personally known three of the candidates for the United States Senate for many years. All of them have had legislative or executive experience as Government servants. We may therefore justly consider their records and their public utterances— and we can justly, also, seek to determine for ourselves what is their inward point of view in relationship to present and future problems of government.

It has been pointed out by writers and speakers who do not analyze public questions very deeply that in passing through the State of Kentucky a month ago I gave as a reason for the reelection of Senator Barkley that he had had very long and successful service in the Congress of the United States and that his opponent did not have that experience. In Kentucky, there was no clear-cut issue between a liberal on the one side and a died-in-the-wool conservative on the other. Neither of the two principals on his record could be classified as a reactionary; and, therefore, the criterion of experience, especially that of the Majority Leadership of the Senate of the United States, weighed heavily, and properly, in favor of Senator Barkley.

Here in Georgia, however, my old friend, the senior Senator [George] from this State, cannot possibly in my judgment be classified as belonging to the liberal school of thought—and, therefore, the argument that he has long served in the Senate, I think, falls by the wayside. Here in Georgia the issue is a different one from that in Kentucky.

I speak seriously and in the most friendly way in terms of liberal and conservative for the very simple fact, and I am sure you will recognize, that on my shoulders rests a responsibility to the people of the United States. In 1932 and again in 1936 I was chosen Chief Executive with the mandate to seek by definite action to correct many evils of the past and of the present; to work for a wider distribution of national income, to improve the conditions of life, especially among those who need it most and, above all, to use every honest effort to keep America in the van of social and economic progress.

To the Congress of the United States I make recommendations—that is all—in most cases recommendations relating to objectives of legislation—leaving it to the Congress to translate the recommendations into law. The majority of the Senate and House have agreed with those objectives and have worked with me and I have worked with them to translate those objectives into action. Some have given "lip service" to some of the objectives but have not raised their little fingers actively to attain the objectives themselves. Too often these few have listened to the dictatorship of a small minority of individuals and corporations who oppose the objectives themselves. That, my friends, is a real dictatorship and one that I am glad to say we have been getting away from slowly but surely during the past five years. And just as long as I live, as long as I live you will find me fighting against any kind of dictatorship—especially the kind of dictatorship that has enslaved many of our fellow citizens for more than half a century.

Now, my friends, what I am about to say will be no news, no startling news to my old friend—and I say it with the utmost sincerity—Senator Walter George. It will be no surprise to him because I have recently had personal correspondence with him and, as a result of it, he fully knows what my views are.

Let me make it clear—let me make something very clear that he is, and I hope always will be, my personal friend. He is beyond question, beyond any possible question, a gentleman and a scholar—but there are other gentlemen in the Senate and in the House for whom I have a real affectionate regard but with whom I differ heartily and sincerely on the principles and policies of how the Government of the United States ought to be run.

For example, I have had an almost lifelong acquaintance and great personal friendship for people like Senator Hale from the State of Maine, for Representative James Wadsworth of New York and for the Minority Leader, Representative Snell. All of these lifelong conservative Republicans are gentlemen and scholars—but they and I learned long ago that our views on public questions were just as wide apart as the North Pole and the South.

And, therefore, I repeat that I trust and am confident that Senator George and I will always be good personal friends even though I am impelled to make it clear that on most public questions he and I do not speak the same language.

To carry out my responsibility as President, it is clear that if there is to be success in our Government there ought to be cooperation between members of my own party and myself,— cooperation, in other words, within the majority party, between one branch of Government, the Legislative branch, and the executive head of the other branch, which is the Executive. That is one of the essentials of a party form of government. It has been going on in this country for nearly a century and a half. The test is not measured, in the case of an individual, by his every vote on every bill—of course not. The test lies rather in the answer to two questions: first, has the record of the candidate shown, while differing perhaps in details, a constant active fighting attitude in favor of the broad objectives of the party and of Government as they are constituted today and, secondly, does the candidate really, in his heart, deep down in his heart, believe in those objectives? And I regret that in the case of my friend, Senator George, I cannot honestly answer either of these questions in the affirmative.

And, my friends, in the case of another candidate in the State of Georgia for the United States Senate—former Governor Talmadge (boos)—I have known him in the State of Georgia for many years. His attitude toward me and toward other members of the Government in 1935 and in 1936 concerns me not at all. But, my friends, in those years and in this year I have read so many of his proposals, so many of his promises, so many of his panaceas that I am very certain in my own mind that his election would contribute very little to practical progress in government. And, my friends, that is all that I can say about him. . . .

## CABLEGRAM TO ADOLPH HITLER

*The White House. September 27, 1938*

*During the Munich Crisis the President chose a moment when Prime Minister Neville Chamberlain of Great Britain promised to reject Hitler's demands for portions of Czechoslovakia to urge the dictator to settle the issue peacefully. But Chamberlain and Premier Daladier of France on September 30 gave in to Hitler's threats for the sake of "peace in our time."*

I desire to acknowledge Your Excellency's reply to my telegram of September 26. I was confident that you would coincide in the opinion I expressed regarding the unforeseeable consequences and the incalculable disaster which would result to the entire world from the outbreak of a European war.

The question before the world today, Mr. Chancellor, is not the question of errors of judgment or of injustices committed in the past. It is the question of the fate of the world today and tomorrow. The world asks of us who at this moment are heads of nations the supreme capacity to achieve the destinies of nations without forcing upon them as a price, the mutilation and death of millions of citizens.

Resort to force in the Great War failed to bring tranquillity. Victory and defeat were alike sterile. That lesson the world should have learned. For that reason above all others I addressed on September 26 my appeal to Your Excellency and to the President of Czechoslovakia and to the Prime Ministers of Great Britain and of France.

The two points I sought to emphasize were, first, that all matters of difference between the German Government and the Czechoslovak Government could and should be settled by pacific methods; and, second, that the threatened alternative of the use of force on a scale likely to result in a general war is as unnecessary as it is unjustifiable. It is, therefore, supremely important that negotiations should continue without interruption until a fair and constructive solution is reached.

My conviction on these two points is deepened because responsible statesmen have officially stated that an agreement in principle has already been reached between the Government of the German Reich and the Government of Czechoslovakia, although the precise time, method and detail of carrying out that agreement remain at issue.

Whatever existing differences may be, and whatever their merits may be—and upon them I do not and need not undertake to pass—my appeal was solely that negotiations be continued until a peaceful settlement is found, and that thereby a resort to force be avoided.

Present negotiations still stand open. They can be continued if you will give the word. Should the need for supplementing them become evident, nothing stands in the way of widening their scope into a conference of all the nations directly interested in the present controversy. Such a meeting to be held immediately—in some neutral spot in Europe—would offer the opportunity for this and correlated questions to be solved in a spirit of justice, of fair dealing, and, in all human probability, with greater permanence.

In my considered judgment, and in the light of the experience of this century, continued negotiations remain the only way by which the immediate problem can be disposed of upon any lasting basis.

Should you agree to a solution in this peaceful manner I am convinced that hundreds of millions throughout the world would recognize your action as an outstanding historic service to all humanity.

Allow me to state my unqualified conviction that history,

and the souls of every man, woman, and child whose lives will be lost in the threatened war will hold us and all of us accountable should we omit any appeal for its prevention.

The Government of the United States has no political involvements in Europe, and will assume no obligations in the conduct of the present negotiations. Yet in our own right we recognize our responsibilities as a part of a world of neighbors.

The conscience and the impelling desire of the people of my country demand that the voice of their government be raised again and yet again to avert and to avoid war.

## ANNUAL MESSAGE TO CONGRESS

*January 4, 1939*

*This Message marked the most important turning point in the twelve-year history of the Roosevelt Administration. Lacking confidence in the Munich Agreement, the President decided that the United States should strengthen opposition of the peaceful nations to the Axis powers, in the first place, repeal the embargo on arms to aggressor and defender nations alike, and substitute a discriminatory embargo against aggressors alone. He decided that this was so important as a possible deterrent to the makers of a second world war that he subordinated the struggle for further domestic reforms to the drive against isolationism. The creative phase of the New Deal ended; its meaning was reinterpreted as a basis for consolidation of national unity and organization of defense; and the struggle for a new foreign policy of collective security began in earnest.*

In reporting on the state of the nation, I have felt it necessary on previous occasions to advise the Congress of disturbance abroad and of the need of putting our own house in order in the face of storm signals from across the seas. As this Seventy-Sixth Congress opens there is need for further warning.

A war which threatened to envelop the world in flames has been averted: but it has become increasingly clear that world peace is not assured.

All about us rage undeclared wars—military and economic. All about us grow more deadly armaments—military and economic. All about us are threats of new aggression—military and economic.

Storms from abroad directly challenge three institutions indispensable to Americans, now as always. The first is religion. Religion is the source of the other two—democracy and international good faith.

Religion, by teaching man his relationship to God, gives the individual a sense of his own dignity and teaches him to respect himself by respecting his neighbors.

Democracy, the practice of self-government, is a covenant among free men to respect the rights and liberties of their fellows.

International good faith, a sister of democracy, springs from the will of civilized nations of men to respect the rights and liberties of other nations of men.

In a modern civilization, all three—religion, democracy and international good faith—complement and support each other.

Where freedom of religion has been attacked, the attack has come from sources opposed to democracy. Where democracy has been overthrown, the spirit of free worship has disappeared. And where religion and democracy have vanished, good faith and reason in international affairs have given way to strident ambition and brute force.

An ordering of society which relegates religion, democracy and good faith among nations to the background can find no place within it for the ideals of the Prince of Peace. The United States rejects such an ordering, and retains its ancient faith.

There comes a time in the affairs of men when they must prepare to defend not their homes alone but the tenets of faith and humanity on which their churches, their governments and their very foundations are set. The defense of religion, of democracy and of good faith among nations is all the same fight. To save one we must now make up our minds to save all.

And we know what might happen to us of the United States if the new philosophies of force were to encompass the other continents and invade our own. We, no more than other nations, can afford to be surrounded by the enemies of our faith and our humanity. Fortunate it is, therefore, that in this Western Hemisphere we have, under a common ideal of democratic government, a rich diversity of resources and of peoples functioning together in mutual respect and peace.

That Hemisphere, that peace, and that ideal we propose to do our share in protecting against storms from any quarter. Our people and our resources are pledged to secure that protection. And from that determination no American flinches.

This by no means implies that the American Republics disassociate themselves from the nations of other continents— it does not mean the Americas against the rest of the world. We as one of the Republics reiterate our willingness to help the cause of world peace. We stand on our long historic offer to take counsel with all other nations of the world to the end that aggression among them may be terminated, that the race of armaments cease and that commerce be renewed.

But the world has grown so small and the weapons of attack so swift that no nation can be safe in its will to peace so long as any other powerful nation refuses to settle its grievances at the council table.

For if any government bristling with implements of war insists on policies of force, weapons of defense give the only safety.

In our foreign relations we have learned from the past what not to do. From new wars we have learned what we must do.

We have learned that effective timing of defense, and the distant points from which attacks may be launched are completely different from what they were twenty years ago.

We have learned that survival cannot be guaranteed by

arming after the attack begins—for there is new range, new speed to offense.

We have learned that long before any overt military act, aggression begins with preliminaries of propaganda, subsidized penetration, the loosening of ties of good will, the stirring of prejudice and the incitement to disunion.

We have learned that God-fearing democracies of the world which observe the sanctity of treaties and good faith in their dealings with other nations cannot safely be indifferent to international lawlessness anywhere. No, they cannot forever let pass, without effective protest, acts of aggression against sister nations—acts which automatically undermine all of us.

Obviously they must proceed along practical, peaceful lines. But the mere fact that we rightly decline to intervene with arms to prevent acts of aggression does not mean that we must act as if there were no aggression at all. Words may be futile, but war is not the only means of commanding a decent respect for the opinions of mankind. There are many methods short of war, but stronger and more effective than mere words, of bringing home to aggressor governments the aggregate sentiments of our own people.

At the very least, we can and should avoid any action, or any lack of action, which will encourage, assist or build up an aggressor. We have learned that when we deliberately try to legislate neutrality, our neutrality laws may operate unevenly and unfairly—may actually give aid to an aggressor and deny it to the victim. The instinct of self-preservation should warn us that we ought not to let that happen any more.

And we have learned something else—the old, old lesson that probability of attack is mightily decreased by the assurance of an ever ready defense. Since 1931, nearly eight years ago, world events of thunderous import have moved with lightning speed. During these eight years many of our people clung to the hope that the innate decency of mankind would protect the unprepared who showed their innate trust in mankind. Today we are all wiser—and sadder.

Under modern conditions what we mean by "adequate defense"—a policy subscribed to by all of us—must be divided into three elements. First we must have armed forces and defenses strong enough to ward off any sudden attack against strategic positions and key facilities essential to ensure sustained resistance and ultimate victory. Secondly we must have the organization and the location of those key facilities so that they may be immediately utilized and rapidly expanded to meet all needs without danger of serious interruption by enemy attack.

In the course of a few days I shall send to you a special message making recommendations for those two essentials of defense against danger which we cannot safely assume will not come.

If these first two essentials are reasonably provided for, we must be able confidently to invoke the third element, the underlying strength of citizenship—the self-confidence, the ability, the imagination and the devotion that give the staying power to see things through.

A strong and united nation may be destroyed if it is unprepared against sudden attack. But even a nation well armed and well organized from a strictly military point of view, may, after a period of time, meet defeat if it is unnerved by self-distrust, endangered by class prejudice, by dissension between capital and labor, by false economy and by other unsolved social problems at home.

In meeting the troubles of the world we must meet them as one people—with a unity born of the fact that for generations those who have come to our shores, representing many kindreds and tongues, have been welded by common opportunity into a united patriotism. If another form of government can present a united front in its attack on a democracy, the attack must and will be met by a united democracy. Such a democracy can and must exist in the United States.

A dictatorship may command the full strength of a regimented nation. But the united strength of a democratic nation can be mustered only when its people, educated by modern standards to know what is going on and where they are going, have conviction that they are receiving as large a share of opportunity for development, as large a share of material success and of human dignity, as they have a right to receive.

Our nation's program of social and economic reform is therefore a part of defense, a part as basic as armaments themselves.

Against the background of events in Europe, in Africa and in Asia during these recent years, the pattern of what we here have accomplished since 1933 appears in even clearer focus.

For the first time we have moved upon deep-seated problems affecting our national strength and have forged national instruments adequate to meet them. . . .

We have now passed the period of internal conflict in the launching of our program of social reform. Our full energies may now be released to invigorate the processes of recovery in order to preserve our reforms, and to give every man and woman who wants to work a real job at a living wage.

But time is of paramount importance. The deadline of danger from within and from without is not within our control. The hour-glass may be in the hands of other nations. Our own hour-glass tells us that we are off on a race to make democracy work, so that we may be efficient in peace and therefore secure in national defense.

This time element forces us to still greater efforts to attain the full employment of our labor and our capital. . . .

I hear some people say "This is all so complicated. There are certain advantages in a dictatorship. It gets rid of labor trouble, it gets rid of unemployment, of wasted motion and of having to do your own thinking".

My answer is "yes, but it also gets rid of some other things which we Americans intend very definitely to keep—and we still intend to do our own thinking."

It will cost us taxes and the voluntary risk of capital to attain some of the practical advantages which other forms of government have acquired.

Dictatorship, however, involves costs which the American people will never pay: The cost of our spiritual values. The cost of the blessed right of being able to say what we please. The cost of freedom of religion. The cost of seeing our capital confiscated. The cost of being cast into a concentration camp. The cost of being afraid to walk down the street with the wrong neighbor. The cost of having our children brought up not as free and dignified human beings, but as pawns molded and enslaved by a machine.

If the avoidance of these costs means taxes on my income; if avoiding these costs means taxes on my estate at death, I would bear those taxes willingly as the price of my breathing and my children breathing the free air of a free country, as the price of a living and not a dead world.

Events across the sea have made it increasingly clear to the American people that dangers within are less to be feared than dangers from without. If therefore a solution of this problem of idle men and idle capital is the price of preserving our liberty, no formless selfish fears can stand in the way.

Once I prophesied that this generation of Americans had a rendezvous with destiny. That prophecy comes true. To us much is given; more is expected.

This generation will "nobly save or meanly lose the last best hope of earth. . . . The way is plain, peaceful, generous, just —a way which if followed the world will forever applaud and God must forever bless".

## PRESS CONFERENCE #523

*The White House. February 3, 1939*

*But isolationists, too, sharpened their weapons, and the President had furthermore to contend against the accumulated distempers of the six strenuous New Deal years. Scare rumors and worse had become standard fare in public debate. For more than three months Roosevelt refrained from bringing to bear on Congress the public pressure that angered his opponents and had failed in the "Court packing" fight. One rumor, however, made him burst out.*

THE PRESIDENT: . . . I had always supposed, and I still believe, that the foreign policy of the United States should not be involved in either legislative or party or newspaper politics. In other words, I do not think that the 1940 campaign should enter into the problem either on foreign policy or American defense in the year 1939. All you have to do is to read stories and headlines to realize that pure guesses dressed up have become, in the next step, statements of fact. I have in front of me, Oh, about eight or ten different newspapers. There isn't one story or one headline in all of those papers that does not give, to put it politely, an erroneous impression—not one. It is a rather interesting fact. These things have been manufactured by deliberate misrepresentation of facts, existing facts. The foreign policy has not changed and it is not going to change. If you want a comparatively simple statement of the policy, I will give it to you and Kannee can copy it out afterwards:

Number 1: We are against any entangling alliances, obviously.

Number 2: We are in favor of the maintenance of world trade for everybody—all nations—including ourselves.

Number 3: We are in complete sympathy with any and every effort made to reduce or limit armaments.

Number 4: As a Nation—as American people—we are sympathetic with the peaceful maintenance of political, economic and social independence of all nations in the world.

Now, that is very, very simple. There is absolutely nothing new in it. The American people are beginning to realize that the things they have read and heard, both from agitators of the legislative variety and the agitators of the newspaper owner variety, have been pure bunk—b-u-n-k, bunk; that these people are appealing to the ignorance, the prejudice and the fears of Americans and are acting in an un-American way.

You will also notice that quite a number of them are receiving the loud acclaim, the applause of those governments in the world which do not believe in the continued independence of all nations.

I think that covers it pretty well.

Q: Mr. President, did the Rome Embassy report to you that the Italian Government is going to change the name of Via Woodrow Wilson to Hamilton Fish?

THE PRESIDENT: All I can say is that that is rather joyous.

Q: Is it possible then, in connection with this, to clarify the differences in interpretations that have been coming from the conferences you have had? In other words, can you now give us exactly what happened there?

THE PRESIDENT: I don't believe I could without asking them on the Hill what they think about it.

Now, on the question of secrecy, that also is 100% bunk.

Q: In what way?

THE PRESIDENT: In this way: I will ask you a question: Do you think that—suppose I had information which came in through the intelligence service, that such and such things were going on in such and such a country. There are no names, no way of proving the information before a court, and yet it is information which, because it has been checked from two or three different sources, looks to be, as far as we can tell now, reasonably true.

Now, suppose I held a press conference every day and gave out information of that kind to the public. In the first place, we are not definitely sure of it; it would be almost like certain stories that you read—many of them are true, many of them turn out later on not to be true. In the second place, giving out information of that kind would completely terminate the getting of future information, because the sources of the information would be immediately blocked.

Now, in that conference the other day, I told them of some things, information of that type, which we at the present time believe to be true but it is not the kind of thing to write a newspaper story about because it may not be true. It is merely our best slant as of today. It may be changed two weeks or a month from now by other information.

That is the only element of secrecy that has entered into either of the conferences, either with the Senate Committee or the House Committee. I told them both one or two pieces of—you would not even call it information—matters that have been reported to us, which we have reason to believe are true. Now, that is the only element of secrecy in either of those conferences. The rest of the conferences related solely to what I have just given you.

Q: One of the principal items of the conference is that you are supposed to have told some of the conferees that the Rhine was our frontier in the battle of democracies versus fascism.

THE PRESIDENT: What shall I say? Shall I be polite or call it by the right name?

Q: Call it by the right name.

THE PRESIDENT: Deliberate lie.

Q: That goes, too, for the French?

THE PRESIDENT: Yes.

Q: May we quote that?

THE PRESIDENT: Yes.

Q: Was there any discussion of the manner in which the purchase of planes by France and Great Britain would be financed?

THE PRESIDENT: Well, they asked in both conferences—the question has been asked about ten times before, "Are they going to be paid for in cash?" I said, "Yes." That is all; there is no further discussion.

Q: Will the R. F. C. help them?

THE PRESIDENT: No. . . .

## LETTER TO JOHN CUDAHY

*The White House. March 4, 1939*

*Roosevelt described what he* had *said in a letter to the United States Minister to Ireland.*

Dear John:

. . .The truth about the newspaper story is, of course, a very simple and obvious one. I never of course mentioned frontiers on the Rhine or in France or anywhere else but I did point out that there are fifteen or sixteen independent nations in Europe whose continued independent political and economic existence is of actual moment to the ultimate defense of the United States. I pointed out that if, for example, the Baltic States went the way of Czechoslovakia and fell completely under German domination, the American position would be to that extent weakened. That if the Scandinavian countries were to lose their present political and economic independence, again the position of the United States would be weakened. That the same thing holds true with regard to Holland and Belgium and Portugal and even Greece, Egypt and Turkey—not to mention Romania, Bulgaria and Yugoslavia. And I pointed out that Czechoslovakia, a year ago could very properly be called a link in American defense against German and Italian aggression in the future; that Czechoslovakia no longer constituted such a link.

All of which was, of course, not only true but proper. The howls and curses that have continued to come from Berlin and Rome convinces me that the general result has been good even if a few silly Senators reported the conversation in a wholly untruthful way.

As ever yours,

## LETTER TO LINDSAY ROGERS

*Warm Springs. April 7, 1939*

*The President invited the King and Queen of England to visit him and Mrs. Roosevelt. The visit was a demonstration of Anglo-American friendship at a moment when the Chamberlain Government, following Hitler's occupation on March 15 of the remainder of Czechoslovakia in violation of his Munich pledge, had finally begun to take a stand against further aggressions. The problem of Their Majesties' visit was to make it reduce*

*anti-British sentiment, which was a chief ingredient of isolation-*
*ism. Professor Rogers of Columbia University wrote to the Presi-*
*dent on April 3: "On page 201 of Mrs. Woodrow Wilson's*
*(somewhat amazing) My Memoir, there is a story which will*
*amuse you. She tells how the Lord Chamberlain and another*
*elderly peer waited on her and President Wilson in their apart-*
*ments in Buckingham Palace and escorted them into the pres-*
*ence of the King and Queen for the state dinner. The two peers*
*waving wands, moving to the rear, bowing low every three*
*paces, took the Wilsons down one long corridor, up a great stair-*
*case, and then backed down another long corridor before the*
*cavalcade debouched into the drawing room. Is your Lord*
*Chamberlain trained to reciprocate? Even though he won't have*
*to do it, you might like to watch him practice." In the event,*
*the Roosevelts organized a picnic for Their Majesties at Hyde*
*Park where they ate hot dogs with sensational political success.*

Dear Lindsay:—

That story of the Wilsons' visit in Buckingham Palace is a
joy. I am inclined to think that when the scene is transferred to
the White House I will have one of the Roosevelt grandchildren rap on the royal doors and sing out "SUPPER'S READY."

> With all good wishes,
> Always sincerely,

## MEMORANDUM FOR CORDELL HULL

*The White House. April 27, 1939*

*The Secretary of State had passed on to the President an in-*
*quiry by the Soviet Government whether Constantine A. Ou-*
*mansky would be acceptable as Soviet Ambassador to the United*
*States.*

Yes, but double the guard!

## LETTER TO NICHOLAS ROOSEVELT

*The White House. June 15, 1939*

*The "famous book" was the notorious smear by Elizabeth Dilling, The Red Network.*

Dear Nick:

Many thanks for that nice note of yours. I wish that you could have met the King and Queen—they are very delightful and understanding people, and, incidentally, know a great deal not only about foreign affairs in general but also about social legislation. Actually they would qualify for inclusion in that famous book, which is constantly quoted by some of *your friends—not mine*—to the effect that Eleanor and I are Communists!

As ever yours,


## PRESS CONFERENCE #564

*Hyde Park. July 21, 1939*

*The Administration held Congress in session to repeal the arms embargo until weary Senators forced the President to give up. But from this, his last important defeat in foreign affairs, Roosevelt extracted full benefit from the fact that the Senators based their final position not on denial of the President's argument that repeal might deter Hitler from starting a second world war, but on a prediction that there would be no war in Europe before Congress reconvened in January.*

Q (MR. DURNO): Mr. President, the isolation group in the Senate is predicting very freely that you are going to carry the neutrality issue to the country in your forthcoming western swing. Can you comment on that?

THE PRESIDENT: On the neutrality issue?

Q: The arms embargo.

THE PRESIDENT: Isn't that closed until January?

Q: Well—

THE PRESIDENT: (interposing) By action of the Senate? I think that is the best way of handling it. There is no and there cannot be any immediate issue before the country because certain groups in the Senate just precluded any action until January, making it perfectly clear, of course,—and they have accepted it—that the responsibility rests wholly on them.

Of course, one of the important things to bring out on that —what was it? Tuesday night—is the fact that they were willing to accept the responsibility. And, as Steve (Mr. Early) told you yesterday, about all we can do between now and January is to pray that there won't be another crisis, and pray awfully hard.

Q (MR. HARKNESS): After the session on Tuesday, various participants, various Senators, gave their version of the meeting, what they had said to you, and more, what you had said to them.

THE PRESIDENT: It is like the old story of the Congressman that went in to see Mr. Hoover, I think it was, and was actually in Mr. Hoover's office by a stop watch for a minute and a half and then went out into the lobby and took ten minutes to tell the Press what he had told President Hoover. I have always loved the story. You remember that?

Q (MR. O'DONNELL): Yes, and I remember the Congressman too.

THE PRESIDENT: Go ahead, I did not mean to interrupt.

Q (MR. HARKNESS): That is a fitting story, and that is the way I meant it. But there was only one side of that conference came out and I wondered if you had anything to say about the conference itself.

THE PRESIDENT: Except this, that any stories that there was any—I do not know—what is the term for it?

Q: I used "clashes," "verbal clashes."

THE PRESIDENT: "Clashes," right. I think it was John (Mr. O'Donnell) that said it was bitter. Did you ever see me bitter, John?

Q (MR. O'DONNELL): No, sir.

THE PRESIDENT: There weren't any clashes. That part is

entirely made up out of whole cloth. There was only one disagreement between two people in the conference and that was the fact—this has been printed—the fact was that Senator Borah did intimate rather clearly and definitely that his information, his private information from Europe was better than the information received by the United States Government from Europe and the Secretary of State asked him if he intended that as a suggestion that the State Department information was not as good as his own private information. He finally said that he had meant to infer that. It was all in very parliamentary language.

Q (MR. HARKNESS): Did Vice President Garner step into that situation?

THE PRESIDENT: No, he did not.

Q (MR. HARKNESS): Did the Vice President use this line, "Captain, we may as well be candid; you haven't got the votes"?

THE PRESIDENT: No. No. When it became perfectly clear from a statement by the Republican Leader that the Republicans would vote en masse for postponement until January, and then Senator Barkley said there would probably be sufficient Democrats to go along with them to prevent a vote being taken if Congress stayed in session, nobody had to say anything more. That was obvious.

No, the thing came down to that simple fact, that the Republicans as a whole were going to work against the taking of a vote until January, one hundred per cent of them, and that about a third of the Democrats were going to do the same thing. That does not even raise the question of whether there was a minority or a majority because, under the Senate rules, any sizeable group can prevent action. And the statement, of course, as written, did show the acceptance of responsibility by the Republicans and by Barkley in the sense that Barkley knew he could not get a vote, but only in that sense.

Q (MR. HARKNESS): Senator McNary did definitely accept?

THE PRESIDENT: Oh, yes. The responsibility? Oh, yes.

Q (MR. HARKNESS): Is there anything at all you can tell us about the Department of State information which was at issue between Secretary Hull and Senator Borah?

THE PRESIDENT: Well, I would say from every capital in Europe, without exception, with respect to evidences of preparing for an eventuality that they believe to be fairly close, for the very simple reason that the preparations are moving at a very fast rate, of course emphasizing always what has been said, has been printed and everything else, that it is not any allegation of probability, it is a statement of definite possibility. There is all the difference in the world between those two words and the members of the Senate who have decided to defer action until January have been gambling that the possibility won't eventuate. Therefore, there is nothing further to discuss. The country understands it. . . .

Disaster in Europe
Third Term Campaign
The Great Arsenal of Democracy
Battle of the Atlantic

SEPTEMBER 1, 1939 — DECEMBER 7, 1941

# RADIO ADDRESS ON OUTBREAK
# OF THE EUROPEAN WAR

*The White House. September 3, 1939*

*The Nazi-Soviet Pact opened the way for Hitler to invade Poland and divide it with Russia. On September 3, Great Britain and France kept their engagements to Poland and declared war on Germany. This was the first European war in American national history whose outbreak led the American President to condemn one side.*

Tonight my single duty is to speak to the whole of America. Until four-thirty this morning I had hoped against hope that some miracle would prevent a devastating war in Europe and bring to an end the invasion of Poland by Germany.

For four long years a succession of actual wars and constant crises have shaken the entire world and have threatened in each case to bring on the gigantic conflict which is today unhappily a fact.

It is right that I should recall to your minds the consistent and at times successful efforts of your Government in these crises to throw the full weight of the United States into the cause of peace. In spite of spreading wars I think that we have every right and every reason to maintain as a national policy the fundamental moralities, the teachings of religion and the continuation of efforts to restore peace—because some day, though the time may be distant, we can be of even greater help to a crippled humanity.

It is right, too, to point out that the unfortunate events of these recent years have, without question, been based on the use of force and the threat of force. And it seems to me clear, even at the outbreak of this great war, that the influence of America should be consistent in seeking for humanity a final peace which will eliminate, as far as it is possible to do so, the continued use of force between nations.

It is, of course, impossible to predict the future. I have my constant stream of information from American representatives and other sources throughout the world. You, the people of this country, are receiving news through your radios and your newspapers at every hour of the day.

You are, I believe, the most enlightened and the best informed people in all the world at this moment. You are subjected to no censorship of news, and I want to add that your Government has no information which it withholds or which it has any thought of withholding from you.

At the same time, as I told my Press Conference on Friday, it is of the highest importance that the press and the radio use the utmost caution to discriminate between actual verified fact on the one hand, and mere rumor on the other.

I can add to that by saying that I hope the people of this country will also discriminate most carefully between news and rumor. Do not believe of necessity everything you hear or read. Check up on it first.

You must master at the outset a simple but unalterable fact in modern foreign relations between nations. When peace has been broken anywhere, the peace of all countries everywhere is in danger.

It is easy for you and for me to shrug our shoulders and to say that conflicts taking place thousands of miles from the continental United States, and, indeed, thousands of miles from the whole American Hemisphere, do not seriously affect the Americas—and that all the United States has to do is to ignore them and go about its own business. Passionately though we may desire detachment, we are forced to realize that every word that comes through the air, every ship that sails the sea, every battle that is fought does affect the American future.

Let no man or woman thoughtlessly or falsely talk of America sending its armies to European fields. At this moment there is being prepared a proclamation of American neutrality. This would have been done even if there had been no neutrality statute on the books, for this proclamation is in accordance with international law and in accordance with American policy.

This will be followed by a Proclamation required by the existing Neutrality Act. And I trust that in the days to come our neutrality can be made a true neutrality.

It is of the utmost importance that the people of this country, with the best information in the world, think things through. The most dangerous enemies of American peace are those who, without well-rounded information on the whole broad subject of the past, the present and the future, undertake to speak with assumed authority, to talk in terms of glittering generalities, to give to the nation assurances or prophecies which are of little present or future value.

I myself cannot and do not prophesy the course of events abroad—and the reason is that because I have of necessity such a complete picture of what is going on in every part of the world, that I do not dare to do so. And the other reason is that I think it is honest for me to be honest with the people of the United States.

I cannot prophesy the immediate economic effect of this new war on our nation but I do say that no American has the moral right to profiteer at the expense either of his fellow citizens or of the men, the women and the children who are living and dying in the midst of war in Europe.

Some things we do know. Most of us in the United States believe in spiritual values. Most of us, regardless of what church we belong to, believe in the spirit of the New Testament—a great teaching which opposes itself to the use of force, of armed force, of marching armies and falling bombs. The overwhelming masses of our people seek peace—peace at home, and the kind of peace in other lands which will not jeopardize our peace at home.

We have certain ideas and certain ideals of national safety and we must act to preserve that safety today and to preserve the safety of our children in future years.

That safety is and will be bound up with the safety of the

Western Hemisphere and of the seas adjacent thereto. We seek to keep war from our own firesides by keeping war from coming to the Americas. For that we have historic precedent that goes back to the days of the Administration of President George Washington. It is serious enough and tragic enough to every American family in every State in the Union to live in a world that is torn by wars on other Continents. And those wars today affect every American home. It is our national duty to use every effort to keep those wars out of the Americas.

And at this time let me make the simple plea that partisanship and selfishness be adjourned; and that national unity be the thought that underlies all others.

This nation will remain a neutral nation, but I cannot ask that every American remain neutral in thought as well. Even a neutral has a right to take account of facts. Even a neutral cannot be asked to close his mind or close his conscience.

I have said not once but many times that I have seen war and that I hate war. I say that again and again.

I hope the United States will keep out of this war. I believe that it will. And I give you assurance and reassurance that every effort of your Government will be directed toward that end.

As long as it remains within my power to prevent, there will be no blackout of peace in the United States.

## LETTER TO ROBERT E. WOOD

*The White House. October 12, 1939*

*A special session of Congress repealed the arms embargo and substituted "cash-and-carry," which was advantageous to Britain and France. General Wood, chairman of the board of Sears Roebuck of Chicago, became head of the America First Committee, spearhead of the isolationist fight against Roosevelt's reorganization of foreign policy.*

Dear Bob:

I really thought that at your age you would have learned to discriminate between newspaper interpretations on the one hand and facts on the other. I do not know anyone in official Washington who, as you say, "feels it inevitable that this country should be drawn into the European conflict." You make all kinds of wild and wholly incorrect statements. "The whole Department of State" is *not* permeated with this feeling, nor are "some of the Ambassadors," neither is "notably the Ambassador to France." Neither do I share this feeling. Neither does Mrs. Roosevelt share this feeling.

I think, too, that you are asking the impossible when you suggest that high officials of the Federal Government should be "neutral in thought." What you mean is, of course, that while they cannot humanly be neutral in thought, they ought not to let this affect their neutrality of action in any shape, manner or form.

So, my dear friend, stop being disturbed and get both of your feet back on the ground.

Always sincerely,

## LETTER TO JOSEPH C. GREW

*The White House. November 30, 1939*

*After Hitler's "blitzkrieg" victory in Poland and the Western Front settled down to "sitzkrieg," the Soviet Government, to round off its takings east of Germany, launched an unprovoked attack against Finland. Grew was Ambassador to Japan.*

Dear Joe:

It is grand to get yours of November sixth on my return this morning from a few days' holiday in Warm Springs. In the meantime, the Finland attack has occurred and the whole of the United States is not only horrified but thoroughly angry. People are asking why one should have anything to do with the present Soviet leaders because their idea of civilization and human happiness is so totally different from ours.

We have not got that feeling about Japan but things might develop into such a feeling if the Japanese government were to fail to speak as civilized twentieth century human beings.

Do keep on writing me from time to time.

As ever yours,

## MEMORANDUM TO HAROLD L. ICKES

*The White House. February 8, 1940*

*A typical row among the President's subordinates brought a letter of resignation from the ardent and rambunctious New Dealer, Secretary of the Interior Ickes. On receipt of this Memorandum, he withdrew his resignation.*

You and I have been married "for better or worse" for too long to get a divorce or for you to break up the home. I continue to need you.

Affectionately,

## LETTER TO HENRY HORNER

*The White House, March 27, 1940*

*Governor Horner of Illinois, like many other Democratic leaders, urged the President to run for a third term. Roosevelt kept his own counsel, was caricatured as a Sphinx, and probably did not make up his mind firmly until after the Fall of France.*

Dear Henry:

That was a mighty nice telegram of yours and I want you to know that I deeply appreciate it as coming from an old friend.

I cannot, of course, be otherwise than complimented by what you say—but I think there is another aspect which we must duly consider.

You and I are, after all, not only liberal Democrats but are convinced of the fact that if our Government in Washington and in a majority of the States should revert to the control of those who frankly put property ahead of human beings instead of working for human beings under a system of government which recognizes property, the nation as a whole would be again in a bad situation.

Essentially, we mean that we are fighting for the ideals of government and not merely for the individual man. Under our political system it would be a great pity if the continuance of liberal government were dependent on one person in the Presidency.

Therefore, it seems to me that we should look at the coming Convention with the following purposes in mind. First we should seek a platform of progressive liberalism and candidates who are progressive liberals at heart and not merely in lip service. This first criterion eliminates a good many people whose names you and I could readily agree on.

The second criterion is the practical one of picking a liberal ticket which can win. Some liberal combinations would obviously be weak, others would be strong—at least as strong as it is possible to find. It is silly to put up, as we have several times in our lifetime, a ticket which is foreordained to defeat.

In this last matter of choice it is too early in my judgment to attempt to make selections. Several people who might be considered available may stub their toes in the next four months—others may say or do something which will bring them to favorable public notice.

Especially do I deprecate the attitude of some of our friends that unless I run, no other Democrat can be elected. That is sheer defeatism.

This stupid flu germ continues with me and although it is nothing serious, it is most annoying and I certainly have a warm fellow feeling for you who have had to go through so much. I do hope that you are really taking excellent care of yourself and that I shall have a chance to see you in the Spring.

As ever yours,

## PRESS CONFERENCE #635

*The White House. April 12, 1940*

*On April 9, Nazi troops burst into Norway and Denmark. The possibility that Greenland and Iceland, on the flank of North Atlantic approaches to the United States, would fall as Danish possessions into Hitler's hands brought the war very close.*

Q: Would the violation of the integrity of Greenland raise the problem of applying the Monroe Doctrine?

THE PRESIDENT: Oh, I think you are about—you are very, very premature.

In regard to Greenland, I have been reading the encyclopaedia and various other works on Greenland and I have also talked to a number of geographers and geologists, et cetera, and from the point of view of very, very ancient history, the Island of Greenland, in its fauna and its flora and its geology, belongs much more closely to the American Continent than it does to the European Continent; that is the very simple fact. Still, at the present time, and I am looking at it more from a humanitarian point of view than a political point of view, there are about, roughly, 17,000 human beings in Greenland and the Danes have—of course nearly all of them are Eskimos, full-blooded or part-blooded, and comparatively few pure white Danes, Europeans, I think only a few hundred. The Danes have done an awfully good job with the Eskimos. They have a system of community governments, where each small settlement of Eskimos and perhaps a few white people among them are self-governing, and the thing has worked awfully well, both from the social angle and also the economic angle. But, in spite of that, Denmark has had to send up, every spring and every summer, a certain number of supply ships to take to the population of Greenland certain necessities of life which they cannot raise or grow among themselves.

I have got the Red Cross looking into the question of fact

as to the needs of these 17,000 people in these small communities on the east coast and the south end and the west coast of Greenland during this coming summer so that we can be reasonably certain that they won't starve through next winter and they will have certain things they ought to have. It will be primarily a question of relief, which should be handled by the Red Cross, and I think the American people— it won't involve any large sum of money because there are 17,000 total population—and I think the American people will be glad to chip in and help those people go through the next winter if their supply ships from Denmark are cut off. I think that covers it.

Q: Thank you.

Q: Suppose Germany occupies Greenland, any part of it? Won't the political question arise—

THE PRESIDENT: (interposing) I think you are awfully hypothetical, Fred (Mr. Essary).

Q: Well, there are a lot more like me. I hear it discussed everywhere and read discussions of it in nearly all the papers I read.

THE PRESIDENT: I think it is grand that the American people are learning something about a subject that very, very few people have thought of before. The number of people in the last three days or two days that have come to me and said, "By gosh, have you looked at the map?" "Sure, I have been looking at the map." Everybody has been pulling out an atlas and they have been reading the Encyclopaedia Britannica, just the way I did, but it is all to the good.

Q: Don't you think a globe is better?

Q: Is this interest of yours in this statement relating to the possible relief of the Eskimos something of your own or was it suggested to you by the Danish Government?

THE PRESIDENT: No, no. I will tell you how it came about. Mrs. Ruth Bryan Owen, Mrs. Rhode, on her way back from Denmark four or five years ago, stopped off in Greenland and took a lot of pictures and showed them to us at the White House one evening and I got quite thrilled. I have been thinking a lot of those people up in Greenland the last few days, thinking in terms of these pictures, the very interesting life they are living. I invented it; it is all right; nobody else.

Q: Iceland is not included?

THE PRESIDENT: No, I am thinking in terms of Greenland.

Q: Do you consider, sir, that Iceland, by its flora and its fauna—

THE PRESIDENT: (interposing) I only had time to do Greenland last night. . . .

# RADIO ADDRESS ON NATIONAL DEFENSE

*The White House. May 26, 1940*

*On May 10, the Nazis broke into Belgium, The Netherlands, and Luxembourg. Panzer divisions broke the French line at Sedan and raced for the Channel coast and Paris. On May 15, Winston Churchill, a few days after he became Prime Minister, wrote to President Roosevelt that Britain needed old American destroyers, airplanes, and much besides. If the United States held back too long, he wrote, it might face a nazified Europe alone. On May 16 the President went to Congress with a defense program geared to these events. Stunned, the public was in danger of falling victim to rumors and hysteria.*

At this moment of sadness throughout most of the world, I want to talk with you about a number of subjects that directly affect the futue of the United States. We are shocked by the almost incredible eyewitness stories that come to us, stories of what is happening at this moment to the civilian populations of Norway and Holland and Belgium and Luxembourg and France.

I think it is right on this Sabbath evening that I should say a word in behalf of women and children and old men who need help—immediate help in their present distress—help from us across the seas, help from us who are still free to give it.

Tonight over the once peaceful roads of Belgium and France

millions are now moving, running from their homes to escape bombs and shells and fire and machine gunning, without shelter, and almost wholly without food. They stumble on, knowing not where the end of the road will be. I speak to you of these people because each one of you that is listening to me tonight has a way of helping them. The American Red Cross, that represents each of us, is rushing food and clothing and medical supplies to these destitute civilian millions. Please —I beg you—please give according to your means to your nearest Red Cross chapter, give as generously as you can. I ask this in the name of our common humanity.

Let us sit down together again, you and I, to consider our own pressing problems that confront us.

There are many among us who in the past closed their eyes to events abroad—because they believed in utter good faith what some of their fellow Americans told them—that what was taking place in Europe was none of our business; that no matter what happened over there, the United States could always pursue its peaceful and unique course in the world.

There are many among us who closed their eyes, from lack of interest or lack of knowledge; honestly and sincerely thinking that the many hundreds of miles of salt water made the American Hemisphere so remote that the people of North and Central and South America could go on living in the midst of their vast resources without reference to, or danger from, other Continents of the world.

There are some among us who were persuaded by minority groups that we could maintain our physical safety by retiring within our continental boundaries—the Atlantic on the east, the Pacific on the west, Canada on the north and Mexico on the south. I illustrated the futility—the impossibility—of that idea in my Message to the Congress last week. Obviously, a defense policy based on that is merely to invite future attack.

And, finally, there are a few among us who have deliberately and consciously closed their eyes because they were determined to be opposed to their government, its foreign policy and every other policy, to be partisan, and to believe that anything that the Government did was wholly wrong.

To those who have closed their eyes for any of these many reasons, to those who would not admit the possibility of the approaching storm—to all of them the past two weeks have meant the shattering of many illusions.

They have lost the illusion that we are remote and isolated and, therefore, secure against the dangers from which no other land is free.

In some quarters, with this rude awakening has come fear, fear bordering on panic. It is said that we are defenseless. It is whispered by some that, only by abandoning our freedom, our ideals, our way of life, can we build our defenses adequately, can we match the strength of the aggressors.

I did not share those illusions. I do not share these fears.

Today we are more realistic. But let us not be calamity-howlers and discount our strength. Let us have done with both fears and illusions. On this Sabbath evening, in our homes in the midst of our American families, let us calmly consider what we have done and what we must do.

In the past two or three weeks all kinds of stories have been handed out to the American public about our lack of preparedness. It has even been charged that the money we have spent on our military and naval forces during the last few years has gone down the rat-hole. I think that it is a matter of fairness to the nation that you hear the facts.

Yes we have spent large sums of money on the national defense. This money has been used to make our Army and Navy today the largest, the best equipped, and the best trained peace-time military establishment in the whole history of this country. . . .

In line with my request the Congress, this week, is voting the largest appropriation ever asked by the Army or the Navy in peace-time; and the equipment and training provided for them will be in addition to the figures I have given you.

The world situation may so change that it will be necessary

to reappraise our program at any time. And in such case I am confident that the Congress and the Chief Executive will work in harmony as a team—work in harmony as they are doing today.

I will not hesitate at any moment to ask for additional funds when they are required.

In this era of swift, mechanized warfare, we all have to remember that what is modern today and up-to-date, what is efficient and practical, becomes obsolete and outworn tomorrow.

Even while the production line turns out airplanes, new airplanes are being designed on the drafting table.

Even as a cruiser slides down the launching ways, plans for improvement, plans for increased efficiency in the next model, are taking shape in the blue prints of designers.

Every day's fighting in Europe, on land, or sea, and in the air, discloses constant changes in methods of warfare. We are constantly improving and redesigning, testing new weapons, learning the lessons of the immediate war, and seeking to produce in accordance with the latest that the brains of science can conceive.

Yes, we are calling upon the resources, the efficiency and the ingenuity of the American manufacturers of war materiel of all kinds—airplanes and tanks and guns and ships, and all the hundreds of products that go into this materiel. The Government of the United States itself manufactures few of the implements of war. Private industry will continue to be the source of most of this materiel; and private industry will have to be speeded up to produce it at the rate and efficiency called for by the needs of the times.

I know that private business cannot be expected to make all of the capital investment required for expansions of plants and factories and personnel which this program calls for at once. It would be unfair to expect industrial corporations or their investors to do this, when there is a chance that a change in international affairs may stop or curtail future orders a year or two hence.

Therefore, the Government of the United States stands ready to advance the necessary money to help provide for the enlargement of factories, the establishment of new plants, the employment of thousands of necessary workers, the development of new sources of supply for the hundreds of raw materials required, the development of quick mass transportation of supplies. And the details of all of this are now being worked out in Washington, day and night.

We are calling on men now engaged in private industry to help us in carrying out this program and you will hear more of this in detail in the next few days. . . .

We must make sure, in all that we do, that there be no breakdown or cancellation of any of the great social gains which we have made in these past years. We have carried on an offensive on a broad front against social and economic inequalities and abuses which had made our society weak. That offensive should not now be broken down by the pincers movement of those who would use the present needs of physical military defense to destroy it.

There is nothing in our present emergency to justify making the workers of our nation toil for longer hours than now limited by statute. As more orders come in and as more work has to be done, tens of thousands of people, who are now unemployed, will, I believe, receive employment.

There is nothing in our present emergency to justify a lowering of the standards of employment. Minimum wages should not be reduced. It is my hope, indeed, that the new speed-up of production will cause many businesses which now pay below the minimum standards to bring their wages up.

There is nothing in our present emergency to justify a breaking down of old age pensions or of unemployment insurance. I would rather see the systems extended to other groups who do not now enjoy them.

There is nothing in our present emergency to justify a retreat from any of our social objectives—from conservation of natural resources, assistance to agriculture, housing, and help to the under-privileged.

Conversely, however, I am sure that responsible leaders will not permit some specialized group, which represents a minority of the total employees of a plant or an industry, to break up the continuity of employment of the majority of the employees. Let us remember that the policy and the laws that provide for collective bargaining are still in force. And I can assure you that labor will be adequately represented in Washington in the carrying out of this program of defense.

And one more point on this: Our present emergency and a common sense of decency make it imperative that no new group of war millionaires shall come into being in this nation as a result of the struggles abroad. The American people will not relish the idea of any American citizen growing rich and fat in an emergency of blood and slaughter and human suffering.

And, last of all, this emergency demands that the consumers of America be protected so that our general cost of living can be maintained at a reasonable level. We ought to avoid the spiral processes of the World War, the rising spiral of costs of all kinds. The soundest policy is for every employer in the country to help give useful employment to the millions who are unemployed. By giving to those millions an increased purchasing power, the prosperity of the whole nation will rise to a much higher level. . . .

For more than three centuries we Americans have been building on this continent a free society, a society in which the promise of the human spirit may find fulfillment. Commingled here are the blood and genius of all the peoples of the world who have sought this promise.

We have built well. We are continuing our efforts to bring the blessings of a free society, of a free and productive economic system, to every family in the land. This is the promise of America.

It is this that we must continue to build—this that we must continue to defend.

It is the task of our generation, yours and mine. But we

build and defend not for our generation alone. We defend the foundations laid down by our fathers. We build a life for generations yet unborn. We defend and we build a way of life, not for America alone, but for all mankind. Ours is a high duty, a noble task.

Day and night I pray for the restoration of peace in this mad world of ours. It is not necessary that I, the President, ask the American people to pray in behalf of such a cause—for I know you are praying with me.

I am certain that out of the hearts of every man, woman and child in this land, in every waking minute, a supplication goes up to Almighty God; that all of us beg that suffering and starving, that death and destruction may end —and that peace may return to the world. In common affection for all mankind, your prayers join with mine—that God will heal the wounds and the hearts of humanity.

## CONFERENCE WITH REPRESENTATIVES OF THE AMERICAN YOUTH CONGRESS

*The White House. June 5, 1940*

*Mrs. Roosevelt had arranged this meeting. Some of those present adhered to the Communist line which lumped the French and the British with the Nazis as "imperialists." Others were genuine representatives of American youth who found it difficult to forget the unfinished business of the New Deal and see the Nazi threat as the chief danger to American democracy. Probably no President has submitted to a more severe raking over, but Roosevelt was very patient with the generation that grew up in the America of mass unemployment and hunger.*

THE PRESIDENT: I suppose I might as well begin by reminding myself that this is the first time I have had a party like this since last April, when I had my annual gathering, about this size—a little bit bigger—of the editors and publishers of America, a very formidable group.

I was scared to death the first time, in 1933, and I have been getting over it bravely ever since.

I told them . . . a remark that was made to me by one of the nationally known commentators. I said to that commentator, "I believe that in your column, three days out of six, you are consistently taking a crack at every known kind of social reform or betterment program of the Government that we have been trying to put through in the last seven years. Why is it?" I said, "I have known you for a great many years and you are not as anti-social or as unsocial personally."

"Well," he said, "of course I am not; of course I am not. But I can sell my column if I take this line that I have been taking now ever since you have been President. I can sell my column to sixty papers and if I commented the way I really feel, I would not have any clients left." . . .

Frankly, I have seen a good deal of the world, probably more than anybody in this room, first and last, and a war. I don't think I would like to live, if I were eighteen or sixteen— I don't think I would like, knowing what I do, what we have, having seen it all—that I would care to live the rest of my life under Communism or under Naziism or under Fascism. If I did want to live that way, I think I would probably go over there and join them. If I wanted to live under our form of government, I think I would stay here and I think I would do what I could—yes, to improve it, but also to support it.

So I think, if there are any questions that do not relate to the too distant past but relate more to things of the immediate—as I said to the editors—I will conduct this just like a Press Conference, in which I have certain formulae. One of them is "off the record." "Off the record" means off the record—

MRS. ROOSEVELT: (*interposing*) I told everybody that before. . . .

Q: I speak from the standpoint of those who share in great concern for the democratic form of government and who come from states where more than half of the citizens who should be voting according to the democratic form of government and our Constitution are denied that right today and, when they try to vote, are in some instances, as some of us know, beaten up by thugs and thrown into jail because they are trying to do the thing which they think they have the responsibility to do, to vote and to get their fellow citizens to vote.

THE PRESIDENT: What are we going to do about it?

Q: What are we going to do about it?

THE PRESIDENT: I will tell you one thing, you can't change it in the year 1940 or you can't change it in the year 1941. I will give you an illustration: I was in Chattanooga two years ago and I drove around Chattanooga with old Judge—I have forgotten his name—an old Tennessean.

We were driving through this street and, if you know your geography, you know the State of Georgia comes right up to the city line of Chattanooga. We were still out in this street, a big wide avenue, in the State of Tennessee, and there was a large portion of the population out in the streets, and they were waving their hats and yelling, "Hello, Mr. President."

I said to the Judge, "Do these people vote?" "Yes, there are about 80 per cent of them vote." I said, "What? In Tennessee?" He said, "Sure, not in every part of Tennessee, but they vote in Chattanooga."

Then we came to a sign, a little sign and it said, "State of Georgia." We went over past the sign, still in the same suburb, and the colored population was standing there, not saying a word. I said to the Judge, "You don't vote in Georgia, in this suburb in the same city?" He said, "No; none vote in Georgia."

I said, "Judge, what is going to happen?" "Well," he said, "there is going to come a time, largely through education."

I said, "How long?" He said, "I think they will begin voting —it is a gradual process—I think in Georgia they will begin voting in perhaps another five years."

I said, "That is a long ways off." I said, "What about the court ruling, the Supreme Court?" He said, "That is a possibility." He said, "I think we have got to pursue all possibilities and bring it along as fast as we can." He said, "I have always worked for it in the State of Tennessee and now we have caught on substantially in most parts of the State and now it is spreading."

There is a time element. You cannot get it in one year or two. We are all working and in time it will happen. Of course, part of it is the problem of education and, as you know, in my State of Georgia what education there is, is not so hot, poor whites or otherwise.

Q: In the Workers' Alliance we were considerably disturbed in January when, in your Budget Message, there was a proposal for approximately a billion dollars more for armaments, for war purposes generally, and about a billion dollars less proposed for relief to the farmers, the youth and the unemployed. . . .

Q: Mr. President. . . . I want to hark back, for a moment, to the first question raised and that was the question about poll taxes.

Now, you said that in your opinion the solution to this problem will come through education?

THE PRESIDENT: Right.

Q: Well, I want to raise the question: Is it not true that the people we have to educate today are Congressmen and Senators? For instance, there is a bill that has been proposed by Representative Geyer of California, the Anti-Poll Tax Bill, which would eliminate the poll tax as a requirement for voting in Federal elections—

THE PRESIDENT: (interposing) And if it is constitutional, it ought to go through. I hope, frankly—I could not give you my opinion as to whether it is constitutional because that has to go through the courts—I hope it is constitutional.

Q: I hope it is too, and I would like to talk, just for a moment, on the assumption that it is constitutional because, at the present stage of the game, the only people of America that are backing this bill are organized, such as the one for which I work, the Southern Negro Youth Council, and there are other organizations—

THE PRESIDENT: (*interposing*) And you ought to get more people because it is a difficult thing, as you know, in our civilization unless you have sentiment. You take the voters in Dutchess County, New York, where that problem of poll taxes does not affect their lives: we are all human and I think probably most of the people of Dutchess County, New York, if it was explained to them would get behind the bill.

Q: The point I am trying to make is that I think the fact that our Senators and Representatives, people in official positions who should be supporting this bill but are not today, is a fact which creates a great deal of uneasiness in the minds of American youth, for the reason that we connect their attitude of lack of activity on this question with the fact that they are concentrating all their efforts on the program for rearmament and are neglecting not only the poll tax effort but it is true also in another case, another piece of legislation that particularly affects the Negroes, the Anti-Lynching Bill, for which we had achieved a majority of signatures in favor of this bill. Now we find that these Senators refuse to take action to bring the bill to the floor and have a vote on it.

Now, it is the general impression, not only of Negroes in America but probably of the majority of people, that one of the dangers inherent in our present rearmament program is that such pieces of legislation as these have not only been sacrificed—they have already been sacrificed—but will continue to be, despite pronouncement that we may make to the contrary, unless we are able to organize our Senators and Representatives and people who have the power to form our national policy so that the security and civil liberties of the American people may be preserved.

THE PRESIDENT: I think it is a very good point. You have to remember on that point that when you get to a crisis of this kind, you also avoid the repeal of a lot of good legislation we already have. Especially in a campaign year, it works both ways. I think we have to keep pushing all our social legislation to improve Government machinery.

Now, you spoke about that Anti-Lynching Bill: You have got a situation up there on the Hill which goes back well over a hundred years, when the Senate began calling itself the greatest debating society in the world—the most exclusive club in the world—"We operate without any rules whatsoever." One of the inherent rights of a Senator is to filibuster just as long as he can stand on his feet. "We operate without rules." Now, one of the things that is a perfectly practical thing for everybody here, and that is to put to every candidate for the United States Senate the question, "Are you in favor of the Senate continuing its right to filibuster and prevent bringing to a vote certain legislation that a minority of the Senators, a rather small minority, is opposing—the majority in favor of it?"

If you can get a vote on the Anti-Lynching Bill in the Senate it would go through—we all know it.

Q: For that reason, the question I want to emphasize, and it is one which should be of particular concern to all who are here, and that is, What can we do, what can you do, Mr. President, in your position as the official representative of our Government, to see that our Congress takes some position, some stand, on these issues, for the very serious reason that, I believe, among a large section of the population, the program for defense and rearmament, in some places, is held in suspicion because they feel that the first line of defense of America should be that of the social needs of the people, and that this is the thing that our Senators should certainly concentrate on with equal ardor as their concentration on our military objectives.

THE PRESIDENT: Nothing more than you would have done right along. It means getting ninety-six Senators to say, "Go out and take a vote on the Anti-Lynching Bill." You have had some rather definite accessions of strength this year. Take the Vice President and several other Southern Senators: they have given up and said, "Yes, we think it is better to take a vote." We are gaining on it but you won't get it this year.

Q: I was very much interested to note in your statement, after the rapid development of the emergency and after your bill for the extended arms program, that the hard won gains of labor should not be lost sight of in the present situation, and then the Congress, by a voice vote passed the Vinson Bill, which would, I think, be an opening wedge for undermining the thing that has been so slowly built up.

THE PRESIDENT: I have been trying to get it eliminated in the Senate. . . .

Q: Mr. President, I am chairman of the Connecticut Youth Council. In our State seven thousand young people are aided by [National Youth Administration] out of 125 thousand people that need it on relief certification. That is still the most important problem for young people within our borders. We know that you, on January fourth, said that the plight of youth was the special concern of Government. We feel that such a tremendous problem must be a constant concern to the leaders of our Government. On February tenth we heard from you that ten, twenty, thirty years ago unemployment had no such worries for young people as now. Since then we have not heard anything to the contrary. Nevertheless, the N.Y.A. and the C.C.C. are at the same figure that they were last year so that the disparity between those that are given and those that need help still continues. We want an answer from you and we want a concrete proposal.

THE PRESIDENT: Well, I think Mr. Hopkins has the general figures and plan on that. We are extending, when we get this bill passed, we are extending the C.C.C. and N.Y.A. and, of course, the C.A.A. employment. What do you suppose the total will be, Harry (Mr. Hopkins)? Have you got any idea of the additional number?

MR. HOPKINS: I think it will probably be about two million young people all together. . . .

Q: Mr. President, I would like to get back to the question

of the rights of the Negro people because I feel that the final test of any group that is interested in extending and preserving democracy is the position of the Negro people. There are 15 million American Negroes who still do not enjoy full citizenship rights and we are in entire agreement on the proposition that the first line of defense is the security and well-being of the citizens of any country.

The Negro people are particularly interested in this theory because they feel that they do not have complete welfare and security in the United States, which is a democracy, and we feel that since defense is the burning question, that certainly the Administration should go out vigorously, even perhaps more vigorously, on the question of the rights of Negroes as being as much a part of the program for defense as any other thing.

Things that have been brought up here are just a small part of the vast question with respect of the rights of Negroes. In the South they are under the system of Jim Crow; in the North it is more subtle but it has its forms and I feel there should be a vigorous indication on the part of the Administration on the stand it takes on the Negro question.

THE PRESIDENT: I think you are dead right. I do not know much about the women's end of the Negro question, but I know a lot about the men's end. I went down to Tuskegee a year and a half ago and at that time, because of our tremendous forestry program, we were looking for two types of trained people. One was the graduate forester. Well, that means just about as much time as it takes to become a bachelor of laws. And I said to Dr. Patterson, "Is there any school in the country that has ever graduated a Negro forester?" He said, "As far as I know, no."

"Have any of them gone to the northern forestry schools?"
"Not that I know of."

Secondly, we need a tremendous number of what is called "working foresters" who have not had the long three-year course but have had the short two-year course, which does not require a college degree. Now, there is no school in the

United States, no Negro school that teaches forestry. Did you know that?

Q. No.

THE PRESIDENT: That is a true thing.

MRS. ROOSEVELT: Would they have been taken on if they had taken the course?

THE PRESIDENT: Yes, and particularly in the South because there is a tremendous need. There is a profession at the present time where there is demand. It is as big, bigger than the supply—graduate foresters and working foresters.

Q: They work in groups, do they not?

THE PRESIDENT: No—what do you mean?

Q: You don't send one lone forester to a special place; you send a group?

THE PRESIDENT: No.

Q: You would have to send a unit of colored workers?

THE PRESIDENT: Not necessarily. Believe me, they are so scarce today that they would take anybody. There are a good many things we have not gone into along that line for definite occupations for Negro men and Negro boys. We are not teaching them. Take simple engineering. Out through the West, on these soil erosion control projects, we have not got enough young engineers that know the practical engineering field work to fill jobs on the different projects that we are running all through the Middle West and the Prairie States. There is no place to train them.

Q: The question I am raising is that there are definite policies that have grown to be such a definite part of our American system that we have come to accept them, that prevent Negroes from taking a full part in the life of America.

THE PRESIDENT: I am not so much interested in the statement of policy as I am interested in the training. What I am trying to do is to get Negro colleges to train people in the work where there is a real need for them. That is practical. . . .

Q: You suggested in your speech at the beginning of the meeting that the choice of the people of the world today was a choice between forms of government, so my questions are these:

First, do you believe that the Allies are defending any particular form of government, whether they are concerned with democracy?

And the second, if that is true, is it borne out by their imperialistic policies?

THE PRESIDENT: I do not think that is the question. I would put it the other way around. Where would you rather live, in France or Germany, today?

Q: You are asking me?

THE PRESIDENT: Yes.

Q: Is there much choice today? I would answer that I would much prefer living in the United States.

THE PRESIDENT: Yes, but between France and Germany I would certainly much rather live in France. After all, the civil liberties in France have always been, on the whole, pretty good. The French people are an extremely independent people, if you know anything about them. I think their form of government is very cumbersome and I think this changing of administration every few months is an extremely bad way of running a government in any country. But they have a pretty free method of life and you will find that the average French family has a great deal of civil liberty. Now, if I had to choose between the two, I would rather live in France than in Germany.

Q: The question now is whether I would enjoy living in the French colonies and I would have to answer, "No."

THE PRESIDENT: I agree with you. I am talking as between France and Germany. I would say this—have you ever been to Martinique?

Q: No.

THE PRESIDENT: Martinique is a French colony and they have a very interesting form of local government for nearly all Negroes. They get on extremely well with the small number of French white people who are down there. They never have any trouble. They have a low standard of living but that is so all through the West Indies. They are a happy, cheerful people and, surprisingly, they have much better education among the Negroes of Martinique than we have in most of our states in the South. Now, that is an interesting fact and that is a French colony. The same thing applies to Guadalupe.

Q: Not in Indo-China?

THE PRESIDENT: Indo-China, no.

Q: I don't want to prolong this discussion but I would like to ask one more—the first question I asked you, whether you believed that the Allies were fighting for democracy, whether they are concerned with—

THE PRESIDENT: (*interposing*) Put it the other way around. They are fighting for a better form of democracy, certainly, than Germany is fighting for. I would say it is an ideal. . . .

Q: If Hitler should win this war, there has been all kinds of talk about readjustments that this country would have to go through, the loss of foreign trade, and building up a tremendous armament machine. Now, has the Administration gone into that? Have you any ideas—can you give us an idea of what sort of readjustment, reorientation, this country may have to go through if Hitler should win the war?

THE PRESIDENT: First of all, I have to ask you to consider yourself Hitler. Suppose you were a victorious Hitler, what would you do? I do not know him, never met him. I know all sorts of stories. I have heard the story that he wanted to go back and paint pictures—that that is his one desire, to go back and paint pictures. He may do it. I don't know. It is anybody's guess. Or he might do like other successful conquerors; he might say, "I have got a third of the world and I have fixed up relations with another third of the world, the Far East. Why should I stop? How about this American third?" I am not saying that is a *probability*, because it would be silly. I am saying it is a *possibility*, which is correct, and therefore, if it is a possibility, which it is, we have got to say to ourselves, "we have got to prepare against it."

And then we go back to Hitler's mind and say, "How is he going to do it if he adopts that thesis?" And we are going to say, "Well, one obvious thing would be to go down to the Argentine, where we have a large German population that has never assimilated with the Argentine people." They are not like our Germans, they have remained by themselves. They have over a million Italians down there.

He would say to the Argentine Government, "Now I have a nice little trade bloc here. It is very nice. Do you want to join it?" Argentine would say, "No. What are the terms?" Hitler would say, "Well, you can't live in the Argentine unless you can export your beef and your corn and your wheat. You will all go broke. We will give you a quota and we will take so many tons of beef and take so many bushels of wheat and corn, and we will tell you where to send them. We will allocate them and you have got to sell them through the Germania Corporation at a charge of two per cent commission on it. And we will tell you where to send it. We don't like the way the Belgians are behaving; now, they can fend for themselves this year." So next year they don't like the Danes, so they will keep Argentine corn out of Denmark. It will be completely in the control of a little group.

"Well," says the Argentine, "how are you going to pay us?" "Well, there is no such thing as gold in the world; we will pay you in steel rails." "Hell, we don't want steel rails." "Hell, you have got to take steel rails." "Well, there is no longer any independence when we do that." And then Germany, the Germania Corporation says to the Argentine, "Take it or leave it. By the way, we forgot, you cannot have planes or an army, except planes and an army and a navy that are run by German officers." Argentine says, "We cannot do that. We will lose our independence. We are Argentinians." The Germania Corporation will say, "Sorry, we can't take it. Sell your surplus products to the United States," knowing darned well that the United States has a surplus of beef and wheat and corn of its own.

Well, that is not infiltration; that is something very, very different. That is highjacking.

Q: It seems to me we are all getting critical, talking about our American way of life, and we have had demonstrated clearly here tonight that democracy does not exist in the United States—

THE PRESIDENT: (*interposing*) That is some statement.

Q: In fact, it does not—the poll tax and such things as that —we know in peacetimes and even in the best times it is not a fact. Well, it is going to be worse in the event of war. And the first thing is that there is much talk now—the Dies Committee—of un-American activities, Communists and fifth columns. Well, I would like to know who is going to define them, what they are and what is happening to them. I think the first indication of what is happening to the American people as a whole is this attack on Communists.

THE PRESIDENT: Well, I think the first definition to put in that class are those people who prefer to live under the Communist system of government instead of the American system.

Q: Isn't that a democratic right?

THE PRESIDENT: Oh, yes.

Q: Then why do we permit laws to be passed which keep such people off the W.P.A. rolls?

THE PRESIDENT: It is a democratic and, incidentally, it is a constitutional thing, but you have not got a chance in these times and you never will have, in my judgment, of establishing the Communist form of Government.

Q: That is not the question.

THE PRESIDENT: I think it is sort of silly to waste time on it.

Q: Isn't it against the Constitution, its provisions?

THE PRESIDENT: You can amend the Constitution any time you want.

Q: Has it been amended?

THE PRESIDENT: You have a swell chance of doing it on that law. . . .

Q: Mr. President, I have come here tonight in order to ask

one very simple and one very basic question and yet it touches rather deeply everything that was said here tonight. I want to go back a little bit, keeping in mind your warning, to the time you came into the Presidency, and it occurs to me as we are sitting here tonight that for a long time we looked to President Roosevelt as a leader who, in the case of civil liberties, in the case of the rights of aliens, in the case of the right to work, in the case of expansion of opportunities for young people for jobs, for training and education, in the case of the health program, was a fighter, was a man who did not offer to us the excuse that such a thing could not be got by the House, that there were forces in the Senate who would not listen to this or that proposal, but a man who carried the fight to the people and from the people he got the support which pushed these bills through the House and pushed them through the Senate.

Now, what has alarmed us and the reason we gather here tonight is that something has happened, that this war has caused the President, has caused the members of his Cabinet to somehow forget this very important, this first line of defense, of social security, the peace and happiness of our people, and has definitely, and I think we may say very positively placed in a secondary position these things that we require, food and housing and clothing, and has placed in front of those things the needs for national defense. . . . And we are becoming very highly suspicious that billions of dollars are forthcoming for rearmaments, guns, battleships, and yet millions of dollars are not forthcoming for a job-training program, are not forthcoming for a program of relief, are not forthcoming for a health program and a housing program.

And also we are . . . a little bit angry that the President and the members of his Cabinet have not carried this fight once again to the people. . . .

THE PRESIDENT: Young man, I think you are very sincere. Have you read Carl Sandburg's *Lincoln?*

Q: No, sir.

THE PRESIDENT: I think the impression was that Lincoln was

a pretty sad man because he could not do all he wanted to do at one time, and I think you will find examples where Lincoln had to compromise to gain a little something. He had to compromise to make a few gains. Lincoln was one of those unfortunate people called a "politician" but he was a politician who was practical enough to get a great many things for this country. He was a sad man because he couldn't get it all at once. And nobody can. Maybe you would make a much better President than I have. Maybe you will, some day. If you ever sit here, you will learn that you cannot, just by shouting from the housetops, get what you want all the time.

MRS. ROOSEVELT: Isn't it true? I would like to elaborate on that a little because I think there is one thing they do not quite get, namely, they think of carrying a fight to the people as carrying it to people who will think as they do, whereas you think a bit in the terms of what you get as the opinion of the people through what Congress reports on as their backing at home and, therefore, you are bound to take that because the people have elected Congress.

THE PRESIDENT: Yes, and so often the individual Congressman or the Senator is way behind the people and the people have got the responsibility of bringing him up to date. . . .

Harry [Hopkins], do you want to come over here? Because I have got to telephone to the Secretary of State. I am awfully sorry. Harry will answer any more questions you have in mind.

It has been a really grand evening and I am glad to meet all of you. I have had a grand time and I hope I have done something to clarify questions in your mind and to point out why we have to keep our feet on the ground and do the best we can if we believe in our system of Government, and I believe everybody in this room does.

Good night. (Applause)

Q: Are you ready to answer questions?

MR. HOPKINS: First, we are going to have some beer. . . .

# ADDRESS AT THE UNIVERSITY
# OF VIRGINIA

*Charlottesville. June 10, 1940*

*The famous "stab in the back" passage was reinserted by the President at the last moment after Under Secretary of State Welles had persuaded him to remove it. "Undiplomatic," it expressed perfectly the anger and contempt of most Americans when Mussolini attacked France after Hitler had broken her. The correlative of this mood was the President's announcement that military supplies would be sent to countries fighting the dictators.*

President Newcome, My Friends of the University of Virginia: . . .

Every generation of young men and women in America has questions to ask the world. Most of the time they are the simple but nevertheless difficult questions, questions of work to do, opportunities to find, ambitions to satisfy.

But every now and then in the history of the Republic a different kind of question presents itself—a question that asks, not about the future of an individual or even of a generation, but about the future of the country, the future of the American people. . . .

Some indeed still hold to the now somewhat obvious delusion that we of the United States can safely permit the United States to become a lone island, a lone island in a world dominated by the philosophy of force.

Such an island may be the dream of those who still talk and vote as isolationists. Such an island represents to me and to the overwhelming majority of Americans today a helpless nightmare, the helpless nightmare of a people without freedom; yes, the nightmare of a people lodged in prison, handcuffed, hungry, and fed through the bars from day to day by the contemptuous, unpitying masters of other continents.

It is natural also that we should ask ourselves how now we

can prevent the building of that prison and the placing of ourselves in the midst of it.

Let us not hesitate—all of us—to proclaim certain truths. Overwhelmingly we, as a nation—and this applies to all the other American nations—are convinced that military and naval victory for the gods of force and hate would endanger the institutions of democracy in the western world, and that equally, therefore, the whole of our sympathies lies with those nations that are giving their life blood in combat against these forces.

The people and the Government of the United States have seen with the utmost regret and with grave disquiet the decision of the Italian Government to engage in the hostilities now raging in Europe. . . .

Not so long ago, recognizing that certain aspirations of Italy might form the basis of discussions between the powers most specifically concerned, I offered, in a message addressed to the Chief of the Italian Government, to send to the Governments of France and of Great Britain such specific indications of the desires of Italy to obtain readjustments with regard to her position as the Chief of the Italian Government might desire to transmit through me. . . .

Unfortunately, to the regret of all of us and to the regret of humanity, the Chief of the Italian Government was unwilling to accept the procedure suggested and he has made no counter proposal. . . .

On this tenth day of June, 1940, the hand that held the dagger has struck it into the back of its neighbor.

On this tenth day of June, 1940, in this University founded by the first great American teacher of democracy, we send forth our prayers and our hopes to those beyond the seas who are maintaining with magnificent valor their battle for freedom.

In our American unity, we will pursue two obvious and simultaneous courses; we will extend to the opponents of force the material resources of this nation and, at the same time, we will harness and speed up the use of those resources in order that we ourselves in the Americas may have equipment and training equal to the task of any emergency and every defense.

All roads leading to the accomplishment of these objectives must be kept clear of obstructions. We will not slow down or detour. Signs and signals call for speed—full speed ahead. . . .

## SPECIAL MESSAGE ON EXCESS PROFITS TAX

*July 1, 1940*

*The President was asking Congress for a Selective Service Act, which he proposed to balance with a "draft of wealth." The former was enacted in September and the latter in October. This and many other safeguards made the current defense program the first one in American history that was not severely exploited for private profit.*

To the Congress of the United States:

We are engaged in a great national effort to build up our national defenses to meet any and every potential attack.

We are asking even our humblest citizens to contribute their mite.

It is our duty to see that the burden is equitably distributed according to ability to pay so that a few do not gain from the sacrifices of the many.

I, therefore, recommend to the Congress the enactment of a steeply graduated excess profits tax, to be applied to all individuals and all corporate organizations without discrimination.

## LETTER TO GEORGE W. NORRIS

*The White House. July 21, 1940*

*On July 19, the President had accepted nomination for a third term. He had been opposed by Vice President Garner and Postmaster General Farley with a minority of conservatives and isolationists.*

Dear George:

Your letter has made me deeply happy because I would rather have that said by you than by anyone else in the country.

Did you know how near you came to being made the vehicle of those thoughts of mine? One week before the Convention opened I wrote out in longhand a letter to you which though not as long as my radio speech to the Convention carried essentially the same thoughts.

I was going to send it to you the day the Convention opened with the belief that, by saying it in letter form to the one outstanding American who has always risen above party, it would be better understood by the people as a whole. The draft of this letter to you had been actually prepared.

However, two days before the Convention opened it became fairly clear that the old line conservative element in the party had, one way or another, obtained a much larger share in the control of the temporary organization of the Convention than it had any right to have from the point of view of public sentiment. Therefore, all or nearly all of the more liberal leaders pleaded with me not to send the letter to you but to withhold speaking until the permanent organization was effected on Tuesday night. They pointed out that obviously I should not address the Convention itself in the first person or through the Chairman until the Permanent Chairman had actually begun to preside.

I was, frankly, amazed by the terrific drive which was put on by the old-line conservatives to make so many things adverse to liberalism occur that I would have to decline and disassociate myself from anything further to do with the restoration of control to the conservative element.

To this conservative element in the Convention was added, for the same objective but on other grounds, the strength of what you and I can privately call "The Hater's Club"—strange bedfellows like Wheeler and McCarran and Tydings and Glass and John J. O'Connor and some of the wild Irishmen from Boston, et cetera.

Essentially this line-up (except for Wheeler and one or two others) was the same as the one-third of the Chicago Convention of 1932. Obviously that crowd had no chance to make a fight in 1936. However, they were greatly heartened by the 1938 elections and thought that this would give them a fighting chance to put the control of the Democratic Party back where it was in 1920, 1924 and 1928.

That is why I feel that, from a purely political point of view, a great victory was won in Chicago.

On the nomination of Wallace they made their final stand. They were sure to be beaten, even by a fairly small margin, but their stupidity in making a violent issue out of Wallace will cost the ticket a great many votes this Autumn.

Wallace is a true liberal—far more so than any of the others suggested for Vice President—with the possible exception of Bill Douglas, who would have been harder to get nominated than Wallace.

I do not need to tell you, my dear friend, what your support has meant, not to me but I honestly believe, to the future of the country through all these years and even though you and I are tired and "want to go home," we are going to see this thing through together.

I am going home for a few days but hope to see you very soon after I get back.

As ever yours,


## RADIO ADDRESS ON SELECTIVE SERVICE REGISTRATION DAY

*October 16, 1940*

*Under the Act of September 16, the first peacetime draft in American history began with the registration of all men between the ages of twenty-one and thirty-six years. By ordinary standards such an operation in the middle of an election campaign would have been considered a political mistake.*

On this day more than sixteen million young Americans are reviving the three hundred year old American custom of the Muster. They are obeying that first duty of free citizenship by which, from the earliest Colonial times, every able-bodied citizen was subject to the call for service in the national defense.

It is a day of deep and purposeful meaning in the lives of all of us. For on this day we Americans proclaim the vitality of our history, the singleness of our will and the unity of our nation.

We prepare to keep the peace in this New World which free men have built for free men to live in. The United States, a nation of one hundred and thirty million people, has today only about five hundred thousand—half a million—officers and men in Army and National Guard. Other nations, smaller in population, have four and five and six million trained men in their armies. Our present program will train eight hundred thousand additional men this coming year and somewhat less than one million men each year thereafter. It is a program obviously of defensive preparation and of defensive preparation only.

Calmly, without fear and without hysteria, but with clear determination, we are building guns and planes and tanks and ships—and all the other tools which modern defense requires. We are mobilizing our citizenship, for we are calling on men and women and property and money to join in making our defense effective. Today's registration for training and service is the key-stone in the arch of our national defense.

In the days when our forefathers laid the foundation of our democracy, every American family had to have its gun and know how to use it. Today we live under threats, threats of aggression from abroad, which call again for the same readiness, the same vigilance. Ours must once again be the spirit of those who were prepared to defend as they built, to defend as they worked, to defend as they worshipped.

The duty of this day has been imposed upon us from without. Those who have dared to threaten the whole world with war—those who have created the name and deed of Total War—have imposed upon us and upon all free peoples the necessity of preparation for total defense.

But this day not only imposes a duty; it provides also an opportunity—an opportunity for united action in the cause of liberty—an opportunity for the continuing creation on this continent of a country where the people alone shall be master, where the people shall be truly free.

To the sixteen million young men who register today, I say that democracy is your cause—the cause of youth.

Democracy is the one form of society which guarantees to every new generation of men the right to imagine and to attempt to bring to pass a better world. Under the despotisms the imagination of a better world and its achievement are alike forbidden.

Your act today affirms not only your loyalty to your country, but your will to build your future for yourselves.

We of today, with God's help, can bequeath to Americans of tomorrow a nation in which the ways of liberty and justice will survive and be secure. Such a nation must be devoted to the cause of peace. And it is for that cause that America arms itself.

It is to that cause—the cause of peace—that we Americans today devote our national will and our national spirit and our national strength.

## CAMPAIGN SPEECH

*Madison Square Garden, New York City. October 28, 1940*

*The President's third-term campaign was limited to some highly visible inspection tours of defense plants and relatively few speeches. Roosevelt feared Wendell Willkie, the Republican nominee, more than any other of the four men he ran against. Late in the campaign Willkie gave up his normal bipartisan support of the Administration's foreign policy and accused Roosevelt of a conspiracy to take the country into war. This led the*

*President to promise "again, and again, and again," that he*
*would not send American boys into foreign wars. When the Re-*
*publicans accused him of neglecting the nation's defenses, he*
*enjoyed answering.*

Mr. Chairman, Governor Lehman, Ladies and Gentlemen:

No campaign can possibly be complete without this great
Garden meeting.

I have had a very wonderful day in New York, all five
boroughs. But, as you know, I have had an anxious day too
because three or four times during the day I have had to be in
touch with the Department of State, with the Secretary of
State, Cordell Hull, because, unfortunately, it seems that
another war has broken out on the other side of the ocean,
and I am quite sure that all of you will feel the same sorrow
in your hearts that I feel—the sorrow in our hearts for the
Italian people and the Grecian people, that they should have
been involved together in conflict.

Tonight it is the second time I take up once more the
public duty—the far from disagreeable duty—of answering
major campaign falsifications with facts. (Applause)

Last week in Philadelphia, which is supposed to be the City
of Brotherly Love, but isn't always—I nailed the falsehood
about some fanciful secret treaties, I nailed them up to dry
on the barn door. (Laughter) I nailed that falsehood and
other falsehoods the way when I was a boy up in Dutchess
County we used to nail up the skins of foxes and weasels.
(Laughter) And I think it was a kinsman of mine, about
thirty years ago, who invented the word, "weasel words."

Tonight I am going to nail up the falsifications that have
to do with our relations with the rest of the world, with the
building up of our Army, our Navy and our air defense. It's
a very dangerous thing for the United States to distort facts
about things like that, because if repeated over and over
again, it is apt to create a sense of fear, a sense of doubt in
the minds of some American people.

And so I now brand as false the statement being made by

Republican campaign orators (boos), day after day and night after night, that the rearming of America was slow, that it is hamstrung and impeded, that it will never be able to meet threats from abroad. Those are the whisperings of appeasers.

That particular misstatement has a history. It came into the world last June, just about the time of the Republican National Convention. (Laughter) Before that, the responsible Republican leaders had been singing an entirely different song. For almost seven years the Republican leaders in the Congress kept on saying that I was placing too much emphasis on national defense.

And now today these men of great vision, they have suddenly discovered that there is a war going on in Europe and another one in Asia. And so, now, always with their eyes on the good old ballot box, they are charging that we have placed too little emphasis on national defense.

But, unlike them, the printed pages of the Congressional Record cannot be changed or suppressed at election time. And based on that permanent record of their speeches and their votes, I make this assertion—that if the Republican leaders had been in control of the Congress of the United States during the past seven years, the important measures for our defenses would not now be law; I make the assertion that the Army and Navy of the United States would still be in almost the same condition in which I found them in 1933.

Remember, I am making those charges against the responsible political leadership of the Republican Party. But there are millions—millions and millions—of patriotic Republicans who have at all times been in sympathy with the efforts of this Administration to arm itself adequately for purposes of defense.

And to Washington in the past few months have come not two or three or a dozen but several hundred of the best business executives in the United States—Republicans and Democrats alike. Not holding company executives or lawyers, I am talking about men experienced in actual production— production of all the types of machines and tools and steel and everything else that have made this nation the industrial leader of the world.

Yes, I have asked Mr. Knudsen and Mr. Stettinius and Mr. Harriman and Mr. Budd and the many others to serve their Government because I certainly believe that they are among the ablest men in the nation in their own fields. I do not know their politics. I do not care about their politics. (Applause) All I know is that they are cooperating one hundred per cent with this Administration in our efforts for national defense. And, the other way around, this Government is cooperating with them—one hundred per cent.

All of these men—all of American industry and American labor—they are all doing magnificent and unselfish work. And the progress of today proves it.

I shall have occasion on Wednesday or Friday or Saturday of this week to tell more about the work they are doing, that they are turning out, and about the progress that has been made in our whole picture of defense.

When the World War, I mean the first World War broke out, we were pretty weak, but by the end of it we were the strongest, one of the strongest naval and military powers in the world. But when this Administration first came into office fifteen years later, we were one of the weakest.

As early as that year of 1933 the storm in Europe was gathering and it was gathering in Asia. Year by year I reported the warnings of danger from our listening posts in foreign lands. But I was only called "an alarmist" by the Republican leadership, and by the great majority of the Republican newspapers of the country. (Boos)

Year by year I asked for more and more defense appropriations. In addition, I allocated hundreds of millions of dollars for defense work from relief funds, the C.C.C. helped, the Public Works helped—as was understood by the Congress when the money was voted by them.

Today our Navy is at a peak of efficiency and fighting strength. Ship for ship, man for man, it is as powerful and efficient as any single navy that ever sailed the seas in history.

(Applause) But, it is not as powerful as combinations of other navies that might be put together in an attack upon us. Our Army and our air forces are now at the highest level that they have ever been in peacetime. But in the light of existing dangers they are not great enough for the absolute safety of America at home.

While this great, constructive work was going forward—what happened?—the Republican leaders were definitely and beyond peradventure of doubt trying to block our efforts toward national defense. They not only voted against these efforts; but they stated time and again through the years that they were unnecessary, that they were extravagant, that our armed strength was sufficient for any emergency.

I propose now to indict these Republican leaders out of their own mouths—these leaders who now disparage our defenses—indict them with what they themselves said in the days before this election year, about how adequate our defenses already were.

Listen to this for instance:

"The facts are that we have the largest and most powerful Navy we ever had, except for two years after the World War, and the greatest air forces we ever had and a match for any nation."

Now, who do you suppose made that statement a little over two years ago? It was not I. It was not even a member of this Administration. It was the ranking Republican member of the House Committee on Foreign Affairs, Republican leader, Hamilton Fish. (Boos)

And now listen to the only living ex-President of the United States. He said in that same year, two years ago:

"We shall be expending nine hundred million dollars more than any other nation on earth.

"We are leading in the arms race."

And now listen to Republican leader Senator Vandenberg, (boos) also speaking at that time. He said that our defense expenditures had already brought us "an imcomparably efficient Navy"; and he said further, "I rise in opposition to this super-super Navy bill. (Laughter) I do not believe it is justified by any conclusive demonstration of national necessity."

And then listen to what Republican leader Senator Taft— the runner-up for the Republican Presidential nomination this year, said: Why, just this past February, 1940, he said:

"The increase of the Army and Navy over the tremendous appropriations of the current year seems to be unnecessary if we are concerned solely with defense." (Laughter and applause)

There is the record on that; the permanent crystal clear record. Until the present political campaign opened, Republican leaders, in and out of the Congress, shouted from the housetops that our defenses were fully adequate.

Today they proclaim that this Administration has starved our armed forces, that our Navy is anemic, (laughter) our Army puny, (laughter) our air forces piteously weak.

Yes, it is a remarkable somersault.

I wonder if the election could have something to do with it. (Laughter) And this seems what they would have called "logic" when I was at school: If the Republican leaders were telling the truth in 1938 and 1939, then—out of their own mouths—they stand convicted of inconsistency today. (Applause) And, as we used to say, per contra, if they are telling the truth today, they stand convicted of inconsistency in 1938.

Why, the simple truth is that the Republican Party, through its leadership, played politics with defense, the defense of the United States, in 1938 and 1939. And they are playing politics with the national security of America today.

That same group would still control their party in Congress at the next session. It is the Congress that passes the laws of the United States. The record of those Republican leaders shows what a slim chance the cause of strong defense would have, if they were in control.

Not only in their statements but in their votes is written their record of sabotage of this Administration's continual efforts to increase our defenses to meet the dangers that loomed ever larger and larger upon the horizon.

For example, deeply concerned over what was happening in Europe, I asked the Congress in January, 1938, for a naval expansion of twenty per cent—forty-six additional ships, nine hundred and fifty new planes.

What did the Republican leaders do when they had this chance to increase our national defense almost three years ago? You would think from their present barrage of verbal pyrotechnics, that they rushed in to pass that bill, or that they even demanded a larger expansion for the Navy.

But, ah! my friends, they were not in a national campaign for votes then. (Laughter)

In those days they were trying to build up a different kind of political fence.

In those days they thought that the way to win votes was by representing this Administration as extravagant in national defense, indeed as hysterical, as manufacturing panics and inventing foreign dangers.

But now, in the serious days of 1940, all is changed! Not only because they are serious days, but because they are election days as well.

To use the old, old example that is always good: On the radio these Republican orators swing through the air with the greatest of ease; but the American people are not voting this year for the best trapeze performer. (Laughter and applause)

The plain fact is that when that naval bill I was speaking about was submitted to the Congress, the Republican leaders jumped in to fight it.

Who were they? There was the present Republican candidate for Vice President, Senator McNary. (Boos) There were Senator Vandenberg and Senator Nye. And there was the man who would be the Chairman of the House Committee on Foreign Affairs, Congressman Fish. (Boos)

The first thing they did was to try to eliminate the battleships from the bill. The Republicans in the House voted sixty-seven to twenty against building them; and in the

Senate, where the Republicans had a much smaller number, the Republicans voted seven to four against building them.

The record is perfectly clear that back in 1938 they were positive in their own minds that we needed no more battle-ships. The naval expansion bill, of course, was passed; but it was passed by Democratic votes in the Congress—in spite of the Republicans.

You see, I am talking by the book. Again, in March, 1939, the Republican Senators voted twelve to four against the bill for one hundred and two million dollars to buy certain strategic war materials that we needed, that we do not have in this country.

In March, 1939, the Republicans in the Senate voted eleven to eight against increasing the authorized number of planes in the Navy.

In June, 1939, Republicans in the House voted one hundred and forty-four to eight in favor of reducing the appropriations for the Army Air Corps. (Boos)

Now that proves this one simple fact: It proves that if the Republican leaders had been in control in the Congress in 1938 and 1939, these measures to increase our Navy and our Army and our Air Forces would have been defeated over-whelmingly.

I say that those leaders played politics with defense in 1938 and I say that they are playing politics with our national security today.

Turn another page:

The Republican campaign orators and leaders are all now yelling "me too" (laughter)—and especially I know in the past few days they are saying "me too" on help to Britain. (Applause) But last fall they had their chance to vote to give aid to Britain and other democracies—and they turned it down.

This chance came when I recommended that the Congress repeal the embargo on the shipment of armaments and munitions to nations at war, and permit such shipment on a "cash-and-carry basis." It is only because of the repeal of the embargo law that we have been able to sell planes and ships and guns and munitions to victims of aggression.

But how did the Republicans vote on the repeal of that embargo?

In the Senate the Republicans voted fourteen to six against it. And in the House, this time, the Republicans voted one hundred and forty to nineteen against it. (Boos)

Yes, the Act was passed by Democratic votes (applause) but it was over the opposition of the Republican leaders. And just to name a few, the following Republican leaders, among many others, voted against the Act—Senators McNary, Vandenberg, Nye and Johnson; now wait, a perfectly beautiful alliteration—Congressmen Martin, Barton and Fish. (Laughter and applause.)

Now, at the eleventh hour, they have discovered what we knew all along—that overseas success in warding off invasion by dictatorship forces means safety of the United States. It means also independence, continued independence, to those smaller nations which still retain their independence. And it means restoration of sovereignty to those smaller nations which have temporarily lost it. As we know, one of the keystones of American policy is the recognition of the right of small nations to survive and prosper.

So, we can well say that Britain and a lot of other nations would never have received one ounce of help from us—if the decision had been left to Martin, Barton and Fish.

And, finally, let me come down to something that happened two months ago.

In the Senate there was an amendment to permit the United States Government to prevent profiteering or unpatriotic obstruction by any corporation in defense work. It permitted the Government to take over, with reasonable compensation, any manufacturing plant which refused to cooperate in national defense. (Applause) And the Republican Senators voted against this Russell-Overton Amendment on August 28, 1940, eight to six.

The bill was adopted all right—by Democratic votes. (Applause) But the opposing vote of those eight Republican leaders showed what would happen if the National Government were turned over to their control. For their vote said, in effect, that they put money rights ahead of human lives— to say nothing of national security.

You and I, and the overwhelming majority of Americans, will never stand for that. (Applause)

Let's go: Outside the halls of Congress eminent Republican candidates began to turn new somersaults. At first they denounced that bill about making corporations do something, to match the obligation of human lives. Yes, at first they denounced the bill, but then, when public opinion rose up to demand it, they seized their trapeze with the greatest of ease, and reversed themselves in mid-air. (Applause and laughter)

This record of Republican leadership—a record of timidity, of weakness, of short-sightedness—is as bad in international as in military affairs.

It is the same record of timidity, of weakness, of short-sightedness which they showed in domestic affairs when they were in control before 1933. (Applause)

But the Republican leaders' memories seem to have been short, in this, as in some other matters. And by the way—who was it said that an elephant never forgets? (Laughter and applause)

Yes, it is the same record of timidity, of weakness and of short-sightedness that governed the policy of the confused, reactionary governments in France and England before the war.

That fact was discovered too late in France.

It was discovered just in time in England. (Applause)

Pray God that, having discovered it, we won't forget it either. (Applause) . . .

## LETTER TO CARL SANDBURG

*Aboard Presidential Special Train. December 3, 1940*

*Speaking for the independent voter, the Illinois poet and biographer of Abraham Lincoln in a radio speech on election eve had called Roosevelt "a not perfect man and yet more precious than fine gold."*

Dear Carl Sandburg:

I have not had a chance since the election to tell you really and truly how much that broadcast of yours closing the 1940 campaign meant to me. You are such a very understanding soul and can make allowances with fairness for the weaknesses and frailties of human nature that you are one of the few people who can truly understand the perplexities, the complications, the failures and the successes of what goes on in Washington today.

It is amazing that the independent voters of America—an increasing number of them—many of them without real education—do have that final ability to decide our fate and the country's fate "in the deep silence of their own minds."

If you are in Washington, do run in and see me.

As ever yours,

## PRESS CONFERENCE #702

*The White House. December 17, 1940*

*After a post-election cruise, the President revealed the thinking that led to the Lend-Lease Act of March, 1941. In a Fireside Chat on December 29, 1940, he proposed that the United States should be "the great arsenal of democracy."*

THE PRESIDENT: . . . I don't think there is any particular news, except possibly one thing that I think is worth my talking about from—what will I call it?—the background method. In the present world situation of course there is absolutely no doubt in the mind of a very overwhelming number of Americans that the best immediate defense of the United States is the success of Great Britain in defending itself, and that, therefore, quite aside from our historic and current interest in the survival of democracy as a whole in the world, it is equally important from a selfish point of view of American defense that we should do everything to help the British Empire to defend itself.

I have read a great deal of nonsense by people who can only think in what we may call traditional terms, in the last few days, about finances. Steve (Mr. Early) was asking me about it this morning, and I thought it was better that I should talk to you than for Steve to talk to you; but I gave him one line which he would have used this morning if anybody had asked him, and that was this: In my memory and your memory and in all history no major war has ever been won or lost through a lack of money. . . .

I go back to the idea that one thing that is necessary for American national defense is additional productive facilities; and the more we increase those facilities—factories, shipbuilding ways, munition plants, et cetera and so on—the stronger American national defense is. Now, orders from Great Britain are therefore a tremendous asset to American national defense, because they create, automatically, additional facilities. I am talking selfishly, from the American point of view—nothing else. Therefore, from the selfish point of view, that production must be encouraged by us; and there are several ways of encouraging it—not just one, the way the narrow-minded fellow I have been talking about might assume, and has assumed. He has assumed that the only way was to repeal certain existing statutes, like the Neutrality Act and the old Johnson Act and a few other things like that, and then lend the money to Great Britain to be spent over here—either lend it through, as was done in the earlier days of the previous war, private banking circles or make it a loan from this Government to another government—the British Government.

Well, that is the—what will I call it? the banal (you will have to find another word for banal) the banal type of mind that can only think of that method.

There is another one which is also somewhat banal—we may come to it, I don't know—and that is a gift; in other words, for us to pay for all these munitions, ships, plants, guns, et cetera, and make a gift of them to Great Britain. I am not at all sure that that is a necessity, and I am not at all sure that Great Britain would care to have a gift from the United States—the taxpayers of the United States. I doubt it very much.

Well, there are other ways, and those ways are being explored; but they are possible. All I can do is to speak in very general terms, because we are in the middle of it. I have been at it now three or four weeks, exploring other methods of continuing the building up of our productive facilities and continuing the flow of munitions to Great Britain automatically; and I will just put it this way, as not a final other method but as one of possibly several other methods that might be devised toward that end. It is possible—I will put it that way—for the United States to take over British orders, and, because they are essentially the same kind of munitions that we use ourselves, turn them into American orders. We have got enough money to do it. And thereupon such portion of them as the military events of the future would determine to be right and proper for us to allow to go to the other side, either lease the materials or sell the materials subject to mortgage to the people on the other side, on the general theory that it may still prove true that the best defense of Great Britain is the best defense of the United States, and therefore that they would be more useful to the defense of the United States if they were used in Great Britain than if they were kept in storage here.

Now, what I am trying to do is to eliminate the dollar sign, and that is something brand new in the thoughts of practically everybody in this room, I think—get rid of the silly, foolish old dollar sign. All right!

Well, let me give you an illustration: Suppose my neighbor's home catches fire, and I have got a length of garden hose four or five hundred feet away; but, by Heaven, if he can take my garden hose and connect it up with his hydrant, I may help him to put out his fire. Now, what do I do? I don't say to him before that operation, "Neighbor, my garden hose cost me $15; you have got to pay me $15 for it." What is the transaction that goes on? I don't want $15—I want my garden hose back after the fire is over. All right. If it goes through the fire all right, intact, without any damage to it, he gives it back to me and thanks me very much for the use of it. But suppose it gets smashed up—holes in it—during the fire; we don't have to have too much formality about it, but I say to him, "I was glad to lend you that hose; I see I can't use it any more, it's all smashed up." He says, "How many feet of it were there?" I tell him, "There were 150 feet of it." He says, "All right, I will replace it." Now, if I get a nice garden hose back, I am in pretty good shape. In others words, if you lend certain munitions and get the munitions back at the end of the war, if they are intact—haven't been hurt—you are all right; if they have been damaged or deteriorated or lost completely, it seems to me you come out pretty well if you have them replaced by the fellow that you have lent them to.

I can't go into details, and there is no use asking legal questions about how you would do it, because that is the thing that is now under study; but the thought—the bright thought —is that we would take over not all but a very large number of future British orders, and when they come off the line, whether they were planes or guns or something else, we would enter into some kind of arrangement for their use by the British on the ground that it was the best thing for American defense, and that when the show was over we would get repaid in kind sometime, thereby leaving out the dollar mark in the form of a dollar debt and substituting for it a gentleman's obligation to repay in kind. I think you all get it. . . .

## ANNUAL MESSAGE TO CONGRESS

*The Capitol. January 6, 1941*

*The Lend-Lease idea was now formally proposed to Congress and supported in several significant ways.*

. . . Let us say to the democracies: "We Americans are vitally concerned in your defense of freedom. We are putting forth our energies, our resources and our organizing powers to give you the strength to regain and maintain a free world. We shall send you, in ever-increasing numbers, ships, planes, tanks, guns. That is our purpose and our pledge."

In fulfillment of this purpose we will not be intimidated by the threats of dictators that they will regard as a breach of international law or as an act of war our aid to the democracies which dare to resist their aggression. Such aid is not an act of war, even if a dictator should unilaterally proclaim it so to be.

And if the dictators are ready to make war upon us, they will not wait for an act of war on our part. They did not wait for Norway or Belgium or the Netherlands to commit an act of war.

Their only interest is in a new one-way international law, which lacks mutuality in its observance, and, therefore, becomes an instrument of oppression.

The happiness of future generations of Americans may well depend on how effective and how immediate we can make our aid felt. No one can tell the exact character of the emergency situations that we may be called upon to meet. The Nation's hands must not be tied when the Nation's life is in danger.

Yes, and we must all prepare—all of us prepare—to make the sacrifices that the emergency—almost as serious as war itself—demands. Whatever stands in the way of speed and efficiency in defense—in defense preparations of any kind—must give way to the national need.

A free nation has the right to expect full cooperation from

all groups. A free nation has the right to look to the leaders of business, of labor, and of agriculture to take the lead in stimulating effort, not among other groups but within their own groups.

The best way of dealing with the few slackers or trouble makers in our midst is, first, to shame them by patriotic example, and, if that fails, to use the sovereignty of government to save government.

As men do not live by bread alone, they do not fight by armaments alone. Those who man our defenses, and those behind them who build our defenses, must have the stamina and the courage which come from unshakeable belief in the manner of life which they are defending. The mighty action that we are calling for cannot be based on a disregard of all the things worth fighting for.

The Nation takes great satisfaction and much strength from the things which have been done to make its people conscious of their individual stake in the preservation of democratic life in America. Those things have toughened the fibre of our people, have renewed their faith and strengthened their devotion to the institutions we make ready to protect.

Certainly this is no time for any of us to stop thinking about the social and economic problems which are the root cause of the social revolution which is today a supreme factor in the world.

For there is nothing mysterious about the foundations of a healthy and strong democracy. The basic things expected by our people of their political and economic systems are simple. They are:

Equality of opportunity for youth and for others.

Jobs for those who can work.

Security for those who need it.

The ending of special privilege for the few.

The preservation of civil liberties for all.

The enjoyment of the fruits of scientific progress in a wider and constantly rising standard of living.

These are the simple, basic things that must never be lost

sight of in the turmoil and unbelievable complexity of our modern world. The inner and abiding strength of our economic and political systems is dependent upon the degree to which they fulfill these expectations.

Many subjects connected with our social economy call for immediate improvement.

As examples:

We should bring more citizens under the coverage of old-age pensions and unemployment insurance.

We should widen the opportunities for adequate medical care.

We should plan a better system by which persons deserving or needing gainful employment may obtain it.

I have called for personal sacrifice. And I am assured of the willingness of almost all Americans to respond to that call.

A part of the sacrifice means the payment of more money in taxes. In my Budget Message I will recommend that a greater portion of this great defense program be paid for from taxation than we are paying for today. No person should try, or be allowed, to get rich out of this program; and the principle of tax payments in accordance with ability to pay should be constantly before our eyes to guide our legislation.

If the Congress maintains these principles, the voters, putting patriotism ahead of pocketbooks, will give you their applause.

In the future days, which we seek to make secure, we look forward to a world founded upon four essential human freedoms.

The first is freedom of speech and expression—everywhere in the world.

The second is freedom of every person to worship God in his own way—everywhere in the world.

The third is freedom from want—which, translated into world terms, means economic understandings which will secure to every nation a healthy peacetime life for its inhabitants—everywhere in the world.

The fourth is freedom from fear—which, translated into world terms, means a world-wide reduction of armaments to such a point and in such a thorough fashion that no nation will be in a position to commit an act of physical aggression against any neighbor—anywhere in the world.

That is no vision of a distant millennium. It is a definite basis for a kind of world attainable in our own time and generation. That kind of world is the very antithesis of the so-called new order of tyranny which the dictators seek to create with the crash of a bomb.

To that new order we oppose the greater conception—the moral order. A good society is able to face schemes of world domination and foreign revolutions alike without fear.

Since the beginning of our American history, we have been engaged in change—in a perpetual peaceful revolution—a revolution which goes on steadily, quietly adjusting itself to changing conditions—without the concentration camp or the quick-lime in the ditch. The world order which we seek is the cooperation of free countries, working together in a friendly, civilized society.

This nation has placed its destiny in the hands and heads and hearts of its millions of free men and women; and its faith in freedom under the guidance of God. Freedom means the supremacy of human rights everywhere. Our support goes to those who struggle to gain those rights and keep them. Our strength is our unity of purpose.

To that high concept there can be no end save victory.


## MEMORANDUM FOR WILLIAM S. KNUDSEN AND SIDNEY HILLMAN

*June 12, 1941*

*This Memorandum to the Co-Directors of the Office of Production Management resulted in the establishment of the Fair Employment Practice Committee on June 25. Although Congress refused to make it permanent, the FEPC by methods of media-*

*tion and persuasion achieved results that made it a significant
"New Deal" measure of the war period.*

Complaints have repeatedly been brought to my attention
that available and much-needed workers are being barred
from defense production solely because of race, religion, or
national origin. It is said that at a time when labor stringencies
are appearing in many areas, fully qualified workers are being
turned from the gates of industry on specifications entirely un-
related to efficiency and productivity. Also that discrimination
against Negro workers has been nation-wide, and other minority racial, national and religious groups have felt its effects in
many localities. This situation is a matter of grave national
importance, and immediate steps must be taken to deal with
it effectively.

I note with satisfaction that the Office of Production Management has recognized the seriousness of this situation, and
that on April 11, 1941, it addressed a letter on the subject to
all holders of defense contracts. As Chief Executive of the
Nation I place the full support of my office behind your statement to the effect that, "All holders of defense contracts are
urged to examine their employment and training policies at
once to determine whether or not these policies make ample
provision for the full utilization of available and competent
Negro workers. Every available source of labor capable of
producing defense materials must be tapped in the present
emergency."

No nation combatting the increasing threat of totalitarianism
can afford arbitrarily to exclude large segments of its population from its defense industries. Even more important is it for
us to strengthen our unity and morale by refuting at home
the very theories which we are fighting abroad.

Our Government cannot countenance continued discrimination against American citizens in defense production. Industry
must take the initiative in opening the doors of employment
to all loyal and qualified workers regardless of race, national
origin, religion or color. American workers, both organized and
unorganized, must be prepared to welcome the general and

much-needed employment of fellow workers of all racial and
nationality origins in defense industries.

In the present emergency, it is imperative that we deal
effectively and speedily with this problem. I shall expect the
Office of Production Management to take immediate steps to
facilitate the full utilization of our productive man-power.

## LETTER TO D. WORTH CLARK

*The White House. August 1, 1941*

*Isolationists like Senator Clark sometimes suggested that the
United States could achieve ample security by abandoning
friends in Europe and Asia and annexing part or all of Latin
America and Canada.*

My dear Senator Clark:

It is as I expected. I felt very certain that your remarks the
other day in regard to a virtual act of aggression against the
other twenty American Republics and the establishment of
puppet governments therein by the United States would result in these remarks being played up and used in Europe by
the Nazis and Fascists.

I said nothing about this, however.

Now, though, I think it is only right that you should know
that my fears have been realized. A dispatch from Rome
quotes the Italian press as alleging that your statement ends
the Good Neighbor Policy and represents the real opinion of
the President and of the State Department. It goes on to say
that your remarks amount to a frank statement made out of
turn and that the Statements of the President and the Acting
Secretary of State are mere camouflage because they are not
yet ready to assume the role of the aggressor in South America.
Finally, the Italian papers plead with the Latin-American
countries to take warning and abandon all cooperation with
this country.

Simultaneously the German newspapers are "congratulating
Senator Clark" on his "touching frankness in letting the cat out

of the bag and that the real aim of the United States is not that of the Good Neighbor but of the Big Stick."

As I said before, I think it is only fair that you should know just what the result has been.

Very sincerely yours,

## PRESS CONFERENCE #761

*On Board* U.S.S. Potomac *at Rockland, Maine. August 16, 1941*

*President Roosevelt and Prime Minister Churchill met at sea off Argentia, Newfoundland, on August 9. Besides discussions of current problems, they stated in the Atlantic Charter their belief that a "permanent system of general security" should be established after the war.*

THE PRESIDENT: I am glad to see you. How are you?

PRESS: Very well, sir. . . .

THE PRESIDENT: Mike says he hasn't got any news.

PRESS: Have you, sir?

THE PRESIDENT: No. Awfully glad to have you see the cabin of the *Potomac*. There is a gentleman over here behind Mike, Harry Hopkins, just back from Moscow. There he is.

PRESS: Could you tell us where this conference with Mr. Churchill was held?

THE PRESIDENT: I cannot, for obvious reasons. I had better make one or two things clear in the beginning. Names of ships are out. I suppose it has been published. The Prime Minister was there on the *Prince of Wales* and I was there on the *Augusta*, but outside of that, nothing about ships, nothing about times, dates, and nothing about locations. All those things for perfectly obvious reasons, which I don't have to explain. Just for example, I wanted to slay a gentleman that said I was coming to Rockland today, because it's merely an invitation.

Things of that kind cause trouble, if you make known the exact location on the high seas of the President and the Prime Minister. However, it was foggy between North Haven and

Rockland, and while it's open season out there, no submarine fired a torpedo at us as far as we could see, and we are here safely.

You want to know certain things, I suppose. The easiest thing to do is to give you what we might call the impressions that stand out. I think the first thing in the minds of all of us was a very remarkable religious service on the quarterdeck of the *Prince of Wales* last Sunday morning. There was their own ship's complement, with three or four hundred bluejackets and marines from American ships, on the quarterdeck, completely intermingled, first one uniform and then another uniform. The service was conducted by two chaplains, one English and one American, and as usual, the lesson was read by the captain of the British ship. They had three hymns that everybody took part in, and a little ship's altar was decked with the American flag and the British flag. The officers were all intermingled on the fantail, and I think the pictures of it have been released. I am not sure. The point is, I think everybody there, officers and enlisted men, felt that it was one of the great historic services. I know I did. . . .

PRESS: We might assume that you have complete understanding with Mr. Churchill on all aspects of the world situation, including the Far East?

THE PRESIDENT: When you come down to localities, I don't suppose there is a single section or a single continent that was not discussed at one time or another, in all the conferences you ever heard of.

PRESS: Are we any closer to entering the war, actually?

THE PRESIDENT: I should say, no.

PRESS: May we quote directly?

THE PRESIDENT: No, you can quote indirectly.

PRESS: Mr. President, is Russia bound to subscribe to this eight point program?

THE PRESIDENT: No.

PRESS: Will she be?

THE PRESIDENT: Nobody ever suggested it until you did.

PRESS: Can you tell us anything about aid to Russia?

THE PRESIDENT: You know just as much about it as I do, or Mr. Churchill, for discussion. Last year two commentators entirely overlooked two factors—one was geography, and the other was goods and munitions.

We did discuss the fitting in of Russian needs to the existing production program, and we also discussed what might be called the fact that the Russian needs might be divided into two categories. The first is material which is immediately available, to get there during this summer's campaign, and on the assumption that winter will bring at least a partial halt to campaigns in Russia. The other part is the materials and munitions which can be got to Russia by the time the spring campaign opens, and the fitting in of all of that to our own domestic needs and other Lease-Lend orders.

PRESS: You have no doubt the Russian resistance will continue into winter?

THE PRESIDENT: I guess from that there is a sort of an assumption in there.

PRESS: Mr. President, do you plan to go on the radio or deliver any message to Congress?

THE PRESIDENT: That depends largely on you fellows.

PRESS: How so, sir?

THE PRESIDENT: If you give the country an exceedingly correct picture, I probably won't go on the radio.

PRESS: You can rely on us, sir.

THE PRESIDENT: I suppose you won't print that.

PRESS: That's what he thinks.

THE PRESIDENT: I think that's all the news. I have to get back to Washington tomorrow. . . .

## LETTER TO POPE PIUS XII

*The White House. September 3, 1941*

*The President worked to prevent religious antagonism against the Soviet Government from interfering with his policy of aid to Russia. Nowhere did he state more definitely his view of the distinction between the Communist and the Nazi dictatorships.*

Your Holiness:

At my request, Mr. Myron Taylor will discuss with Your Holiness certain matters with regard to which I am very desirous that he explain my feelings and American opinion. These are matters in regard to which I feel very strongly.

The first of these relates to the problem of the attitude of the Russian Government and the Russian people toward religion. In so far as I am informed, churches in Russia are open. I believe there is a real possibility that Russia may as a result of the present conflict recognize freedom of religion in Russia, although, of course, without recognition of any official intervention on the part of any church in education or political matters within Russia. I feel that if this can be accomplished it will put the possibility of the restoration of real religious liberty in Russia on a much better footing than religious freedom is in Germany.

There are in the United States many people in *all* churches who have the feeling that Russia is governed completely by a communistic form of society. In my opinion, the fact is that Russia is governed by a dictatorship, as rigid in its manner of being as is the dictatorship in Germany. I believe, however, that this Russian dictatorship is less dangerous to the safety of other nations than is the German form of dictatorship. The only weapon which the Russian dictatorship uses outside of its own borders is communist propaganda which I, of course, recognize has in the past been utilized for the purpose of breaking down the form of government in other countries, religious belief, et cetera. Germany, however, not only has utilized, but is utilizing, this kind of propaganda as well and has also undertaken the employment of every form of military aggression outside of its borders for the purpose of world conquest by force of arms and by force of propaganda. I believe that the survival of Russia is less dangerous to religion, to the church as such, and to humanity in general than would be the survival of the German form of dictatorship. Furthermore, it is my belief that the leaders of all churches in the United States should recognize these facts clearly and should not close their eyes to these basic questions and by their present attitude on this question directly assist Germany in her present objectives.

Bearing in mind the common desire which Your Holiness and I share that a firm basis for lasting concord between men and nations founded on the principles of Christianity can again be established, I have asked Mr. Taylor to explain my feelings in this matter in order that Your Holiness may understand my position in this respect.

Believe me, with the assurances of my highest regard,

Yours very sincerely,

## RADIO ADDRESS ON THE BATTLE
## OF THE ATLANTIC

*The White House. September 11, 1941*

*This address announced limited, undeclared, naval war in Atlantic waters west of combat zones. The Navy was ordered to "shoot on sight" German and Italian submarines and raiders south and west of Iceland.*

My fellow Americans:

The Navy Department of the United States has reported to me that on the morning of September fourth the United States destroyer *Greer*, proceeding in full daylight towards Iceland, had reached a point southeast of Greenland. She was carrying American mail to Iceland. She was flying the American flag. Her identity as an American ship was unmistakable.

She was then and there attacked by a submarine. Germany admits that it was a German submarine. The submarine deliberately fired a torpedo at the *Greer*, followed later by another torpedo attack. In spite of what Hitler's propaganda Bureau has invented, and in spite of what any American obstructionist organization may prefer to believe, I tell you the blunt fact that the German submarine fired first upon this American destroyer without warning, and with deliberate design to sink her

Our destroyer, at the time, was in waters which the Government of the United States had declared to be waters of self-defense—surrounding outposts of American protection in the Atlantic.

In the North of the Atlantic, outposts have been established by us in Iceland, in Greenland, in Labrador and in Newfoundland. Through these waters there pass many ships of many flags. They bear food and other supplies to civilians; and they bear materiel of war, for which the people of the United States are spending billions of dollars, and which, by Congressional action, they have declared to be essential for the defense of our own land.

The United States destroyer, when attacked, was proceeding on a legitimate mission.

If the destroyer was visible to the submarine when the torpedo was fired, then the attack was a deliberate attempt by the Nazis to sink a clearly identified American warship. On the other hand, if the submarine was beneath the surface of the sea and, with the aid of its listening devices, fired in the direction of the sound of the American destroyer without even taking the trouble to learn its identity—as the official German communique would indicate—then the attack was even more outrageous. For it indicates a policy of indiscriminate violence against any vessel sailing the seas—belligerent or non-belligerent.

This was piracy—piracy legally and morally. It was not the first nor the last act of piracy which the Nazi Government has committed against the American flag in this war. For attack has followed attack.

A few months ago an American flag merchant ship, the *Robin Moor*, was sunk by a Nazi submarine in the middle of the South Atlantic, under circumstances violating long-established international law and violating every principle of humanity. The passengers and the crew were forced into open boats hundreds of miles from land, in direct violation of international agreements signed by nearly all nations including the Government of Germany. No apology, no allegation of mistake, no offer of reparations has come from the Nazi Government.

In July, 1941, nearly two months ago an American battleship in North American waters was followed by a submarine which for a long time sought to maneuver itself into a position of attack upon the battleship. The periscope of the submarine was clearly seen. No British or American submarines were within hundreds of miles of this spot at the time, so the nationality of the submarine is clear.

Five days ago a United States Navy ship on patrol picked up three survivors of an American-owned ship operating under the flag of our sister Republic of Panama—the S.S. *Sessa*. On August seventeenth, she had been first torpedoed without warning, and then shelled, near Greenland, while carrying civilian supplies to Iceland. It is feared that the other members of her crew have been drowned. In view of the established presence of German submarines in this vicinity, there can be no reasonable doubt as to the identity of the flag of the attacker.

Five days ago, another United States merchant ship, the *Steel Seafarer* was sunk by a German aircraft in the Red Sea two hundred and twenty miles south of Suez. She was bound for an Egyptian port.

So four of the vessels sunk or attacked flew the American flag and were clearly identifiable. Two of these ships were warships of the American Navy. In the fifth case, the vessel sunk clearly carried the flag of our sister Republic of Panama.

In the face of all this, we Americans are keeping our feet on the ground. Our type of democratic civilization has outgrown the thought of feeling compelled to fight some other nation by reason of any single piratical attack on one of our ships. We are not becoming hysterical or losing our sense of proportion. Therefore, what I am thinking and saying tonight does not relate to any isolated episode.

Instead, we Americans are taking a long-range point of view in regard to certain fundamentals—a point of view in regard to a series of events on land and on sea which must be considered as a whole—as a part of a world pattern.

It would be unworthy of a great nation to exaggerate an isolated incident, or to become inflamed by some one act of violence. But it would be inexcusable folly to minimize such incidents in the face of evidence which makes it clear that the incident is not isolated, but is part of a general plan.

The important truth is that these acts of international lawlessness are a manifestation of a design that has been made clear to the American people for a long time. It is the Nazi design to abolish the freedom of the seas, and to acquire absolute control and domination of these seas for themselves.

For with control of the seas in their own hands, the way can obviously become clear for their next step—domination of the United States—domination of the Western Hemisphere by force of arms. Under Nazi control of the seas, no merchant ship of the United States or of any other American Republic would be free to carry on any peaceful commerce, except by the condescending grace of this foreign and tyrannical power. The Atlantic Ocean which has been, and which should always be, a free and friendly highway for us would then become a deadly menace to the commerce of the United States, to the coasts of the United States, and even to the inland cities of the United States.

The Hitler Government, in defiance of the laws of the sea, in defiance of the recognized rights of all other nations, has presumed to declare, on paper, that great areas of the seas—even including a vast expanse lying in the Western Hemisphere—are to be closed, and that no ships may enter them for any purpose, except at peril of being sunk. Actually they are sinking ships at will and without warning in widely separated areas both within and far outside of these far-flung pretended zones.

This Nazi attempt to seize control of the oceans is but a counterpart of the Nazi plots now being carried on throughout the Western Hemisphere—all designed toward the same end. For Hitler's advance guards—not only his avowed agents but also his dupes among us—have sought to make ready for him footholds, bridgeheads in the New World, to be used as soon as he has gained control of the oceans.

His intrigues, his plots, his machinations, his sabotage in this New World are all known to the Government of the United States. Conspiracy has followed conspiracy.

For example, last year a plot to seize the Government of Uruguay was smashed by the prompt action of that country, which was supported in full by her American neighbors. A like plot was then hatching in Argentina, and that government has carefully and wisely blocked it at every point. More recently, an endeavor was made to subvert the government of Bolivia. And within the past few weeks the discovery was made of secret air-landing fields in Colombia, within easy range of the Panama Canal. I could multiply instance upon instance.

To be ultimately successful in world mastery, Hitler knows that he must get control of the seas. He must first destroy the bridge of ships which we are building across the Atlantic and over which we shall continue to roll the implements of war to help destroy him, to destroy all his works in the end. He must wipe out our patrol on sea and in the air if he is to do it. He must silence the British Navy.

I think it must be explained over and over again to people who like to think of the United States Navy as an invincible protection, that this can be true only if the British Navy survives. And that, my friends, is simple arithmetic.

For if the world outside of the Americas falls under Axis domination, the shipbuilding facilities which the Axis powers would then possess in all of Europe, in the British Isles, and in the Far East would be much greater than all the shipbuilding facilities and potentialities of all of the Americas—not only greater, but two or three times greater, enough to win. Even if the United States threw all its resources into such a situation, seeking to double and even redouble the size of our Navy, the Axis powers, in control of the rest of the world, would have the man-power and the physical resources to outbuild us several times over.

It is time for all Americans, Americans of all the Americas to stop being deluded by the romantic notion that the Americas can go on living happily and peacefully in a Nazi-dominated world.

Generation after generation, America has battled for the general policy of the freedom of the seas. And that policy is a very simple one—but a basic, a fundamental one. It means that no nation has the right to make the broad oceans of the world at great distances from the actual theatre of land war, unsafe for the commerce of others.

That has been our policy, proved time and again, in all of our history.

Our policy has applied from the earliest days of the Republic—and still applies—not merely to the Atlantic but to the Pacific and to all other oceans as well.

Unrestricted submarine warfare in 1941 constitutes a defiance—an act of aggression—against that historic American policy.

It is now clear that Hitler has begun his campaign to control the seas by ruthless force and by wiping out every vestige of international law, every vestige of humanity.

His intention has been made clear. The American people can have no further illusions about it.

No tender whisperings of appeasers that Hitler is not interested in the Western Hemisphere, no soporific lullabies that a wide ocean protects us from him—can long have any effect on the hard-headed, farsighted and realistic American people.

Because of these episodes, because of the movements and operations of German warships, and because of the clear, repeated proof that the present government of Germany has no respect for treaties or for international law, that it has no decent attitude toward neutral nations or human life—we Americans are now face to face not with abstract theories but with cruel, relentless facts.

This attack on the *Greer* was no localized military operation in the North Atlantic. This was no mere episode in a struggle between two nations. This was one determined step towards creating a permanent world system based on force, on terror and on murder.

And I am sure that even now the Nazis are waiting, waiting to see whether the United States will by silence give them the green light to go ahead on this path of destruction.

The Nazi danger to our western world has long ceased to be a mere possibility. The danger is here now—not only from a military enemy but from an enemy of all law, all liberty, all morality, all religion. . . .

This is the time for prevention of attack.

If submarines or raiders attack in distant waters, they can attack equally well within sight of our own shores. Their very presence in any waters which America deems vital to its defense constitutes an attack.

In the waters which we deem necessary for our defense, American naval vessels and American planes will no longer wait until Axis submarines lurking under the water, or Axis raiders on the surface of the sea, strike their deadly blow—first.

Upon our naval and air patrol—now operating in large number over a vast expanse of the Atlantic Ocean—falls the duty of maintaining the Americn policy of freedom of the seas—now. That means, very simply, very clearly, that our patrolling vessels and planes will protect all merchant ships—not only American ships but ships of any flag—engaged in commerce in our defensive waters. They will protect them from submarines; they will protect them from surface raiders.

This situation is not new. The second President of the United States, John Adams, ordered the United States Navy to clean out European privateers and European ships of war which were infesting the Caribbean and South American waters, destroying American commerce.

The third President of the United States, Thomas Jefferson, ordered the United States Navy to end the attacks being made upon American and other ships by the corsairs of the nations of North Africa.

My obligation as President is historic; it is clear. Yes, it is inescapable.

It is no act of war on our part when we decide to protect the seas that are vital to American defense. The aggression is not ours. Ours is solely defense.

But let this warning be clear. From now on, if German or Italian vessels of war enter the waters, the protection of which is necessary for American defense, they do so at their own peril.

The orders which I have given as Commander-in-Chief of the United States Army and Navy are to carry out that policy —at once.

The sole responsibility rests upon Germany. There will be no shooting unless Germany continues to seek it.

That is my obvious duty in this crisis. That is the clear right of this sovereign nation. This is the only step possible, if we would keep tight the wall of defense which we are pledged to maintain around this Western Hemisphere.

I have no illusions about the gravity of this step. I have not taken it hurriedly or lightly. It is the result of months and months of constant thought and anxiety and prayer. In the protection of your nation and mine it cannot be avoided.

The American people have faced other grave crises in their history—with American courage, with American resolution. They will do no less today.

They know the actualities of the attacks upon us. They know the necessities of a bold defense against these attacks. They know that the times call for clear heads and fearless hearts.

And with that inner strength that comes to a free people conscious of their duty, conscious of the righteousness of what they do, they will—with Divine help and guidance—stand their ground against this latest assault upon their democracy, their sovereignty, and their freedom.

## MEMORANDUM FOR FREDERIC A. DELANO

*The White House. September 26, 1941*

*Roosevelt shared with his favorite uncle many hobbies, but not this one.*

I think you should tell Mr. Key-Smith that, in my judgment, we should let sleeping heroes lie. The District is pock-marked with generals, statesmen, foreigners, visiting firemen, etc., on horseback, standing and sitting—all without any particular reference to a plan.

Personally I want to see old man Jackson and the horse which is balanced on its tail, in front of the White House as long as I am here. How the General is able to wave without holding onto his pommel, I have never known. I am still fascinated—and I think almost everyone else is too.

From the practical point of view, we should spend no money these days in re-distributing heroes round the parks and squares of Washington.

## MEMORANDUM FOR STEPHEN T. EARLY

*The White House. October 1, 1941*

*Many conservatives hoped that the defense program could be used to clamp down on labor.*

I notice that the Navy is still giving out strike information based on the number of man-days lost. For instance, it is said by the Navy that in September up to the 27th, 109,000 man-days were lost on strikes.

Tell the Navy that no layman knows what 109,000 man-days constitute. What percentage does that figure bear to the total number of man-days worked on Navy contracts of all kinds all over the country.

# PRESS CONFERENCE #787

*The White House. November 28, 1941*

*On November 20, the Japanese Government had proposed to the United States a "modus vivendi" which would require the United States to aid Japan in its program of conquest in China. The Japanese authorities privately regarded this proposal as their ultimatum. On November 22, they ordered the task force that bombed Pearl Harbor to proceed to Hawaii. On November 26, Secretary of State Hull rejected most of the terms of the modus vivendi and proposed instead that negotiations should continue on the basis of an American offer to aid Japan if it would abandon aggression.*

. . . Q: Is there anything you can tell us sir, about these Japanese situations—I mean negotiations?

THE PRESIDENT: I think it's better not.

MR. GODWIN: If you have read newspapers carefully, I think you would come to the conclusion that we have been getting news based on Tokio, to a large extent, in that respect. I just simply throw that out.

THE PRESIDENT: I think that probably is true, Earl, and it has been based on an American policy of infinite patience.

Q: Well, Mr. President, could you say, sir, whether these negotiations have broken down temporarily?

THE PRESIDENT: No. They have not.

Q: Mr. President, did the Japanese yesterday bring any response to the memorandum—the document presented by Mr. Hull?

THE PRESIDENT: No, no.

Q: Mr. President, can you tell when the next meeting will be held with the Japanese?

THE PRESIDENT: I don't know.

Q: Can you tell us, sir, if there were any new developments in your talks with the Japanese different from those that they have had from Mr. Hull?

THE PRESIDENT: No. I would say just exactly the same.

I think I could tell you, for background—but only for background—that the situation seems serious, because our one desire has been peace in the Pacific, and the taking of no steps to alter the prospects of peace, which of course has meant non-aggression. Really boils down to that.

And also—as background—I was, last spring, talking along the line of general peace for the Pacific, based on a settlement of the war between China and Japan—the restoration of peace there, plus a permanent arrangement for non-aggression in the Pacific, and the restoration of normal economic relations, access to raw materials.

And as you know, the Secretary of State, with even more patience than I have—which is saying a whole lot—had been holding conversations from, I think it was April. And in the middle of them came the Japanese expedition to Indo-China, which is very far afield, and caused us very great concern, because it seemed to be a reasonable—to show a reasonable parallel with the Hitler methods in Europe. As for example, the infiltration, over a period of several months, of the German armies into Roumania and Hungary, placing themselves in the position where strategically they were all set to attack Yugoslavia and Greece.

And of course the—the drawing of the parallel made peacefully-inclined people over here to wonder whether this occupation, with a limited number of troops in Indo-China, was the beginning of a similar action in the Far East, placing obvious American interests in great jeopardy if the drawing of such a parallel was justified.

The American flag, of course, does fly from the Philippines. And even before the Japanese went into Indo-China, one might almost say that the Philippines were located in a horseshoe, with Japanese military control over the coasts of China, all the way down to the southern border of China, and Japanese military control on the opposite side—the east—over the mandated islands, so called.

You look at a map closely, that is a sort of a horseshoe, open at the southern end, and the Philippines in the middle of it.

I think a study of the map would be advisable for all of us, because the Hitler method has always been aimed at a little move here and a little move there, by which complete encirclement, or the obtaining of essential military points, was merely—that was a prelude to the extension of aggression to other places. It's a perfectly obvious historical fact today. And we are of course thinking not only about the American flag in the Philippines, not only about certain vital defense needs which come from that open end of the horseshoe, but we are thinking about the—something even more important, and that is the possible extension of control by aggression into the whole of the Pacific area. And we are thinking about what it would mean to this country if that policy were to be used against us in the whole Pacific area. I don't think that anything more can be said at this time. We are—we are waiting. . . .

## MEMORANDUM FOR CORDELL HULL AND SUMNER WELLES

*The White House. December 1, 1941*

*The Japanese expedition to bomb Pearl Harbor proceeded northward of regular sea lanes and kept radio silence. Decoded Japanese diplomatic and espionage messages ("Magic" intercepts) were circulated among the highest officials in Washington and made them aware that the Japanese Government planned a crisis while delaying an answer to the United States proposals of November 26. Intelligence reports of a Japanese military expedition moving southwards along the coast of Indo-China seemed to the President the reason for Japanese expectation of trouble with the United States.*

I have received reports during the past days of continuing Japanese troop movements to southern Indo-China. These reports indicate a very rapid and material increase in the forces of all kinds stationed by Japan in Indo-China.

It was my clear understanding that by the terms of the agreement—and there is no present need to discuss the nature of that agreement—between Japan and the French Government at Vichy that the total number of Japanese forces permitted by the terms of that agreement to be stationed in Indo-China was very considerably less than the total amount of the forces already there.

The stationing of these increased Japanese forces in Indo-China would seem to imply the utilization of these forces by Japan for purposes of further aggression, since no such number of forces could possibly be required for the policing of that region. Such aggression could conceivably be against the Philippine Islands; against the many islands of the East Indies; against Burma; against Malaya or either through coercion or through the actual use of force for the purpose of undertaking the occupation of Thailand.

Please be good enough to request the Japanese Ambassador and Ambassador Kurusu to inquire at once of the Japanese Government what the actual reasons may be for the steps already taken, and what I am to consider is the policy of the Japanese Government as demonstrated by this recent and rapid concentration of troops in Indo-China. This Government has seen in the last few years in Europe a policy on the part of the German Government which has involved a constant and steady encroachment upon the territory and rights of free and independent peoples through the utilization of military steps of the same character. It is for that reason and because of the broad problem of American defense that I should like to know the intention of the Japanese Government.

## MESSAGE TO EMPEROR HIROHITO

*The White House. December 6, 1941*

*Thinking that a Japanese attack on non-American territory was most likely, the President and his advisers pondered whether he should in that case break his antiwar pledge and ask Congress for a declaration of war. They were desperately anxious to avoid a diversion from the Battle of the Atlantic. Such a diversion was precisely the purpose of Hitler, who thought that Russia was*

*now defeated and planned to concentrate next on Britain, where-
fore he urged his Japanese Axis partners to attack the United
States. The American leaders decided that the President should
send a personal appeal to the Emperor Hirohito. If this failed,
he would send a warning to the Japanese Government that the
United States would be compelled to fight if the Japanese expedition attacked a third country, and a message to Congress
explaining the necessity for the warning. The President thought
also of making an address to the American people. He did not
finally decide on the ultimate step of asking for a declaration of
war if all these efforts failed. On December 5, the Japanese Government sent an evasive reply to the President's request for information about the intentions of the Japanese expedition. On
Saturday, December 6, before noon, United States intelligence
reports indicated that the Japanese expedition was heading west
for Thailand. That afternoon the President prepared this message
to Hirohito and it was sent by nine o'clock. The warning to the
Japanese Government and the message to Congress were planned
for Tuesday, December 9, if the appeal to the Emperor failed
to stay the war lords' hands. But on Sunday, December 7, before the Japanese Ambassadors in Washington had delivered
the reply of their Government to the United States offer of November 26, bombs began to fall on Pearl Harbor.*

Almost a century ago the President of the United States addressed to the Emperor of Japan a message extending an offer
of friendship of the people of the United States to the people
of Japan. That offer was accepted, and in the long period of
unbroken peace and friendship which has followed, our respective nations, through the virtues of their peoples and the
wisdom of their rulers have prospered and have substantially
helped humanity.

Only in situations of extraordinary importance to our two
countries need I address to Your Majesty messages on matters of state. I feel I should now so address you because of the
deep and far-reaching emergency which appears to be in
formation.

Developments are occurring in the Pacific area which
threaten to deprive each of our nations and all humanity of

the beneficial influence of the long peace between our two countries. Those developments contain tragic possibilities.

The people of the United States, believing in peace and in the right of nations to live and let live, have eagerly watched the conversations between our two Governments during these past months. We have hoped for a termination of the present conflict between Japan and China. We have hoped that a peace of the Pacific could be consummated in such a way that nationalities of many diverse peoples could exist side by side without fear of invasion; that unbearable burdens of armaments could be lifted for them all; and that all peoples would resume commerce without discrimination against or in favor of any nation.

I am certain that it will be clear to Your Majesty, as it is to me, that in seeking these great objectives both Japan and the United States should agree to eliminate any form of military threat. This seemed essential to the attainment of the high objectives.

More than a year ago Your Majesty's Government concluded an agreement with the Vichy Government by which five or six thousand Japanese troops were permitted to enter into Northern French Indo-China for the protection of Japanese troops which were operating against China further north. And this Spring and Summer the Vichy Government permitted further military forces to enter into Southern French Indo-China for the common defense of French Indo-China. I think I am correct in saying that no attack has been made upon Indo-China, nor that any has been contemplated.

During the past few weeks it has become clear to the world that Japanese military, naval and air forces have been sent to Southern Indo-China in such large numbers as to create a reasonable doubt on the part of other nations that this continuing concentration in Indo-China is not defensive in its character.

Because these continuing concentrations in Indo-China have reached such large proportions and because they extend now to the southeast and southwest corners of that Peninsula, it is only reasonable that the people of the Philippines, of the hundreds of Islands of the East Indies, of Malaya and of Thailand itself are asking themselves whether these forces of Japan are preparing or intending to make attack in one or more of these many directions.

I am sure that Your Majesty will understand that the fear of all these peoples is a legitimate fear in as much as it involves their peace and their national existence. I am sure that Your Majesty will understand why the people of the United States in such large numbers look askance at the establishment of military, naval and air bases manned and equipped so greatly as to constitute armed forces capable of measures of offense.

It is clear that a continuance of such a situation is unthinkable.

None of the peoples whom I have spoken of above can sit either indefinitely or permanently on a keg of dynamite.

There is absolutely no thought on the part of the United States of invading Indo-China if every Japanese soldier or sailor were to be withdrawn therefrom.

I think that we can obtain the same assurance from the Governments of the East Indies, the Governments of Malaya and the Government of Thailand. I would even undertake to ask for the same assurance on the part of the Government of China. Thus a withdrawal of the Japanese forces from Indo-China would result in the assurance of peace throughout the whole of the South Pacific area.

I address myself to Your Majesty at this moment in the fervent hope that Your Majesty may, as I am doing, give thought in this definite emergency to ways of dispelling the dark clouds. I am confident that both of us, for the sake of the peoples not only of our own great countries but for the sake of humanity in neighboring territories, have a sacred duty to restore traditional amity and prevent further death and destruction in the world.

**Part**
*Seven*

Disaster in the Pacific
Invasion of North Africa

DECEMBER 7, 1941 — JANUARY 1, 1944

# WAR MESSAGE TO CONGRESS

*The Capitol. December 8, 1941*

*Within thirty-three minutes after the President had delivered this Message the Senate unanimously and the House of Representatives by a vote of 388-1 passed a joint resolution that war existed by act of Japan. Similar resolutions were passed unanimously on December 11 after Germany and Italy had declared war against the United States. These were the first evidences that the Axis leaders had miscalculated: American isolationism in its original form was dead.*

Yesterday, December 7, 1941—a date which will live in infamy—the United States of America was suddenly and deliberately attacked by naval and air forces of the Empire of Japan.

The United States was at peace with that nation and, at the solicitation of Japan, was still in conversation with its Government and its Emperor looking toward the maintenance of peace in the Pacific. Indeed, one hour after Japanese air squadrons had commenced bombing in the American Island of Oahu, the Japanese Ambassador to the United States and his colleague delivered to our Secretary of State a formal reply to a recent American message. And while this reply stated that it seemed useless to continue the existing diplomatic negotiations, it contained no threat or hint of war or of armed attack.

It will be recorded that the distance of Hawaii from Japan makes it obvious that the attack was deliberately planned many days or even weeks ago. During the intervening time the Japanese Government has deliberately sought to deceive the United States by false statements and expressions of hope for continued peace.

The attack yesterday on the Hawaiian Islands has caused severe damage to American naval and military forces. I regret to tell you that very many American lives have been lost. In addition American ships have been reported torpedoed on the high seas between San Francisco and Honolulu.

Yesterday the Japanese Government also launched an attack against Malaya.

Last night Japanese forces attacked Hong Kong.

Last night Japanese forces attacked Guam.

Last night Japanese forces attacked the Philippine Islands.

Last night the Japanese attacked Wake Island.

And this morning the Japanese attacked Midway Island.

Japan has, therefore, undertaken a surprise offensive extending throughout the Pacific area. The facts of yesterday and today speak for themselves. The people of the United States have already formed their opinions and well understand the implications to the very life and safety of our nation.

As Commander-in-Chief of the Army and Navy I have directed that all measures be taken for our defense.

But always will our whole nation remember the character of the onslaught against us.

No matter how long it may take us to overcome this premeditated invasion, the American people in their righteous might will win through to absolute victory.

I believe that I interpret the will of the Congress and of the people when I assert that we will not only defend ourselves to the uttermost but will make it very certain that this form of treachery shall never again endanger us.

Hostilities exist. There is no blinking at the fact that our people, our territory and our interests are in grave danger.

With confidence in our armed forces—with the unbounding determination of our people—we will gain the inevitable triumph—so help us God.

I ask that the Congress declare that since the unprovoked and dastardly attack by Japan on Sunday, December seventh, 1941, a state of war has existed between the United States and the Japanese Empire.

## PRESS CONFERENCE #796

*The White House. January 2, 1942*

*In several speeches after Pearl Harbor the President rallied patriotic determination to a high pitch. But he also worked with marked success to prevent repetition of the chauvinism, amateur spying and persecutions for which the Wilson Administration bore some responsibility during the First World War.*

THE PRESIDENT: The Attorney General and I got up a statement that is intended to correct the misapprehension of a great many people in the country in regard to the employment of aliens. I think you will regard it necessary that this be spread as widely as possible throughout the country, because there are a great many injustices that are being committed at the present time. I might as well read it to you. Steve can give it to you afterwards.

(*reading*): "I am deeply concerned over the increasing number of reports of employers discharging workers who happen to be aliens or even foreign-born citizens. This is a very serious matter. It is one thing to safeguard American industry, and particularly defense industry, against sabotage; but it is very much another to throw out of work honest and loyal people who, except for the accident of birth, are sincerely patriotic.

"Such a policy is as stupid as it is unjust, and on both counts it plays into the hands of the enemies of American democracy. By discharging loyal, efficient workers simply because they were born abroad or because they have 'foreign-sounding' names or by refusing to employ such men and women, employers are engendering the very distrust and disunity on which our enemies are counting to defeat us.

"Remember the Nazi technique: 'Pit race against race, religion against religion, prejudice against prejudice. Divide and conquer!'

"We must not let that happen here. We must not forget what we are defending: liberty, decency, justice. We cannot afford the economic waste of services of all loyal and patriotic citizens and non-citizens in defending our land and our liberties.

"I urge all private employers to adopt a sane policy regarding aliens and foreign-born citizens, and to remember that the sons of the 'foreigners' they discharged may be among those who fought and are fighting so valiantly at Pearl Harbor or in the Philippines.

"There is no law providing against employment of aliens except in special defense work of a secret nature, and even in such work the employer may hire an alien with the permission of the Army or Navy, depending on the contract."

I think it is pretty important to get that out, because there are a great many people in this country that are discharging people because they have a foreign name.

And this is—what I am going to say is off the record. It is literally true there would be no Notre Dame football team ——. You see the point? . . .

## RADIO ADDRESS ON WASHINGTON'S BIRTHDAY

*The White House. February 23, 1942*

*To help the country face tragic news from the Philippines, the President explained the strategic problems of global war.*

My Fellow Americans:

Washington's Birthday is a most appropriate occasion for us to talk with each other about things as they are today and things as we know they shall be in the future.

For eight years, General Washington and his Continental Army were faced continually with formidable odds and recurring defeats. Supplies and equipment were lacking. In a sense, every winter was a Valley Forge. Throughout the thirteen states there existed fifth columnists—and selfish men, jealous men, fearful men, who proclaimed that Washington's cause was hopeless, and that he should ask for a negotiated peace.

Washington's conduct in those hard times has provided the

model for all Americans ever since—a model of moral stamina. He held to his course, as it had been charted in the Declaration of Independence. He and the brave men who served with him knew that no man's life or fortune was secure, without freedom and free institutions.

The present great struggle has taught us increasingly that freedom of person and security of property anywhere in the world depend upon the security of the rights and obligations of liberty and justice everywhere in the world.

This war is a new kind of war. It is different from all other wars of the past, not only in its methods and weapons but also in its geography. It is warfare in terms of every continent, every island, every sea, every air-lane in the world.

That is the reason why I have asked you to take out and spread before you a map of the whole earth, and to follow with me in the references which I shall make to the world-encircling battle lines of this war. Many questions will, I fear, remain unanswered tonight; but I know you will realize that I cannot cover everything in any one short report to the people.

The broad oceans which have been heralded in the past as our protection from attack have become endless battlefields on which we are constantly being challenged by our enemies.

We must all understand and face the hard fact that our job now is to fight at distances which extend all the way around the globe.

We fight at these vast distances because that is where our enemies are. Until our flow of supplies gives us clear superiority we must keep on striking our enemies wherever and whenever we can meet them, even if, for a while, we have to yield ground. Actually, though, we are taking a heavy toll of the enemy every day that goes by.

We must fight at these vast distances to protect our supply lines and our lines of communication with our allies—protect these lines from the enemies who are bending every ounce of their strength, striving against time, to cut them. The object of the Nazis and the Japanese is to of course separate the United States, Britain, China and Russia, and to isolate them one from another, so that each will be surrounded and cut off from sources of supplies and reinforcements. It is the old familiar Axis policy of "divide and conquer".

There are those who still think, however, in terms of the days of sailing-ships. They advise us to pull our warships and our planes and our merchant ships into our own home waters and concentrate solely on last ditch defense. But let me illustrate what would happen if we followed such foolish advice.

Look at your map. Look at the vast area of China, with its millions of fighting men. Look at the vast area of Russia, with its powerful armies and proven military might. Look at the Islands of Britain, Australia, New Zealand, the Dutch Indies, India, the Near East and the Continent of Africa, with their resources of raw materials, and of peoples determined to resist Axis domination. Look too at North America, Central America and South America.

It is obvious what would happen if all of these great reservoirs of power were cut off from each other either by enemy action or by self-imposed isolation:

(1) First, in such a case, we could no longer send aid of any kind to China—to the brave people who, for nearly five years, have withstood Japanese assault, destroyed hundreds of thousands of Japanese soldiers, and vast quantities of Japanese war munitions. It is essential that we help China in her magnificent defense and in her inevitable counter-offensive—for that is one important element in the ultimate defeat of Japan.

(2) Secondly, if we lost communication with the southwest Pacific, all of that area, including Australia and New Zealand and the Dutch Indies, would fall under Japanese domination. Japan in such a case could release great numbers of ships and men to launch attacks on a large scale against the coasts of the Western Hemisphere—South America and Central America, and North America—including Alaska. At the same time, she could immediately extend her conquests in the other direction toward·India, through the Indian Ocean,

to Africa, to the Near East, and try to join forces with Germany and Italy.

(3) Third, if we were to stop sending munitions to the British and the Russians in the Mediterranean area, in the Persian Gulf and the Red Sea, we would be helping the Nazis to overrun Turkey, and Syria, and Iraq, and Persia—that is now called Iran—Egypt and the Suez Canal, the whole coast of North Africa itself and with that inevitably the whole coast of West Africa—putting Germany within easy striking distance of South America—fifteen hundred miles away.

(4) Fourth, if by such a fatuous policy, we ceased to protect the North Atlantic supply line to Britain and to Russia, we would help to cripple the splendid counter-offensive by Russia against the Nazis, and we would help to deprive Britain of essential food-supplies and munitions.

Those Americans who believed that we could live under the illusion of isolationism wanted the American eagle to imitate the tactics of the ostrich. Now, many of those same people, afraid that we may be sticking our necks out, want our national bird to be turned into a turtle. But we prefer to retain the eagle as it is—flying high and striking hard. . . .

This generation of Americans has come to realize, with a present and personal realization, that there is something larger and more important than the life of any individual or of any individual group—something for which a man will sacrifice, and gladly sacrifice, not only his pleasures, not only his goods, not only his associations with those he loves, but his life itself. In time of crisis when the future is in the balance, we come to understand, with full recognition and devotion, what this nation is, and what we owe to it.

The Axis propagandists have tried in various evil ways to destroy our determination and our morale. Failing in that, they are now trying to destroy our confidence in our own allies. They say that the British are finished—that the Russians and the Chinese are about to quit. Patriotic and sensible Amer-

icans will reject these absurdities. And instead of listening to
any of this crude propaganda, they will recall some of the
things that Nazis and Japanese have said and are still saying
about us.

Ever since this nation became the arsenal of democracy—
ever since enactment of Lend-Lease—there has been one persistent theme through all Axis propaganda.

This theme has been that Americans are admittedly rich,
that Americans have considerable industrial power—but that
Americans are soft and decadent, that they cannot and will
not unite and work and fight.

From Berlin, Rome and Tokyo we have been described
as a nation of weaklings—"playboys"—who would hire British
soldiers, or Russian soldiers, or Chinese soldiers to do our
fighting for us.

Let them repeat that now!

Let them tell that to General MacArthur and his men.

Let them tell that to the sailors who today are hitting hard
in the far waters of the Pacific.

Let them tell that to the boys in the Flying Fortresses.

Let them tell that to the Marines!

The United Nations constitute an association of independent
peoples of equal dignity and equal importance. The United
Nations are dedicated to a common cause. We share equally
and with equal zeal the anguish and the awful sacrifices of
war. In the partnership of our common enterprise, we must
share in a unified plan in which all of us must play our several parts, each of us being equally indispensable and dependent one on the other.

We have unified command and cooperation and comrade-
ship.

We Americans will contribute unified production and unified
acceptance of sacrifice and of effort. That means a national
unity that can know no limitations of race or creed or selfish
politics. The American people expect that much from themselves. And the American people will find ways and means of

expressing their determination to their enemies, including the Japanese Admiral who has said that he will dictate the terms of peace here in the White House.

We of the United Nations are agreed on certain broad principles in the kind of peace we seek. The Atlantic Charter applies not only to the parts of the world that border the Atlantic but to the whole world; disarmament of aggressors, self-determination of nations and peoples, and the four freedoms—freedom of speech, freedom of religion, freedom from want, and freedom from fear.

The British and the Russian people have known the full fury of Nazi onslaught. There have been times when the fate of London and Moscow was in serious doubt. But there was never the slightest question that either the British or the Russians would yield. And today all the United Nations salute the superb Russian Army as it celebrates the twenty-fourth anniversary of its first assembly.

Though their homeland was overrun, the Dutch people are still fighting stubbornly and powerfully overseas.

The great Chinese people have suffered grievous losses; Chungking has been almost wiped out of existence—yet it remains the capital of an unbeatable China.

That is the conquering spirit which prevails throughout the United Nations in this war.

The task that we Americans now face will test us to the uttermost.

Never before have we been called upon for such a prodigious effort. Never before have we had so little time in which to do so much.

"These are the times that try men's souls."

Tom Paine wrote those words on a drum-head, by the light of a campfire. That was when Washington's little army of ragged, rugged men was retreating across New Jersey, having tasted naught but defeat.

And General Washington ordered that these great words written by Tom Paine be read to the men of every regiment in the Continental Army, and this was the assurance given to the first American armed forces:

"The summer soldier and the sunshine patriot will, in this crisis, shrink from the service of their country; but he that stands it now, deserves the love and thanks of man and woman. Tyranny, like hell, is not easily conquered; yet we have this consolation with us, that the harder the sacrifice, the more glorious the triumph."

So spoke Americans in the year 1776.

So speak Americans today!

# MEMORANDUM FOR SECRETARY OF WAR HENRY L. STIMSON AND SECRETARY OF THE NAVY FRANK KNOX

*The White House. March 16, 1942*

*The Army and the Navy were quarreling.*

I wish you would confer on this.

I have only one objective in mind. The crux of the use of aerial torpedoes in the Southwest Pacific is from now for the next ninety days. I do not care who fires the torpedoes— Army fliers or Navy fliers. The point is that they must be fired at Japanese ships. This is the critical time for the use of these torpedoes. I do not give a continental about the use of these torpedoes after the next ninety days. I cannot work that out. But I want you both to plan immediately—Army and Navy or both—this use being based, not on use or availability after ninety days, but on use and availability for the next ninety days.

I am sending this as Commander-in-Chief of both Services and I require that it be carried out by both Services. In other words, this is a directive for joint action.

# *LETTER TO RUSSELL C. LEFFINGWELL*

*The White House. March 16, 1942*

*This correspondent, a Morgan partner, like many who remembered the First World War, was disturbed by the contrast in the national mood during the Second. Neither the President nor anyone else succeeded in reviving the parade and flag-waving spirit. The people had evidently decided that war is not glamorous but evil. They were thoroughly determined to win, but they did the work as policemen do their job rather than like knights in search of glory. Perhaps this attitude was more appropriate to the President's own policy of collective security, with its corollary that aggression is a crime to be put down by forces of law and order, than he himself realized. It sufficed also to overcome all the noisy recalcitrants at home.*

Dear Russell:

Sometimes I wish I could carry out your thought of more frequent talking on the air on my part but the one thing I dread is that my talks should be so frequent as to lose their effectiveness. And incidentally, I suppose you know that every time I talk over the air it means four or five days of long, overtime work in the preparation of what I say. Actually, I cannot afford to take this time away from more vital things.

There is apathy, though frankly I think it is lessening.

But you are dead right about the parades and the brass bands and the meetings and the waving of the flag. I am trying to get that started all over.

Honestly, the real trouble is not in the people or the leaders, but in a gang which unfortunately survives—made up mostly of those who were isolationists before December seventh and who are actuated today by various motives in their effort to instill disunity in the country. Some are publishers like Bertie McCormick and the Pattersons and the Roy Howard papers. The hearts of these people are not in unity and some of them still want a negotiated peace. Some of them are columnists or radio commentators who are actuated by the same motives. Some of them are politically minded and seek election gains. Some of them are anti-racial and anti-religious like the K.K.K. crowd and some are extreme nationalists like some of the wild Irish.

The best comment I have heard was by Elmer Davis after I spoke at the end of February. He said: "Some people want the United States to win so long as England loses. Some people want the United States to win so long as Russia loses. And some people want the United States to win so long as Roosevelt loses."

I think we must avoid too much personal leadership—my good friend Winston Churchill has suffered a little from this. It must grow more slowly—remembering always that we have only been in the war for three months.

But you are dead right about more enthusiasm and I am starting on that line. I do hope to see you one of these days soon.

As ever yours,

## PRESS CONFERENCE #815

*The White House. March 31, 1942*

*Life on the home front sometimes reverted to normal.*

Q: Mr. President, have you anything to say on the international cartels that have been discussed on the Hill—the Standard Oil agreements, and the others?

THE PRESIDENT: No. Don't think—don't know what it was.

Q: I mean the charge has been made, and later denied, that the United States has been deprived of certain products, such as buna rubber and others, through the Standard Oil of New Jersey.

THE PRESIDENT: To tell you the truth, I haven't looked into that. I thought you were going to talk about the nudist problem?

Q: Let's discuss that too.

Q: Have you anything to say on that, sir?

THE PRESIDENT: No. All I can say about that nudist problem is that—of course this has got to be off the record, so stop writing—I would have to be too careful if it was on the record.

This is off the record. Of course, it is a very serious thing, these charges about the old gentleman [Maurice Parmelee, Board of Economic Warfare economist] having written a book on nudism eleven or twelve years ago, because of its— it has entirely disrupted production in this country. It has slowed us down terribly—everybody. You know, the circulation of the newspapers has almost doubled in the last forty-eight hours. But of course the worst is yet to come—this is off the record—you are soon going to find out—in fact some of you here never thought of it—that there is a much more serious thing, which is almost going to stop the production of airplanes, and tanks, and ships, and things like that.

We have discovered that in the House of Representatives itself, we have got something far worse than a nudist—we have got an exhibitionist! (loud laughter)

Q: Is there just one, Mr. President?

## PRESS CONFERENCE #842

*The White House. August 21, 1942*

*The President laid the groundwork for the War Crimes Trials.*

THE PRESIDENT: I will give you the most important thing first, which is a warning to the enemy nations. I am making it in the form of a statement, because I think probably that is as good a way as any.

"The Secretary of State recently forwarded to me a communication signed by the Ambassador of The Netherlands, and the Ministers of Yugoslavia and Luxembourg, on behalf of the governments of Belgium, Greece, Luxembourg, Norway, Netherlands, Poland, Czechoslovakia, Yugoslavia, and the French National Committee in London, calling attention to the barbaric crimes against civilization—civilian populations that are being committed in Occupied countries, particularly on the Continent of Europe."

Of course, we had hoped that the—this is not in the statement—we had hoped that the barbaric acts against civilian populations would decrease. On the contrary, they seem to be increasing. And I just give you the example of the—the shooting of hostages, not only in France but very recently five or six very important citizens in—in The Netherlands, and a good many people in Norway. Well, it's just an illustration. We don't get much news out of the other countries, but it is probable that similar—I call them atrocities on the part of Germany still exist in those other countries like Poland and Czechoslovakia that we don't get much news out of.

(*continuing reading*): "In this communication, attention was invited to the declaration signed in London, January 13 this year, by the representatives of nine governments whose countries are under German occupation. This declaration affirmed that acts of violence thus perpetrated against the civilian populations are at variance with accepted ideas concerning acts of war and political offenses, as these are understood by civilized nations; stated that the punishment, through the channels of organized justice of those guilty and responsible for these crimes, is one of the principal war aims of the contracting governments; and recorded the determination of the contracting governments, in a spirit of international solidarity, to see to it that those guilty and responsible, whatever their nationality, are handed over to justice and tried, and that the sentences pronounced are carried out.

"The communication which I have just received from the chiefs of mission of The Netherlands, Yugoslavia, and Luxembourg, states that these acts of oppression and terror have taken proportions and forms, giving rise to the fear that as the defeat of the enemy countries approaches, the barbaric and unrelenting character of the occupational regime will become more marked, and may even lead to the extermination of certain populations.

"As I stated on October 25 last:

" 'The practice of executing scores of innocent hostages in reprisal for isolated attacks on Germans in countries temporarily under the Nazi heel revolts a world already inured to suffering and brutality. Civilized peoples long ago adopted the basic principle that no man should be punished for the deed of another. Unable to apprehend the persons involved in these attacks, the Nazis characteristically slaughter fifty or a hundred innocent persons. Those who would 'collaborate' with Hitler or try to appease him cannot ignore this ghastly warning.

" 'The Nazis might have learned from the last war the impossibility of breaking men's spirit by terrorism. Instead they develop their 'lebensraum' and 'new order' by deeds of frightfulness which even they have never approached before. These are the acts of desperate men who know in their hearts that they cannot win. Frightfulness can never bring peace to Europe. It only sows the seeds of hatred which will one day bring fearful retribution.' "

And this is new—

(continuing reading): "The Government of the United States has been aware for some time of these crimes. Our Government has constantly received additional information from dependable sources, and it welcomes reports from any trustworthy source which would assist in keeping our Government—our growing fund of information and evidence up to date and reliable."

In other words, we want news—from any source that is reliable—of the continuation of atrocities.

(continuing reading): "The United Nations are going to win the war. When victory has been achieved, it is the purpose of the Government of the United States, as I know it is the purpose of each of the United Nations, to make appropriate use of the information and evidence in respect to these barbaric crimes of the invaders, in Europe and in Asia. It seems only fair that they should have this warning: that the time will come when they shall have to stand in courts of law, in the very countries which they are now oppressing, and answer for their acts."

Well, I think that's clear enough. I don't think it needs much comment. . . .

Q: Mr. President, have you heard the remark of some of the representatives of the Occupied countries: "Give us one week"?

THE PRESIDENT: I have. And I hope that they won't carry that idea out. I think sober judgment would be distinctly—all over the world—in favor of the judicial processes, when we win the war and can give it back. We don't want to kill innocent people. . . .

## MEMORANDUM FOR ELEANOR ROOSEVELT

*The White House. October 7, 1942*

*The President had proposed and obtained broader and steeper income taxes to help pay for the war.*

In view of the new income tax law, it will, of course, result in such a cut in the net I receive from the Government that we shall have to take some steps to reduce the White House food bill, to which I pay $2,000 a month, or $24,000 a year. Next year the taxes on $75,000 will leave me only about $30,000 net and SOMETHING HAS TO BE DONE! I do not think I can contribute more than $1,500 a month—leaving a total of $18,000 for Mrs. Nesbitt for the year.

The only thing I can think of is to reduce the number of servants whom we feed. Because they have a Civil Service status we should, of course, see that they get employment elsewhere in the Government. We must remember, too, that I am away on an average of about ten days out of each month, not counting the more extended trips like the last, which I take at least once a year. When you are away my entertaining very rarely amounts to more than a dinner party of four or five people.

I do realize that the cost of food has gone up. However, I would suggest that something drastic be done about the size of the portions served.

For instance, for my luncheons I have pleaded—when it is an egg dish—for only one egg apiece, yet four eggs for two people constantly appear. In the same way in the evenings, vegetables and meat keep coming up to the Study when night after night more than half of the dish goes back to the pantry. I know of no instance where anybody has taken a second help—except occasionally when I do—and it would be much better if I did not take a second help anyway.

## MESSAGE TO THE FRENCH PEOPLE

*November 7, 1942*

*Among the myriad preparations for the landing of American forces in North Africa, the President had recorded a message in French which was broadcast during the invasion.*

My friends, who suffer day and night, under the crushing yoke of the Nazis, I speak to you as one who was with your Army and Navy in France in 1918. I have held all my life the deepest friendship for the French people—for the entire French people. I retain and cherish the friendship of hundreds of French people in France and outside of France. I know your farms, your villages, and your cities. I know your soldiers, professors, and workmen. I know what a precious heritage of the French people are your homes, your culture, and the principles of democracy in France. I salute again and reiterate my faith in Liberty, Equality, and Fraternity. No two Nations exist which are more united by historic and mutually friendly ties than the people of France and the United States.

Americans, with the assistance of the United Nations, are striving for their own safe future as well as the restoration of the ideals, the liberties, and the democracy of all those who have lived under the Tricolor.

We come among you to repulse the cruel invaders who would remove forever your rights of self-government, your rights to religious freedom, and your rights to live your own lives in peace and security.

We come among you solely to defeat and rout your enemies. Have faith in our words. We do not want to cause you any harm.

We assure you that once the menace of Germany and Italy is removed from you, we shall quit your territory at once.

I am appealing to your realism, to your self-interest and national ideals.

Do not obstruct, I beg of you, this great purpose.

Help us where you are able, my friends, and we shall see again the glorious day when liberty and peace shall reign again on earth.

*Vive la France eternelle!*


## PRESS CONFERENCE #861

*The White House. November 17, 1942*

*In some quarters cries of "appeasement" and "pro-fascism" were raised against the arrangement in French Africa whereby the American authorities recognized Admiral Darlan, agent of the Vichy Government, in return for his cooperation. The conflict in American opinion eased somewhat when Darlan was presently assassinated.*

Q: Mr. President, is any effort being made to change or modify the anti-Jewish laws and regulations now in effect in North Africa?

THE PRESIDENT: Yes. . . .

It is included in this:

(*reading*): "I have accepted General Eisenhower's political arrangements made for the time being in North Africa and Western Africa.

"I thoroughly understand and approve the feeling in the United States and Great Britain, and among all the other

United Nations, that in view of the history of the past two years no permanent arrangement should be made with Admiral Darlan. People in the United Nations likewise would never understand the recognition of a reconstituting of the Vichy government in France, or in any French territory."

I am afraid I am cutting a lot of good stuff out of the feet —from under the feet of people who don't think things through.

"We are opposed to Frenchmen who support Hitler and the Axis. No one in our Army has any authority to discuss the future government of France or the French Empire.

"The future French government will be established not by any individual in metropolitan France or over-seas, but by the French people themselves, after they have been set free by the victory of the United Nations."

It's all words of one syllable stuff—but it's powerful. . . .

"The present temporary arrangement in North and West Africa is only a temporary expedient, justified solely by the stress of battle.

"The present temporary arrangement has accomplished two military objectives. The first was to save American and British lives on the one hand, and French lives on the other." . . .

I thought—I thought of putting in there, but I didn't, an old Balkan proverb, which I cannot have even attributed to me, because at the present time I don't like to call names any more than one has to. It's rather a nice old proverb of the Balkans that has, as I understand it—has the full sanction of the Orthodox Church.

And it runs—this is off the record . . . look it up in an encyclopedia of Balkan proverbs if you want to—it runs something like this. The—mind you, this is okayed by the Church.

It says, "My children, you are permitted in time of great danger to walk with the Devil until you have crossed the bridge." . . .

## PRESS CONFERENCE #875

*Anfa Camp, Casablanca, French Morocco. January 24, 1943*

*This was a joint press conference with Prime Minister Church-
ill. Later the President told a group of newspaper editors the
essential purpose of the Casablanca meeting: "You can't leave
things to the military, otherwise nothing gets done. . . . On the
other hand, if you get certain laymen to stick pins into them all
the time—prod them, if you like—and say you have got to have
an answer to this, that, and the other thing within so many days,
you get an answer." The major decision was to postpone the
cross-Channel invasion of France until 1944 and proceed to
invade Sicily in the period of "the favorable July moon," 1943.
While these things could not be discussed at this press conference, the President did announce the "unconditional surrender" policy which was widely criticized as prolonging the resistance of the Axis powers. The announcement came as a surprise to Churchill, but this does not mean that he had no convictions in favor of it.*

THE PRESIDENT: This meeting goes back to the successful
landing operations last November, which as you all know were
initiated as far back as a year ago, and put into definite shape
shortly after the Prime Minister's visit to Washington in June.

After the operations of last November, it became perfectly
clear, with the successes, that the time had come for another
review of the situation, and a planning for the next steps, especially steps to be taken in 1943. That is why we came here,
and our respective staffs came with us, to discuss the practical
steps to be taken by the United Nations for prosecution of the
war. We have been here about a week.

I might add, too, that we began talking about this after the
first of December, and at that time we invited Mr. Stalin to
join us at a convenient meeting place. Mr. Stalin very greatly
desired to come, but he was precluded from leaving Russia because he was conducting the new Russian offensive against the
Germans along the whole line. We must remember that he is
Commander in Chief, and that he is responsible for the very

wonderful detailed plan which has been brought to such a successful conclusion since the beginning of the offensive.

In spite of the fact that Mr. Stalin was unable to come, the results of the staff meeting have been communicated to him, so that we will continue to keep in very close touch with each other.

I think it can be said that the studies during the past week or ten days are unprecedented in history. Both the Prime Minister and I think back to the days of the first World War when conferences between the French and British and ourselves very rarely lasted more than a few hours or a couple of days. The Chiefs of Staffs have been in intimate touch; they have lived in the same hotel. Each man has become a definite personal friend of his opposite number on the other side.

Furthermore, these conferences have discussed, I think for the first time in history, the whole global picture. It isn't just one front, just one ocean, or one continent—it is literally the whole world; and that is why the Prime Minister and I feel that the conference is unique in the fact that it has this global aspect.

The Combined Staffs, in these conferences and studies during the past week or ten days, have proceeded on the principle of pooling all of the resources of the United Nations. And I think the second point is that they have re-affirmed the determination to maintain the initiative against the Axis Powers in every part of the world.

These plans covering the initiative and maintenance of the initiative during 1943 cover certain things, such as united operations conducted in different areas of the world. Secondly, the sending of all possible material aid to the Russian offensive, with the double object of cutting down the manpower of Germany and her satellites, and continuing the very great attrition of German munitions and materials of all kinds which are being destroyed every day in such large quantities by the Russian armies.

And, at the same time, the Staffs have agreed on giving all possible aid to the heroic struggle of China—remembering that China is in her sixth year of the war—with the objective, not only in China but in the whole of the Pacific area, of ending any Japanese attempt in the future to dominate the Far East.

Another point. I think we have all had it in our hearts and our heads before, but I don't think that it has ever been put down on paper by the Prime Minister and myself, and that is the determination that peace can come to the world only by the total elimination of German and Japanese war power.

Some of you Britishers know the old story—we had a General called U. S. Grant. His name was Ulysses Simpson Grant, but in my, and the Prime Minister's, early days he was called "Unconditional Surrender" Grant. The elimination of German, Japanese and Italian war power means the unconditional surrender by Germany, Italy, and Japan. That means a reasonable assurance of future world peace. It does not mean the destruction of the population of Germany, Italy, or Japan, but it does mean the destruction of the philosophies in those countries which are based on conquest and the subjugation of other people.

While we have not had a meeting of all of the United Nations, I think that there is no question—in fact we both have great confidence that the same purposes and objectives are in the minds of all of the other United Nations—Russia, China, and all the others.

And so the actual meeting—the main work of the Committee—has been ended, except for a certain amount of resultant paper work—has come to a successful conclusion. I call it a meeting of the minds in regard to all military operations, and, thereafter, that the war is going to proceed against the Axis Powers according to schedule, with every indication that 1943 is going to be an even better year for the United Nations than 1942.

THE PRIME MINISTER: I agree with everything that the President has said. . . .

## MEMORANDUM FOR
## SAMUEL I. ROSENMAN

(n.p.) *March 19, 1943*

*This illustrates how the President accumulated material for his speeches. It also suggests that he sometimes got things off his chest which, on second thoughts, as apparently in this case, he left buried in Judge Rosenman's files or in early drafts of speeches.*

In my next speech, I would like to say something like the following:

I get very many letters—too many—from boys in the Army and Navy who are under instruction and who complain that some of their instructors are hardboiled reactionaries—exuding the spirit of isolationism, who pooh pooh any idea of establishing a world *peace,* and scoff at any American attempt so to improve the lot of other nations that they will [not], in the future, resort to arms against their neighbors. I am told that these instructors talk of crackpot idealism and speak of giving away our prosperity.

In the conduct of any great war it is, of course, necessary to employ many thousands of instructors in the mechanics of war. In the course of such instruction, it is inevitable that we find a certain proportion of men who are so hardboiled that they have not changed their ideas in any way since the "get-rich-quick" days of fifteen years ago.

I like to think and believe that these are the exception to the rule. The best advice I can give to the boys in our services is to pay little attention to instructors who have never had a thought of a better world in which America can live in the future.

# PRESS CONFERENCE #888

*The White House. March 30, 1943*

*Roosevelt was haunted by the memory of missteps by President Wilson which deserved some of the blame for the failure of the peace after the First War. One of his many efforts to avoid Wilson's mistakes was the preparation of an international organization for collective security during the war while national and inter-Allied unity was at a maximum. A visit to the United States of Foreign Secretary Anthony Eden marked an important stage in planning.*

THE PRESIDENT: . . . Mr. Eden has left, and we decided that it was probably better not to give out one of those formal statements by the two of us. And he asked me to just talk to you all informally about it.

We are in entire agreement. He has had these series of conferences with a lot of people—the Secretary of State and his advisers, and the Members of the Senate and the House; and he took a little trip to see some of the camps.

We talked about everything—might be put down as current military and political affairs, and other questions arising out of the war relating to the present and the future.

I think I can say for both of us that they disclose very close similarity of outlook on the part of the two governments, and a very fruitful meeting of the minds on all the matters that came under discussion.

We talked about the practical problems that will arise on the surrender of the enemy—problems that will face the governments of the United States, and United Kingdom, and China, and Russia, and all of the other United Nations, primarily in safeguarding the world from future aggression.

I think I ought to make it clear that—I think you should all make it clear that these conversations are exploratory. The object of them was *not* to reach final decisions, which were, of course, impossible at this stage; but to reach a large measure of general agreement on objectives. So as to take time by the forelock, and as a result of these conferences, they will be of great aid in further conferences between all of the United Nations.

I also want to make it very clear that these conferences are by no means confined to the United Kingdom and the United States. They are merely one small part of the long series of conferences between the other United Nations.

We have talked, for example, already rather intimately about these various subjects, with China, and with one or two of the South American Republics. Mr. Eden himself has been to Russia and talked in regard to many of these problems with Mr. Stalin, Mr. Molotov, and other members of the Russian government.

I hope and expect that we will be continuing discussions along these lines with the Russian government in the very near future, and with other members of the United Nations. And therefore, these are—you might put it this way: that these conversations constitute one method of working toward the unity of the United Nations, which is going along extremely well.

Some people ought to take note of that.

And the other method, of course, is through the more formal gathering, such as we will have next month with the United Nations, in regard to the subject of food, to be followed a little later by a similar one in regard to relief; and possibly a little later by another exploratory conference in regard to finances; and possibly another one in regard to things out of the ground. The—the food thing will probably include things that grow out of the ground, and the other one would refer to things that come out from under the surface—minerals, metals, oil, and so forth.

So you see, the thing is progressing in a very satisfactory way.

If some of you go back—some of you can, like myself—go back to 1918, the war came to a rather sudden end in November, 1918. And actually it's a fact that there had been very little work done on the post-war problems before Armistice Day. Well, between Armistice Day and the time that the nations met in Paris early in 1919, everybody was rushing around trying to dig up things.

And the simile I used to Mr. Eden the other day was that— I was here at the time—the tempo seemed to be that of the lady who is told at noon that she is to accompany her husband on a month's trip on the three o'clock train that afternoon. Well, I have seen ladies trying to pack for a month's trip in three hours, and that was a little bit the situation over here, and everywhere else, in making preparations for the Versailles conference. Everybody was rushing around grabbing things out of closets and throwing them into suitcases. Some of the large portions of things out of the cupboards were not needed at all.

I have forgotten how many experts we took to Versailles at that time, but everybody who had a "happy thought," or who thought he was an expert got a free ride.

And that is why I think that this whole method that is going on now is a very valuable thing, in an exploratory way, and incidentally—as I remarked the other day—in the process of getting to know each other.

I would say—if you want to be didactic and put it in terms of figures, I would say that so far, in all of the conferences that we have held with other members of the United Nations—this is not just the British—they come into it too—but we are about 95 percent together. Well, that's—that's an amazing statement. It happens to be true. I wish some people would put that in their pipes and smoke it.

So it was a very good conference.

Q: Can we quote that last part directly? Why don't you let us have that part about the "amazing statement," and so forth?

THE PRESIDENT: The 95 percent?

Q: Yes, sir.

THE PRESIDENT: Yes, I think so. That's all right.

Q: Also about the "amazing statement"?

THE PRESIDENT: No, no. It will only stir up controversy. You wouldn't do that (laughter). . . .

Q: Mr. President, when you say it applies to the others as well, that includes Russia, does it not?

THE PRESIDENT: Yes.

Q: And China?

THE PRESIDENT: And China.

Q: Mr. President, you spoke of plans to have conversations with Russia in the near future. Is there anything more specific we can have on that? This summer, do you plan—

THE PRESIDENT: (interposing) No—not today.

Q: Is hope still "springing eternal" about [a meeting with] Mr. Stalin?

THE PRESIDENT: Yes. . . .

## STATEMENT ON THE ORDER TO "HOLD THE LINE" ON PRICES AND WAGES

*April 8, 1943*

*In managing the domestic economy also the experience of the First War was used as a bad example. Against powerful business, farmer and labor pressures, Roosevelt worked to prevent inflation from the point of view of the consumer: if the cost of living could be held down, other inflationary pressures could be successfully resisted. The Hold-the-Line Order was the turning point. Since August, 1939, the Consumers' Price Index of the Bureau of Labor Statistics had risen by 25 per cent; after this Order until July, 1946, it rose only 10 more per cent. During the First War the same Index rose 108 per cent from 1914 to 1920.*

The Executive Order I have signed today is a Hold-the-Line order.

To hold the line we cannot tolerate further increases in prices affecting the cost of living or further increases in general wage or salary rates except where clearly necessary to correct substandard living conditions. The only way to hold the line is to stop trying to find justifications for not holding it here or not holding it there.

No one straw may break a camel's back, but there is always a last straw. We cannot afford to take further chances in relaxing the line. We already have taken too many.

On the price front, the directions in the Order are clear and specific.

All items affecting the cost of living are to be brought under control. No further price increases are to be sanctioned unless imperatively required by law. . . .

On the wage front the directions in the Order are equally clear and specific.

There are to be no further increases in wage rates or salaries' scales beyond the Little Steel formula, except where clearly necessary to correct substandards of living. . . .

Some groups have been urging increased prices for farmers on the ground that wage earners have unduly profited. Other groups have been urging increased wages on the ground that farmers have unduly profited. A continuance of this conflict will not only cause inflation but will breed disunity at a time when unity is essential.

Under the Act of October 2, 1942, Congress directed that so far as is practicable, wages, salaries and prices should be stabilized as of the level of September 15. Under that direction inflation has been slowed up. Now we must stop it.

We cannot stop inflation solely by wage and price ceilings. We cannot stop it solely by rationing. To complete the job, Congress must act to reduce and hold in check the excess purchasing power. We must be prepared to tax ourselves more, to spend less and save more. . . .

## LETTER TO HENRY A. WALLACE
## AND JESSE H. JONES

*The White House. July 15, 1943*

*These, the most liberal and the most conservative Administration leaders, had taken to slugging out in public a natural antagonism which was nourished by the overlapping jurisdictions of the former's Board of Economic Warfare and the latter's Reconstruction Finance Corporation. There resulted a rare example of the President losing patience with his own administrative methods. His actual preference between the two men became clear on January 20, 1945 (see Letter to Jones of that date).*

Gentlemen:—

I have come to the conclusion that the unfortunate controversy and acrimonious public debate which has been carried on between you in the public press concerning the administration of foreign economic matters make it necessary, in the public interest, to transfer these matters to other hands.

In the midst of waging a war so critical to our national security and to the future of all civilization, there is not sufficient time to investigate and determine where the truth lies in your conflicting versions as to transactions which took place over a year and a half ago.

My action today is not intended to decide that question. The important thing is to clear the decks and to get on with the war at once. To do this requires a fresh start with new men, unencumbered by inter-agency dissension and bitterness.

I am persuaded that the present controversy indicates that future cooperative action between your two agencies is impossible, and that without full cooperation between you the program of economic warfare cannot be carried out. . . .

Very sincerely yours,

# RADIO ADDRESS ON WAR AND PEACE PLANS

*The White House. July 28, 1943*

*Mussolini resigned on July 25. This provided an encouraging set-
ting for a speech in which the President had planned to bolster
the morale of civilians and the armed forces. He announced the
policy which resulted in one of the most successful examples of
what conservatives denounced as starry-eyed postwar planning:
the "G.I. Bill of Rights."*

My fellow Americans:

Over a year and a half ago I said this to the Congress: "The
militarists in Berlin, and Rome and Tokyo started this war,
but the massed angered forces of common humanity will finish
it."

Today that prophecy is in the process of being fulfilled. The
massed, angered forces of common humanity are on the
march. They are going forward—on the Russian front, in the
vast Pacific area, and into Europe—converging upon their
ultimate objectives: Berlin and Tokyo.

I think the first crack in the Axis has come. The criminal,
corrupt Fascist regime in Italy is going to pieces.

The pirate philosophy of the Fascists and the Nazis cannot
stand adversity. The military superiority of the United Nations—on sea and land, and in the air—has been applied in
the right place and at the right time.

Hitler refused to send sufficient help to save Mussolini. In
fact, Hitler's troops in Sicily stole the Italians' motor equipment, leaving Italian soldiers so stranded that they had no
choice but to surrender. Once again the Germans betrayed
their Italian allies, as they had done time and time again on
the Russian front and in the long retreat from Egypt, through
Libya and Tripoli, to the final surrender in Tunisia.

And so Mussolini came to the reluctant conclusion that the
"jig was up;" he could see the shadow of the long arm of justice.

But he and his Fascist gang will be brought to book, and

punished for their crimes against humanity. No criminal will be allowed to escape by the expedient of "resignation."

So our terms to Italy are still the same as our terms to Germany and Japan—"unconditional surrender."

We will have no truck with Fascism in any way, in any shape or manner. We will permit no vestige of Fascism to remain. . . .

In every country conquered by the Nazis and the Fascists, or the Japanese militarists, the people have been reduced to the status of slaves or chattels.

It is our determination to restore these conquered peoples to the dignity of human beings, masters of their own fate, entitled to freedom of speech, freedom of religion, freedom from want, and freedom from fear.

We have started to make good on that promise.

I am sorry if I step on the toes of those Americans who, playing party politics at home, call that kind of foreign policy "crazy altruism" and "starry-eyed dreaming." . . .

The United Nations are substantially agreed on the general objectives for the post-war world. They are also agreed that this is not the time to engage in an international discussion of all the terms of peace and all the details of the future. Let us win the war first. We must not relax our pressure on the enemy by taking time out to define every boundary and settle every political controversy in every part of the world. The important thing—the all-important thing now is to get on with the war—and to win it.

While concentrating on military victory, we are not neglecting the planning of the things to come, the freedoms which we know will make for more decency and greater justice throughout the world.

Among many other things we are, today, laying plans for the return to civilian life of our gallant men and women in the armed services. They must not be demobilized into an environment of inflation and unemployment, to a place on a bread line, or on a corner selling apples. We must, this time, have plans ready—instead of waiting to do a hasty, inefficient, and ill-considered job at the last moment.

I have assured our men in the armed forces that the American people would not let them down when the war is won.

I hope that the Congress will help in carrying out this assurance, for obviously the Executive Branch of the Government cannot do it alone. May the Congress do its duty in this regard. The American people will insist on fulfilling this American obligation to the men and women in the armed forces who are winning this war for us.

Of course, the returning soldier and sailor and marine are a part of the problem of demobilizing the rest of the millions of Americans who have been working and living in a war economy since 1941. That larger objective of reconverting wartime America to a peacetime basis is one for which your government is laying plans to be submitted to the Congress for action.

But the members of the armed forces have been compelled to make greater economic sacrifice and every other kind of sacrifice than the rest of us, and they are entitled to definite action to help take care of their special problems.

The least to which they are entitled, it seems to me, is something like this:

*First* Mustering-out pay to every member of the armed forces and merchant marine when he or she is honorably discharged, *mustering-out pay* large enough in each case to cover a reasonable period of time between his discharge and the finding of a new job.

*Secondly* In case no job is found after diligent search, then unemployment insurance if the individual registers with the United States Employment Service.

*Third* An opportunity for members of the armed services to get further education or trade training at the cost of their government.

*Fourth* Allowance of credit to all members of the armed forces, under unemployment compensation and Federal old-age and survivors' insurance, for their period of service. For these purposes they ought to be treated as if they had continued their employment in private industry.

*Fifth* Improved and liberalized provisions for hospitalization, for rehabilitation, for medical care of disabled members of the armed forces and the merchant marine.

*And finally,* sufficient pensions for disabled members of the armed forces.

Your Government is drawing up other serious, constructive plans for certain immediate forward moves. They concern food, manpower, and other domestic problems that tie in with our armed forces.

Within a few weeks I shall speak with you again in regard to definite actions to be taken by the Executive Branch of the Government, together with specific recommendations for new legislation by the Congress.

All our calculations for the future, however, must be based on clear understanding of the problems involved. And that can be gained only by straight thinking—not guess work, not political manipulation.

I confess that I myself am sometimes bewildered by conflicting statements that I see in the press. One day I read an "authoritative" statement that we will win the war this year, 1943—and the next day comes another statement equally "authoritative," that the war will still be going on in 1949.

Of course, both extremes—of optimism and pessimism—are wrong.

The length of the war will depend upon the uninterrupted continuance of all-out effort on the fighting fronts and here at home, and that effort is all one.

The American soldier doesn't like the necessity of waging war. And yet—if he lays off for a single instant he may lose his own life and sacrifice the lives of his comrades.

By the same token—a worker here at home may not like the driving, wartime conditions under which he has to work and live. And yet—if he gets complacent or indifferent and slacks on his job, he too may sacrifice the lives of American soldiers and contribute to the loss of an important battle.

The next time anyone says to you that this war is "in the bag," or says "it's all over but the shouting," you should ask him these questions:

"Are you working full time on your job?"

"Are you growing all the food you can?"

"Are you buying your limit of war bonds?"

"Are you loyally and cheerfully cooperating with your Government in preventing inflation and profiteering, and in making rationing work with fairness to all?"

"Because—if your answer is 'No'—then the war is going to last a lot longer than you think."

The plans we made for the knocking out of Mussolini and his gang have largely succeeded. But we still have to knock out Hitler and his gang, and Tojo and his gang. No one of us pretends that this will be an easy matter.

We still have to defeat Hitler and Tojo on their own home grounds. But this will require a far greater concentration of our national energy and our ingenuity and our skill.

It isn't too much to say that we must pour into this war the entire strength and intelligence and will power of the United States. We are a great nation—a rich nation—but we are not so great or so rich that we can afford to waste our substance or the lives of our men by relaxing along the way.

We shall not settle for less than total victory. That is the determination of every American on the fighting fronts. That must be, and will be, the determination of every American here at home.


# LETTER TO THE PRESIDENT OF THE SENATE ON JAPANESE RELOCATION CENTERS

*The White House. September 14, 1943*

*In the emergency created by the Pearl Harbor attacks, under heavy pressure from California groups, the Administration had consented to remove all persons of Japanese ancestry from "military areas" to Relocation Centers in the interior. Those born in the United States were citizens, but their constitutional rights were temporarily ignored. This was the only important contradiction of the Administration's record of preserving civil liberties in war time. The President soon began to correct the situation. The excellent performance of Japanese-American troops in the war helped to reduce public prejudice.*

. . . With the segregation of the disloyal evacuees in a separate center, the War Relocation Authority proposes now to redouble its efforts to accomplish the relocation into normal homes and jobs in communities throughout the United States, but outside the evacuated areas, of those Americans of Japanese ancestry whose loyalty to this country has remained unshaken through the hardships of the evacuation which military necessity made unavoidable. We shall restore to the loyal evacuees the right to return to the evacuated areas as soon as the military situation will make such restoration feasible.

Americans of Japanese ancestry, like those of many other ancestries, have shown that they can, and want to, accept our institutions and work loyally with the rest of us, making their own valuable contribution to the national wealth and well being. In vindication of the very ideals for which we are fighting this war it is important to us to maintain a high standard of fair, considerate and equal treatment for the people of this minority as of all other minorities.

Respectfully,

## LETTER TO MACKENZIE KING

*Hyde Park. November 1, 1943*

*The intimacy of Roosevelt's relations with the Canadian Prime Minister equaled that with Churchill.*

Dear Mackenzie:

It is good indeed to get your letter of October twenty-sixth. It finds me at Hyde Park where I am spending a few days before the Election and getting the last of the "flu" bugs out of me. Also, it gives me a chance to give quiet review to the past

six months—landings in Sicily and Italy, the Quebec Conference and the coming conference with Winston. I still hope
that we can see "Uncle Joe." Apparently, however, my constitutional problems weigh lightly with him, though I have
tried a dozen times to explain to him that while my Congress is
in session I must be in a position to receive bills, act on them,
and get them back to the Congress physically within ten days.

The labor problem is again to the fore—but then scarcely
six months have ever gone by since I have been in office, the
past ten and a half years, without a "labor crisis." This time
it is very much involved with the cost of living and inflation
difficulties. I am definitely on the minority side and it will be
quite clear that if they force my hand on inflation, wages and
food prices will have to go up too.

All of this will, of course, affect Canada also because so far,
with great success, we have managed to tie both our dollars
together.

The general attitude seems to be that a little inflation would
not do any harm, in spite of the fact that I am telling them
that a pill or two of opium would not do much harm except
for the fact that in most cases it leads to drug addiction.

I like your little Address to the Liberal Federation—and
there is much in it which I may use in forthcoming statements
or speeches. It is everlastingly worthwhile to emphasize that
the winning of the war is for us, as it is for you, the one great
objective. . . .

                                    Affectionately yours,

World Leader
D-Day
Fourth Term Campaign
Yalta

JANUARY 1, 1944 — APRIL 12, 1945

# ANNUAL MESSAGE TO CONGRESS

*The Capitol. January 11, 1944*

*With war production and the strength of the Army, Navy, and Air Forces reaching their astonishing peaks, and plans for victory over the Axis and establishment of a world collective security organization well advanced, President Roosevelt now reached his final stature as a world leader. It was from this standpoint that he criticized civilian shortcomings, insisted on all-out effort to win the war, advocated American entry into a permanent world organization, and proposed an Economic Bill of Rights which, had he lived, might have amounted to a Third New Deal.*

This Nation in the past two years has become an active partner in the world's greatest war against human slavery.

We have joined with like-minded people in order to defend ourselves in a world that has been gravely threatened with gangster rule.

But I do not think that any of us Americans can be content with mere survival. Sacrifices that we and our Allies are making impose upon us all a sacred obligation to see to it that out of this war we and our children will gain something better than mere survival.

We are united in determination that this war shall not be followed by another interim which leads to new disaster—that we shall not repeat the tragic errors of ostrich isolationism—that we shall not repeat the excesses of the wild twenties when this Nation went for a joy-ride on a roller coaster which ended in a tragic crash.

When Mr. Hull went to Moscow in October, and when I went to Cairo and Teheran in November, we knew that we were in agreement with our Allies in our common determination to fight and win this war. But there were many vital questions concerning the future peace, and they were discussed in an atmosphere of complete candor and harmony.

In the last war such discussions, such meetings, did not even

begin until the shooting had stopped and the delegates began
to assemble at the peace table. There had been no previous
opportunities for man-to-man discussions which lead to meetings of minds. The result was a peace which was not a peace.

That was a mistake which we are not repeating in this war.

And right here I want to address a word or two to some suspicious souls who are fearful that Mr. Hull or I have made
"commitments" for the future which might pledge this Nation
to secret treaties, or to enacting the role of Santa Claus.

To such suspicious souls—using a polite terminology—I
wish to say that Mr. Churchill, and Marshal Stalin, and Generalissimo Chiang Kai-shek are all thoroughly conversant with
the provisions of our Constitution. And so is Mr. Hull. And so
am I.

Of course we made some commitments. We most certainly
committed ourselves to very large and very specific military
plans which require the use of all allied forces to bring about
the defeat of our enemies at the earliest possible time.

But there were no secret treaties or political or financial
commitments.

The one supreme objective for the future, which we discussed for each nation individually, and for all the United
Nations, can be summed up in one word: Security.

And that means not only physical security which provides
safety from attacks by aggressors. It means also economic security, social security, moral security—in a family of nations.

In the plain down-to-earth talks that I had with the Generalissimo and Marshal Stalin and Prime Minister Churchill,
it was abundantly clear that they are all most deeply interested
in the resumption of peaceful progress by their own peoples—
progress toward a better life. All our Allies want freedom to
develop their lands and resources, to build up industry, to increase education and individual opportunity, and to raise
standards of living.

All our Allies have learned by bitter experience that real development will not be possible if they are to be diverted from
their purpose by repeated wars—or even threats of war.

China and Russia are truly united with Britain and America in recognition of this essential fact:

The best interests of each nation, large and small, demand that all freedom-loving nations shall join together in a just and durable system of peace. In the present world situation, evidenced by the actions of Germany, Italy and Japan, unquestioned military control over disturbers of the peace is as necessary among nations as it is among citizens in a community. And an equally basic essential to peace is a decent standard of living for all individual men and women and children in all nations. Freedom from fear is eternally linked with freedom from want.

There are people who burrow through our Nation like unseeing moles, and attempt to spread the suspicion that if other nations are encouraged to raise their standards of living, our own American standard of living must of necessity be depressed.

The fact is the very contrary. It has been shown time and again that if the standard of living of any country goes up, so does its purchasing power—and that such a rise encourages a better standard of living in neighboring countries with whom it trades. That is just plain common sense—and it is the kind of plain common sense that provided the basis for our discussions at Moscow, Cairo and Teheran.

Returning from my journeyings, I must confess to a sense of "let-down" when I found many evidences of faulty perspectives here in Washington. The faulty perspective consists in overemphasizing lesser problems and thereby under-emphasizing the first and greatest problem.

The overwhelming majority of our people have met the demands of this war with magnificent courage and understanding. They have accepted inconveniences; they have accepted hardships; they have accepted tragic sacrifices. And they are ready and eager to make whatever further contributions are needed to win the war as quickly as possible—if only they are given the chance to know what is required of them.

However, while the majority goes on about its great work

without complaint, a noisy minority maintains an uproar of demands for special favors for special groups. There are pests who swarm through the lobbies of the Congress and the cocktail bars of Washington, representing these special groups as opposed to the basic interests of the nation as a whole. They have come to look upon the war primarily as a chance to make profits for themselves at the expense of their neighbors— profits in money or in terms of political or social preferment.

Such selfish agitation can be highly dangerous in wartime. It creates confusion. It damages morale. It hampers our national effort. It muddies the waters and therefore prolongs the war.

If we analyze American history impartially, we cannot escape the fact that in our past we have not always forgotten individual and selfish and partisan interests in time of war—we have not always been united in purpose and direction. We cannot overlook the serious dissensions and the lack of unity in our war of the Revolution, in our War of 1812, or in our War Between the States, when the survival of the Union itself was at stake.

In the first World War we came closer to national unity than in any previous war. But that war lasted only a year and a half, and increasing signs of disunity began to appear during the final months of the conflict.

In this war, we have been compelled to learn how interdependent upon each other are all groups and sections of the population of America.

Increased food costs, for example, will bring new demands for wage increases from all war workers, which will in turn raise all prices of all things including those things which the farmers themselves have to buy. Increased wages or prices will each in turn produce the same results. They all have a particularly disastrous result on all fixed income groups.

And I hope you will remember that all of us in this Government represent the fixed income group just as much as we represent business owners, workers and farmers. This group of fixed-income people include: teachers, clergy, policemen, firemen, widows and minors on fixed incomes, wives and dependents of our soldiers and sailors, and old age pensioners. They and their families add up to one quarter of our one hundred and thirty million people. They have few or no high pressure representatives at the Capitol. In a period of gross inflation they would be the worst sufferers.

If ever there was a time to subordinate individual or group selfishness to the national good, that time is now. Disunity at home—bickerings, self-seeking partisanship, stoppages of work, inflation, business as usual, politics as usual, luxury as usual—these are the influences which can undermine the morale of the brave men ready to die at the front for us here.

Those who are doing most of the complaining are not deliberately striving to sabotage the national war effort. They are laboring under the delusion that the time is past when we must make prodigious sacrifices—that the war is already won and we can begin to slacken off. But the dangerous folly of that point of view can be measured by the distance that separates our troops from their ultimate objectives in Berlin and Tokyo —and by the sum of all the perils that lie along the way.

Over-confidence and complacency are among our deadliest enemies. Last Spring—after notable victories at Stalingrad and in Tunisia and against the U-boats on the high seas—over-confidence became so pronounced that war production fell off. In two months, June and July, 1943, more than a thousand airplanes that could have been made and should have been made were not made. Those who failed to make them were not on strike. They were merely saying, "The war's in the bag—so let's relax".

That attitude on the part of anyone—Government or management or labor—can lengthen this war. It can kill American boys.

Let us remember the lessons of 1918. In the Summer of that year the tide turned in favor of the Allies. But this Government did not relax. In fact, our national effort was stepped up. In August, 1918, the draft age limits were broadened from 21-31 to 18-45. The President called for "force to the utmost", and his call was heeded. And in November, only three months later, Germany surrendered.

That is the way to fight and win a war—all out—and not with half-an-eye on the battlefronts abroad and the other eye-and-a-half on personal, selfish, or political interests here at home.

Therefore, in order to concentrate all our energies and resources on winning the war, and to maintain a fair and stable economy at home, I recommend that the Congress adopt:

(1) A realistic tax law—which will tax all unreasonable profits, both individual and corporate, and reduce the ultimate cost of the war to our sons and daughters. The tax bill now under consideration by the Congress does not begin to meet this test.

(2) A continuation of the law for the renegotiation of war contracts—which will prevent exorbitant profits and assure fair prices to the Government. For two long years I have pleaded with the Congress to take undue profits out of war.

(3) A cost of food law—which will enable the Government (a) to place a reasonable floor under the prices the farmer may expect for his production; and (b) to place a ceiling on the prices a consumer will have to pay for the food he buys. This should apply to necessities only; and will require public funds to carry out. It will cost in appropriations about one per cent of the present annual cost of the war.

(4) Early reenactment of the stabilization statute of October 1942. This expires June 30th, 1944, and if it is not extended well in advance, the country might just as well expect price chaos by Summer.

We cannot have stabilization by wishful thinking. We must take positive action to maintain the integrity of the American dollar.

(5) A national service law—which, for the duration of the war, will prevent strikes, and, with certain appropriate exceptions, will make available for war production or for any other essential services every able-bodied adult in this nation.

These five measures together form a just and equitable

whole. I would not recommend a national service law unless the other laws were passed to keep down the cost of living, to share equitably the burdens of taxation, to hold the stabilization line, and to prevent undue profits.

The Federal Government already has the basic power to draft capital and property of all kinds for war purposes on a basis of just compensation.

As you know, I have for three years hesitated to recommend a national service act. Today, however, I am convinced of its necessity. Although I believe that we and our Allies can win the war without such a measure, I am certain that nothing less than total mobilization of all our resources of manpower and capital will guarantee an earlier victory, and reduce the toll of suffering and sorrow and blood.

I have received a joint recommendation for this law from the heads of the War Department, the Navy Department and the Maritime Commission. These are the men who bear responsibility for the procurement of the necessary arms and equipment, and for the successful prosecution of the war in the field. They say:

"When the very life of the nation is in peril the responsibility for service is common to all men and women. In such a time there can be no discrimination between the men and women who are assigned by the Government to its defense at the battlefront and the men and women assigned to producing the vital materials essential to successful military operations. A prompt enactment of a National Service Law would be merely an expression of the universality of this responsibility".

I believe the country will agree that those statements are the solemn truth.

National service is the most democratic way to wage a war. Like selective service for the armed forces, it rests on the obligation of each citizen to serve his nation to his utmost where he is best qualified.

It does not mean reduction in wages. It does not mean loss of retirement and seniority rights and benefits. It does not mean that any substantial numbers of war workers will be disturbed in their present jobs. Let these facts be wholly clear.

Experience in other democratic nations at war—Britain, Canada, Australia and New Zealand—has shown that the very existence of national service makes unnecessary the widespread use of compulsory power. National service has proven to be a unifying moral force—based on an equal and comprehensive legal obligation of all people in a nation at war.

There are millions of American men and women who are not in this war at all. It is not because they do not want to be in it. But they want to know where they can best do their share. National service provides that direction. It will be a means by which every man and woman can find that inner satisfaction which comes from making the fullest possible contribution to victory.

I know that all civilian war workers will be glad to be able to say many years hence to their grandchildren: "Yes, I, too, was in service in the great war. I was on duty in an airplane factory, and I helped make hundreds of fighting planes. The Government told me that in doing that I was performing my most useful work in the service of my country."

It is argued that we have passed the stage in the war where national service is necessary. But our soldiers and sailors know that this is not true. We are going forward on a long, rough road—and, in all journeys, the last miles are the hardest. And it is for that final effort—for the total defeat of our enemies— that we must mobilize our total resources. The national war program calls for the employment of more people in 1944 than in 1943.

It is my conviction that the American people will welcome this win-the-war measure which is based on the eternally just principle of "fair for one, fair for all."

It will give our people at home the assurance that they are standing four-square behind our soldiers and sailors. And it will give our enemies demoralizing assurance that we mean business—that we, 135,000,000 Americans, are on the march to Rome, Berlin and Tokyo.

I hope that the Congress will recognize that, although this is a political year, national service is an issue which transcends politics. Great power must be used for great purposes.

As to the machinery for this measure, the Congress itself should determine its nature—but it should be wholly non-partisan in its make-up.

Our armed forces are valiantly fulfilling their responsibilities to our country and our people. Now the Congress faces the responsibility for taking those measures which are essential to national security in this the most decisive phase of the nation's greatest war.

Several alleged reasons have prevented the enactment of legislation which would preserve for our soldiers and sailors and marines the fundamental prerogative of citizenship—the right to vote. No amount of legalistic argument can becloud this issue in the eyes of these ten million American citizens. Surely the signers of the Constitution did not intend a document which, even in wartime, would be construed to take away the franchise of any of those who are fighting to preserve the Constitution itself.

Our soldiers and sailors and marines know that the overwhelming majority of them will be deprived of the opportunity to vote, if the voting machinery is left exclusively to the States under existing state laws—and that there is no likelihood of these laws being changed in time to enable them to vote at the next election. The Army and Navy have reported that it will be impossible effectively to administer forty-eight different soldier-voting laws. It is the duty of the Congress to remove this unjustifiable discrimination against the men and women in our armed forces—and to do it as quickly as possible.

It is our duty now to begin to lay the plans and determine the strategy for the winning of a lasting peace and the establishment of an American standard of living higher than ever before known. We cannot be content, no matter how high that general standard of living may be, if some fraction of our

people—whether it be one-third or one-fifth or one-tenth—
is ill-fed, ill clothed, ill housed, and insecure.

This Republic had its beginning, and grew to its present
strength, under the protection of certain inalienable political
rights—among them the right of free speech, free press, free
worship, trial by jury, freedom from unreasonable searches and
seizures. They were our rights to life and liberty.

As our nation has grown in size and stature, however—as our
industrial economy expanded—these political rights proved
inadequate to assure us equality in the pursuit of happiness.

We have come to a clear realization of the fact that true
individual freedom cannot exist without economic security
and independence. "Necessitous men are not free men." People
who are hungry and out of a job are the stuff of which
dictatorships are made.

In our day these economic truths have become accepted as
self-evident. We have accepted, so to speak, a second Bill of
Rights under which a new basis of security and prosperity can
be established for all—regardless of station, race or creed.

Among these are:

The right to a useful and remunerative job in the industries,
or shops or farms or mines of the nation;

The right to earn enough to provide adequate food and
clothing and recreation;

The right of every farmer to raise and sell his products at a
return which will give him and his family a decent living;

The right of every business man, large and small, to trade
in an atmosphere of freedom from unfair competition and
domination by monopolies at home or abroad;

The right of every family to a decent home;

The right to adequate medical care and the opportunity to
achieve and enjoy good health;

The right to adequate protection from the economic fears
of old age, sickness, accident and unemployment;

The right to a good education.

All of these rights spell security. And after this war is won we must be prepared to move forward, in the implementation of these rights, to new goals of human happiness and well-being.

America's own rightful place in the world depends in large part upon how fully these and similar rights have been carried into practice for our citizens. For unless there is security here at home there cannot be lasting peace in the world.

One of the great American industrialists of our day—a man who has rendered yeoman service to his country in this crisis—recently emphasized the grave dangers of "rightist reaction" in this Nation. All clear-thinking business men share his concern. Indeed, if such reaction should develop—if history were to repeat itself and we were to return to the so-called "normalcy" of the 1920's—then it is certain that even though we shall have conquered our enemies on the battlefields abroad, we shall have yielded to the spirit of fascism here at home.

I ask the Congress to explore the means for implementing this economic bill of rights—for it is definitely the responsibility of the Congress so to do. Many of these problems are already before committees of the Congress in the form of proposed legislation. I shall from time to time communicate with the Congress with respect to these and further proposals. In the event that no adequate program of progress is evolved, I am certain that the Nation will be conscious of the fact.

Our fighting men abroad—and their families at home—expect such a program and have the right to insist upon it. It is to their demands that this Government should pay heed rather than to the whining demands of selfish pressure groups who seek to feather their nests while young Americans are dying.

The foreign policy that we have been following—the policy that guided us at Moscow, Cairo and Teheran—is based on the common sense principle which was best expressed by Benjamin Franklin on July 4, 1776: "We must all hang together, or assuredly we shall all hang separately."

I have often said that there are no two fronts for America in this war. There is only one front. There is one line of unity which extends from the hearts of the people at home to the men of our attacking forces in our farthest outposts. When we speak of our total effort, we speak of the factory and the field and the mine as well as of the battleground—we speak of the soldier and the civilian, the citizen and his Government.

Each and every one of us has a solemn obligation under God to serve this Nation in its most critical hour—to keep this Nation great—to make this Nation greater in a better world.

## MEMORANDUM FOR THE SECRETARY OF STATE

*The White House. January 24, 1944*

*As he had liquidated American imperialism during the days of peace, now he used his influence as leader of the anti-Axis world to liquidate all the old empires.*

I saw [British Ambassador Lord] Halifax last week and told him quite frankly that it was perfectly true that I had, for over a year, expressed the opinion that Indo-China should not go back to France but that it should be administered by an international trusteeship. France has had the country—thirty million inhabitants for nearly one hundred years, and the people are worse off than they were at the beginning.

As a matter of interest, I am wholeheartedly supported in this view by Generalissimo Chiang Kai-shek and by Marshal Stalin. I see no reason to play in with the British Foreign Office in this matter. The only reason they seem to oppose it is that they fear the effect it would have on their own possessions and those of the Dutch. They have never liked the idea of trusteeship because it is, in some instances, aimed at future independence. This is true in the case of Indo-China.

Each case must, of course, stand on its own feet, but the case of Indo-China is perfectly clear. France has milked it for

one hundred years. The people of Indo-China are entitled to
something better than that.

# PRESS CONFERENCE #933: FOR THE
# NEGRO NEWSPAPER PUBLISHERS
# ASSOCIATION

*The White House. February 5, 1944*

*More and more the President developed the view that American
problems were integral with world problems.*

THE PRESIDENT: Well, I hope you get to the Senate and
House press galleries. That will be the next step, but this is a
White House (press) conference that I think is all arranged,
that is working out all right.

There is one thing that I think we could mention—I see you
are taking notes, don't publish them—and that is this, . . .
I think it would be a good thing if your Association could
come in once a year . . . and talk off the record for a half-
hour or an hour. It seems to work pretty well.

MR. THEODORE POSTON (O.W.I.): That would be swell. . . .

MR. JOHN SENGSTACKE: Mr. President, on behalf of the Negro
Newspapers Association, may I thank you for your courtesy
in seeing this committee from our Association. Our Association,
which represents Negro newspapers with over ninety-five percent of Negro press coverage, is resolved to do everything that
it can to help win the war and the peace that follows.

In this connection, we are asking Mr. Prattis to read a
statement which is representative of the thinking of our Association and membership.

THE PRESIDENT: All right.

MR. P. L. PRATTIS (*Pittsburgh Courier*): Mr. President, we
are Americans. Our allegiance to the ideals and guarantees and
principles of the Declaration of Independence and the Constitution of the United States is unlimited and unsullied.

This is our country, to share with all other Americans. We

have purchased our stake, in this our native land, with our blood and toil during more than three hundred years. We have a right and a duty to share its blessings, its sacrifices and its sufferings.

This is our war. Negro Americans on every battlefront are giving their lives to defend the soil, the homes and the democratic ideals of their native land. They, and we, are fighting for the freedom of America and of all oppressed and exploited peoples. . . .

We maintain that the Federal Government should begin now to use its authority and powers of persuasion to end abridgement of the Negro's citizenship, so as to bring about a more truly democratic America. Such action would support our claim that we fight for a world order in which economic equality, political self-determination, and social justice both prevail.

It is our resolve to work for the abolition of the color bar in industry, still maintained by many employers and labor unions to the detriment of our war effort.

For equal opportunity to Negroes for employment and advancement in public services.

For equality in all public educational facilities.

For unrestricted suffrage in national, state and municipal elections, including all primary elections.

For full protection by government in the enjoyment of all civil rights and liberties established by law.

For the principle that government should not impose, enforce or sanction patterns of racial segregation.

For full protection and equality of treatment and opportunity for Negroes in the armed forces of the United States, according them the respect which the uniform should command.

For extension of the system of social security, which recognizes the right of the individual to self-development, protection against the hazards of illness, unemployment and want, and promotes the orderly development of the nation's resources.

For application of the Atlantic Charter to all colonial and other exploited peoples, not only Europeans and Asiatics, but also Africans and peoples of African descent throughout the world.

For full participation by the United States in establishing and maintaining such international machinery as may be necessary to establish a world order in which economic equality, political self-determination, and social justice will prevail.

This statement is respectfully submitted by our Association.

We desire to bring to your attention one specific matter concerning our boys in the armed services. Mr. Lewis will bring that to your attention.

THE PRESIDENT: I think it's an awfully good statement.

MR. IRA LEWIS (*Pittsburgh Courier*): Mr. President, may I go back, first, to your statement inviting us to come in once a year to have an off the record talk with you. I appreciate your optimism, and I would say January 22 (1945), in so far as I am concerned. (laughter)

THE PRESIDENT: Well, I'll probably be down in Georgia then. (more laughter)

MR. IRA LEWIS: Candidly, Mr. President, we are, of course, very thankful for this audience and this opportunity to speak to you.

Mr. President, Prattis's statement started out, "We are Americans." That is the way we look at it. I don't think there is any group of citizens in this country who love this country more—

THE PRESIDENT: (*interjecting*) That's right.

MR. IRA LEWIS: (*continuing*)—than the Negro people. This is the only home they know. Now, the question in their minds is as to whether they are expressing—whether they are giving their full share of the contribution not only to the war but what is due to come.

There is one very pressing question that is causing the colored people lots of concern. I think that we represent here perhaps five or six million readers, and that question is posed to us at all times. It is a grievous and vexing one. It has to do with the treatment of our boys in the armed services. They haven't been treated right by civilian police, and by the MPs. We know of instances where soldiers on furlough have come home and taken off their uniform, on account of intimidation.

And they think, Mr. President, that that is your responsibility. They think that you alone can correct that. I think you can put your hand right on the question, which will do more towards strengthening morale and making more for unity and making the Negro citizen believe that he is a part of this great commonwealth. Just one word from you, we all feel, would do that.

Thank you.

THE PRESIDENT: I am glad you brought that up, because I have been in touch with it. It is perfectly true, there is definite discrimination in the actual treatment of the colored engineer troops, and others. And you are up against—you know perfectly well—I have talked about it—I had the Secretary of War and the Assistant—everybody in on it. The trouble lies fundamentally in the attitude of certain white people—officers down the line—

MR. IRA LEWIS: That's right.

THE PRESIDENT:—who haven't got very much more education, many of them, than the colored troops and the Seabees and the engineers, for example. And they—well, you know—you know the kind of person it is. We all do. We don't have to do more than think of a great many people that we know. And it has become not a question of orders—they are repeated fairly often, I think, in all the camps of colored troops—it's a question of the personality of the individual. And we are up against it, absolutely up against it. I always think of the fact that it probably is improving. I like to think that mere association helps things along. . . .

And there is just one thing in here—(indicating the statement)—the only thing I didn't agree with, and that is a thing which your Association, I think, could do something about. You talk about people in other countries. We all know that they are very different from Americans in every way. You can't, for example—I will give you one example—something has got to be done about it in time.

Last year I went to a place called Gambia in Africa, at the mouth of the Gambia River. Bathurst is the capital. I think there are about three million inhabitants, of whom one hundred and fifty are white. And it's the most horrible thing I have ever seen in my life. I was there twice. The natives are five thousand years back of us. Disease is rampant, absolutely. It's a terrible place for disease.

And I looked it up, with a little study, and I got to the point of view that for every—the British have been there for two hundred years—for every dollar that the British have put into Gambia, they have taken out ten. It's just plain exploitation of those people. There is no education whatsoever. A few missionaries. With all due deference to the missionaries, if they wouldn't try to live in the best houses in town, they would be better off. (laughter) . . .

Now, because of your traditional, historic—way back—association, it would be a perfectly grand thing if your Association could send two or three people out there, as a committee, to write stories about what is needed.

I am taking up with Churchill at the present time—he doesn't see the point yet—I think he will—(laughter)—the general thought that the United Nations ought to have an inspection committee of all these colonies that are way, way down the line, that are not ready to have anything to say yet because the owning country has given them no facilities.

And if we sent—sent a committee from the United Nations, and I used the example of Gambia, to go down to Gambia, "If you Britishers don't come up to scratch—toe the mark—then we will let all the world know."

Well, Churchill doesn't like that idea. And his comeback was, "All right, the United Nations will send an inspection committee to your own South in America." (laughter)

He thought he had me.

I said, "Winston, that's all right with me. Go ahead and do

it. Tell the world. But—what you people were talking about —we call it freedom of the press, and you also call it 'pitiless publicity'—you can right a lot of wrongs with 'pitiless publicity.'"

It would be a grand thing. I wouldn't mind if we had a committee of the United Nations come here and make a report on us. Why not?

Q: That's right.

THE PRESIDENT: We have got some things to be ashamed of, and other things that are not as bad as they are painted. It wouldn't hurt at all—bring it all out.

Q: That's right.

THE PRESIDENT: So, if your Association could do something like that, to teach us a little bit more about the world. . . .

## TELEGRAM TO ALBEN W. BARKLEY

*The White House. February 23, 1944*

*To reduce inflationary purchasing power and hold down the national debt, the President asked Congress for ten billion dollars of additional tax revenue. When it passed a bill providing less than one billion, he returned it with a sharp veto message. The Democratic Majority Leader, Senator Barkley, was offended and resigned. The anti-Administration press built this up into a major split in the President's Party. Following publication of this telegram, Barkley was unanimously re-elected Majority Leader of the Senate.*

Dear Alben:

As I am out of the City I am unable to have a personal talk with you. If I were there, of course, that is the first thing I would do.

I regret to learn from your speech in the Senate on the tax veto that you thought I had in my message attacked the integrity of yourself and other members of the Congress. Such you must know was not my intention. You and I may differ, and have differed on important measures, but that does not mean we question one another's good faith.

In working together to achieve common objectives we have always tried to accommodate our views so as not to offend the other whenever we could conscientiously do so. But neither of us can expect the other to go further.

When on last Monday I read to you portions of my tax message and you indicated your disagreement, I made certain changes as a result of our talk. You did not however try to alter my basic decision when you realized how strongly I felt about it. While I did not realize how very strongly you felt about that basic decision, had I known, I should not have tried to dissuade you from exercising your own judgment in urging the overriding of the veto.

I sincerely hope you will not persist in your announced intention to resign as Majority Leader of the Senate. If you do, however, I hope your colleagues will not accept your resignation; but if they do, I sincerely hope they will immediately and unanimously reelect you.

With the many serious problems daily confronting us, it is inevitable that at times you should differ with your colleagues and differ with me. I am sure that your differing with your colleagues does not lessen their confidence in you as Leader. Certainly, your differing with me does not affect my confidence in your leadership nor in any degree lessen my respect and affection for you personally.

Very sincerely yours,


## PRESS CONFERENCE #954

*The White House. June 6, 1944*
*This press conference developed very little substance besides the emotions of D-Day.*

(The President called in the Administrative Assistants and Secretaries, and so forth, to make themselves comfortable around his desk, before the press came in)

THE PRESIDENT: (*as they filed in*) My Lord!—all smiles—all smiles. Look at these two coming in! (laughter)

MR. DANIELS: You don't look like you're so solemn yourself, Mr. President.

THE PRESIDENT: No, I'm not so solemn, I suppose. Where's "Pa"? And, where's Steve? (then upon seeing him) Have you got anything for me?

MR. EARLY: Several suggestions, Mr. President.

THE PRESIDENT: What? (*to those on the couch*): He's always full of suggestions, and he always gets turned down. Doesn't make any difference. (laughter)

MR. EARLY: I'm used to it. . . .

THE PRESIDENT: All right, Charlie (Fredericks), bring in the "wolves." (laughter) (then seeing Grace Tully and Dorothy Brady standing against the wall): You're going to get "squished" there. . . .

(long pause here, as the newspapermen filed in quickly and silently. The President pulled at his sleeves to go to work on the material before him)

MR. DONALDSON: All in.

THE PRESIDENT: Well, I think this is a very happy conference today. Looking at the rows of you coming in, you have the same expressions as the anonymous and silent people this side of the desk who came in just before you—all smiles!

I have very little more news that I can tell you than what you all got in your offices.

I think it's all right to use this, which has not been published yet. It came in a dispatch from Eisenhower on the progress of the operations, as of about 12 o'clock today. The American naval losses were two destroyers and one LST. And the losses incident to the air landing were relatively light— about one percent.

Q: That's the air-borne troops, sir?

THE PRESIDENT: Well, air losses as a whole.

And, of course, there's a great deal of reports coming in all the time, but it's being given out over there just as fast as it possibly can. I think the arrangements seem to be going all right. I think that's all that I have over here. You are getting it just as fast as we are.

Q: Mr. President, how do you feel about the progress of the invasion?

THE PRESIDENT: Up to schedule. And, as the Prime Minister said, "That's a mouthful." (laughter)

Q: May we quote "up to schedule"? . . .

Q: Mr. President, when the Paris broadcaster heard the first German report of the invasion, he said it couldn't be true, because you were going to London at the end of June. Was he altogether wrong? (laughter)

THE PRESIDENT: Well, I am going to ask *you,* is that summer or spring? (more laughter)

MR. GODWIN: Mr. President, at Teheran you took this subject up, and as you know, there were constant cries from Russian sources, among them Mr. Willkie—(laughter)—demanding—demanding—

THE PRESIDENT: (*interposing*) When did Wendell change his citizenship? (more laughter)

MR. GODWIN: Well, I don't want to be too rough, but you know what I mean. There were constant—

THE PRESIDENT: (*interjecting*) Oh, of course.

MR. GODWIN: (*continuing*)—you were aware of that, and can you say whether or not Mr. Stalin was aware of what was going on?

THE PRESIDENT: (*interjecting*) Well,—

MR. GODWIN: (*continuing*) Marshal Stalin, for instance—it seemed to come from there that Stalin was yelling for a second front—

THE PRESIDENT: (*interposing*) Not—not after Teheran.

MR. GODWIN: Not after Teheran?

THE PRESIDENT: Not after Teheran.

MR. GODWIN: He understood thoroughly?

THE PRESIDENT: Absolutely. Mr. Stalin's mind was entirely cleared up at Teheran, when he understood the problem of going across the Channel; and when this particular time was arrived at and agreed on at Teheran, he was entirely satisfied.

Q: Mr. President, when you said that the time was fixed at Teheran approximately, did the—was the position also fixed at the same time?

THE PRESIDENT: Was the what?

Q: The place—point of attack?

THE PRESIDENT: Oh No. Oh No.

Q: When did that develop?

THE PRESIDENT: That was—that was a matter which was—well, I can't—I can't tell you the exact date, but it was always open to change. In other words, may have been half a dozen different places.

Q: That is—that was a matter of strategy?

THE PRESIDENT: A matter of strategy, Yes.

Q: Mr. President, may there still be a half-dozen different places?

THE PRESIDENT: Gosh! What an awful question! You know they are all improper, highly improper. (much laughter)

Q: Mr. President, on this date and point of attack then, as I understand it, that was all left up to the high command?

THE PRESIDENT: Oh Yes.

Q: And has been decided comparatively recently?

THE PRESIDENT: Decided by General Eisenhower.

Q: Comparatively recently?

THE PRESIDENT: Oh Yes—Yes.

Q: Mr. President,—

THE PRESIDENT: It's a long—it's a long, long coast from Spain to Norway, you know. . . .

Q: Mr. President, can you tell us anything about the impact of this invasion on the home front—the population here?

THE PRESIDENT: Here?

Q: Yes.

THE PRESIDENT: No. It has all been—all been coming across the ocean. I haven't heard anything except—

Q: (interposing) Mr. President,—

THE PRESIDENT: (continuing)—that the whole country is tremendously thrilled; and I would say on that that I think that it is a very reasonable thrill, but that I hope very much that there will not be again too much over-confidence, because over-confidence destroys the war effort.

A fellow came in the other day whom I have known for quite a while—near home—and he had come—oh, this was several months ago, at the time we took Sicily—and he had had a mighty good job out on the Pacific coast. I don't know what he was—a welder or something like that.

I said, "What are you doing back home?"

"Oh," he said, "the war's over. I am going to try and get a permanent job before everybody quits working on munitions."

He just walked out, quit his job—and he was a good man, he was a munitions worker—because when we took Sicily he said to himself the war's over.

Now, that's the thing we have got to avoid in this country. The war isn't over by any means. This operation isn't over. You don't just land on a beach and walk through—if you land successfully without breaking your leg—walk through to Berlin. And the quicker this country understands it the better. Again, a question of learning a little geography.

Q: Mr. President, could you tell us something of your hopes for the future on this great day?

THE PRESIDENT: Well, you know what it is, it's win the war.

Q: What?

THE PRESIDENT: Win the war, and win it a hundred percent.

Q: Thank you, Mr. President.

Q: (*interposing*) One last question, Mr. President. How are you feeling?

THE PRESIDENT: What?

Q: How are you feeling?

THE PRESIDENT: I'm feeling fine. I'm a little sleepy. (laughter)

Q: (*loudly*) Thank you, Mr. President.

(more laughter)

# LETTER TO CORDELL HULL

*The White House. September 6, 1944*

*The deepest questions of international life were now preoccupying the President.*

Dear Mr. Secretary:

During the past half century the United States has developed a tradition in opposition to private monopolies. The Sherman and Clayton Acts have become as much a part of the American way of life as the due process clause of the Constitution. By protecting the consumer against monopoly these statutes guarantee him the benefits of competition.

This policy goes hand in glove with the liberal principles of international trade for which you have stood through many years of public service. The trade agreement program has as its objective the elimination of barriers to the free flow of trade in international commerce; the anti-trust statutes aim at the elimination of monopolistic restraints of trade in inter-state and foreign commerce.

Unfortunately, a number of foreign countries, particularly in continental Europe, do not possess such a tradition against cartels. On the contrary, cartels have received encouragement from some of these governments. Especially is this true with respect to Germany. Moreover, cartels were utilized by the Nazis as governmental instrumentalities to achieve political ends. The history of the use of the I. G. Farben trust by the Nazis reads like a detective story. The defeat of the Nazi armies will have to be followed by the eradication of these weapons of economic warfare. But more than the elimination of the political activities of German cartels will be required. Cartel practices which restrict the free flow of goods in foreign commerce will have to be curbed. With international trade involved this end can be achieved only through collaborative action by the United Nations.

I hope that you will keep your eye on this whole subject of international cartels because we are approaching the time when discussions will almost certainly arise between us and other nations.

Very sincerely yours,

## LETTER TO SHAH MOHAMMED REZA PAHLEVI

*The White House. September 2, 1944*

*He tried to do for the country of ancient Persia what he had learned on his land at Hyde Park and had applied in the state of New York as its Governor and in the United States as its President.*

My dear Shah Mohammed Reza:

Of course, I do not pretend to know Iran well on account of the shortness of my visit, but may I write you about one of the impressions which I received on my air trip to Teheran?

It relates to the lack of trees on the mountain slopes and the general aridity of the country which lies above the plains.

All my life I have been very much interested in reforestation and the increase of the water supply which goes with it.

May I express a hope that your Government will set aside a small amount for a few years to test out the possibility of growing trees or even shrubs on a few selected areas [and] to test out the possibility of trees which would hold the soil with their roots and, at the same time, hold back floods? We are doing something along this line in our western dry areas and, though it is a new experiment, it seems to be going well.

It is my thought that if your Government would try similar small experiments along this line it would be worthwhile for the future of Iran.

I do not need to tell you how much interested I am in that future, and the future of the people of Iran.

With my warm regards,

Cordially yours,

# CAMPAIGN SPEECH TO THE
# TEAMSTERS UNION

*Washington. September 23, 1944*

*As pure virtuosity this was probably the greatest political speech he ever made.*

Mr. Tobin—I should say Dan, I always have—ladies and gentlemen. I am very much touched, and I am very happy in your applause, and very happy at the informalities of this dinner with old friends of mine. You know, this is not the first time that we have met together on this basis, and I am particularly happy that this national campaign opens in your presence as it did four years ago. And I don't mind mentioning the fact that Dan Tobin and I are just a little bit superstitious.

Well, here we are—here we are again—after four years—and what years they have been! You know, I am actually four years older—(laughter)—which is a fact that seems to annoy some people. In fact, in the mathematical field there are millions of Americans who are more than eleven years older than when we started in to clear up the mess that was dumped in our laps in 1933.

We all know that certain people who make it a practice to depreciate the accomplishments of labor—who even attack labor as unpatriotic—they keep this up usually for three years and six months in a row. But then, for some strange reason—(laughter)—they change their tune—every four years—just before election day. When votes are at stake, they suddenly discover that they really love labor—and that they are anxious to protect labor from its old friends.

I got quite a laugh, for example—and I am sure that you did—when I read this plank in the Republican platform adopted at their National Convention in Chicago last July:

"The Republican party accepts the purposes of the National Labor Relations Act, the Wage and Hour Act, the Social Security Act and all other Federal statutes designed to promote and protect the welfare of American working men and women, and we promise a fair and just administration of these laws." (laughter)

You know, many of the Republican leaders and Congressmen and candidates, who shouted enthusiastic approval of that plank in that Convention Hall would not even recognize these progressive laws, if they met them in broad daylight. Indeed, they have personally spent years of effort and energy—and much money—in fighting every one of those laws in the Congress, and in the press, and in the courts, ever since this Administration began to advocate them and enact them into legislation. That is a fair example of their insincerity and of their inconsistency.

The whole purpose of Republican oratory these days seems to be to switch labels. The object is to persuade the American people that the Democratic party was responsible for the 1929 crash and the depression, and that the Republican party was responsible for all social progress under the New Deal. (continued laughter)

Now, imitation may be the sincerest form of flattery—but I am afraid that in this case it is the most obvious common or garden variety of fraud. (more laughter, and applause)

Of course, it is perfectly true that there are enlightened, liberal elements in the Republican party, and they have fought hard and honorably to bring the party up to date and to get it in step with the forward march of American progress. But these liberal elements were not able to drive the Old Guard Republicans from their entrenched positions.

Can the Old Guard pass itself off as the New Deal? (laughter)

I think not.

We have all seen many marvelous stunts in the circus, but no performing elephant could turn a hand-spring without falling flat on his back. (laughter, cheers and applause)

I need not recount to you the centuries of history which have been crowded into these four years since I saw you last. There were some—in the Congress and out—who raised their voices against our preparations for defense—before and after 1939—objected to them, raised their voices against them as hysterical war mongering, who cried out against our help to the Allies as provocative and dangerous. We remember the voices. They would like to have us forget them now. But in 1940 and 1941—my, it seems a long time ago—they were loud voices. Happily they were a minority and—fortunately for ourselves, and for the world—they could not stop America.

There are some politicians who kept their heads buried deep in the sand while the storms of Europe and Asia were headed our way, who said that the lend-lease bill "would bring an end"—and I am quoting—"to free government in the United States," and who said, and I am quoting, "only hysteria entertains the idea that Germany, Italy or Japan contemplate war on us." These men—these very men are now asking the American people to intrust to them the conduct of our foreign policy and our military policy.

What the Republican leaders are now saying in effect is this: "Oh, just forget what we used to say, we have changed our minds now—we have been reading the public opinion polls about these things—(laughter)—and now we know what the American people want." And they say: "Don't leave the task of making the peace to those old men who first urged it and who have already laid the foundations for it, and who have had to fight all of us inch by inch during the last five years to do it. Why, just turn it all over to us. We'll do it so skilfully—that we won't lose a single isolationist vote or a single isolationist campaign contribution." (laughter, cheers and applause)

I think there is one thing that you know, I am too old for that. I cannot talk out of both sides of my mouth at the same time.

The Government of the United States welcomes all sincere supporters of the cause of effective world collaboration in the making of a lasting peace. Millions of Republicans all over the nation are with us—and have been with us—in our unshakeable determination to build the solid structure of peace.

And they too will resent this campaign—this campaign talk by those who first woke up to the facts of international life a few short months ago—(laughter)—when they began to study the polls of public opinion. (more laughter, cheers and applause)

Those who today have the military responsibility for waging this war in all parts of the globe are not helped by the statements of men who, without responsibility and without the knowledge of the facts, lecture the Chiefs of Staff of the United States as to the best means of dividing our armed forces and our military resources between the Atlantic and Pacific, between the Army and the Navy, and among the Commanding Generals of the different theatres of war. And I may say that those Commanding Generals are making good in a big way. (cheers and applause)

When I addressed you four years ago, I said this. I said, "I know that America will never be disappointed in its expectation that labor will always continue to do its share of the job—the job we now face, and do it patriotically and effectively and unselfishly."

Today we know that America has not been disappointed. In his Order of the Day when the Allied Armies first landed in Normandy two months ago, General Eisenhower said: "Our home fronts have given us overwhelming superiority in weapons and munitions of war." (cheers and applause)

The country knows that there is a breed of cats, luckily not too numerous, called labor-baiters. I know that those labor-baiters among the opposition are there, who instead of calling attention to the achievements of labor in this war, prefer to pick on the occasional strikes that have occurred—strikes that have been condemned by every responsible national labor leader. I ought to say, parenthetically, all but one [John L. Lewis of the United Mine Workers]. And that one labor leader, incidentally, is not conspicuous among my supporters. (more laughter)

Labor-baiters forget that at our peak American labor and management have turned out airplanes at the rate of 109,000 a year; tanks—57,000 a year; combat vessels—573 a year; landing vessels, to get the troops ashore—31,000 a year; cargo ships —19 million tons a year—(cheers and applause)—and Henry Kaiser is here tonight, I am glad to say—(more cheers and applause); and small arms ammunition—oh, I can't understand it, I don't believe you can, either—23 billion rounds a year.

But a strike is news, and generally appears in shrieking headlines—and, of course, they say labor is always to blame. The fact is that since Pearl Harbor only one-tenth of one percent of manhours have been lost by strikes. Can you beat that? (prolonged cheers and applause)

But, you know, even those candidates who burst out in election-year affection for social legislation and for labor in general, still think that you ought to be good boys and stay out of politics. (laughter) And above all, they hate to see any working man or woman contribute a dollar bill to any wicked political party. (more laughter) Of course, it is all right for large financiers and industrialists and monopolists to contribute tens of thousands of dollars—but their solicitude for that dollar which the men and women in the ranks of labor contribute is always very touching.

They are, of course, perfectly willing to let you vote—unless you happen to be a soldier or a sailor overseas, or a merchant seaman carrying the munitions of war. In that case they have made it pretty hard for you to vote at all—for there are some political candidates who think that they may have a chance of election, if only the total vote is small enough. (laughter and applause)

And while I am on the subject of voting, let me urge every American citizen—man and woman—to use your sacred privilege of voting, no matter which candidate you expect to support. Our millions of soldiers and sailors and merchant seamen have been handicapped or prevented from voting by those politicians, those candidates who think that they stand to lose by such votes. You here at home have the freedom of the ballot. Irrespective of party, you should register and vote this November. I think that is a matter of plain good citizenship.

Words come easily, but they do not change the record. You

are, most of you, old enough to remember what things were like for labor in 1932.

You remember the closed banks and the breadlines and the starvation wages; the foreclosures of homes and farms, and the bankruptcies of business; the "Hoovervilles," and the young men and women of the nation facing a hopeless, jobless future; the closed factories and mines and mills; the ruined and abandoned farms; the stalled railroads, the empty docks; the blank despair of a whole nation—and the utter impotence of the Federal Government.

You remember the long hard road, with its gains and its setbacks, which we have traveled together ever since those days.

Now there are some politicians who do not remember that far back—(laughter)—and there are some who remember but find it convenient to forget. No, the record is not to be washed away that easily.

The opposition in this year has already imported into this campaign a very interesting thing, because it is foreign. They have imported the propaganda technique invented by the dictators abroad. Remember, a number of years ago, there was a book *Mein Kampf* written by Hitler himself. The technique was all set out in Hitler's book—and it was copied by the aggressors of Italy and Japan. According to that technique, you should never use a small falsehood; always a big one for its very fantastic nature would make it more credible—if only you keep repeating it over and over and over again.

Well, let us take some simple illustrations that come to mind. For example, although I rubbed my eyes when I read it, we have been told that it was not a Republican depression, but a Democratic depression from which this nation was saved in 1933—that this Administration—this one—today—is responsible for all the suffering and misery that the history books and the American people have always thought had been brought about during the twelve ill-fated years when the Republican party was in power.

Now, there is an old and somewhat lugubrious adage which says: "Never speak of a rope in the house of a man who has been hanged." (laughter) In the same way, if I were a Republican leader speaking to a mixed audience, the last word in the whole dictionary that I think I would use is that word "depression." (more laughter, and applause)

You know, they pop up all the time. For another example, I learned—much to my amazement—that the policy of this Administration was to keep men in the Army when the war was over, because there might be no jobs for them in civil life.

Well, the very day that this fantastic charge was first made, a formal plan for the method of speedy discharge from the Army had already been announced by the War Department— a plan based on the wishes of the soldiers themselves.

This callous and brazen falsehood about demobilization did, of course, a very simple thing, it was an effort to stimulate fear among American mothers and wives and sweethearts. And, incidentally, it was hardly calculated to bolster the morale of our soldiers and sailors and airmen who are fighting our battles all over the world.

But perhaps the most ridiculous of these campaign falsifications is the one that this Administration failed to prepare for the war that was coming. I doubt whether even Goebbels would have tried that one. (laughter and applause) For even he would never have dared hope that the voters of America had already forgotten that many of the Republican leaders in the Congress and outside the Congress tried to thwart and block nearly every attempt that this Administration made to warn our people and arm our nation. (cheers and applause) Some of them called our 50,000 airplane program fantastic. Many of those very same leaders who fought every defense measure that we proposed are still in control of the Republican party—look at their names—were in control of its National Convention in Chicago, and would be in control of the machinery of the Congress and of the Republican party, in the event of a Republican victory this fall.

These Republican leaders have not been content with attacks on me, or my wife, or on my sons. No, not content with that they now include my little dog, Fala. (prolonged laughter, cheers and applause) Well, of course, I don't resent attacks, and my family don't resent attacks, but Fala *does* resent them. (more laughter, cheers and applause) You know—you know, Fala is Scotch, and being a Scottie, as soon as he learned that the Republican fiction-writers in Congress and out had concocted a story that I had left him behind on the Aleutian Islands and had sent a destroyer back to find him—at a cost to the taxpayers of two or three, or eight or twenty million dollars—his Scotch soul was furious. (continued laughter and applause) He has not been the same dog since. (more laughter and applause) I am accustomed to hearing malicious falsehoods about myself—such as that old, worm-eaten chestnut that I have represented myself as indispensable. But I think I have a right to resent, to object to libelous statements about my dog. (more laughter and applause)

Well, I think we all recognize the old technique. The people of this country know the past too well to be deceived into forgetting. Too much is at stake to forget. There are tasks ahead of us which we must now complete with the same will and the same skill and intelligence and devotion that have already led us so far along the road to victory.

There is the task of finishing victoriously this most terrible of all wars as speedily as possible and with the least cost in lives.

There is the task of setting up international machinery to assure that the peace, once established, will not again be broken.

And there is the task that we face here at home—the task of reconverting our economy from the purposes of war to the purposes of peace.

These peace-building tasks were faced once before, nearly a generation ago. They were botched by a Republican administration. That must not happen this time. We will not let it happen this time.

Fortunately, we do not begin from scratch. Much has been done. Much more is under way. The fruits of victory this time will not be apples sold on street corners. (cheers and applause)

Many months ago this Administration set up necessary machinery for an orderly peace-time demobilization. The Congress has passed much more legislation continuing the agencies needed for demobilization—with additional powers to carry out their functions.

I know that the American people—business and labor and agriculture—have the same will to do for peace what they have done for war. (cheers and applause) And I know that they can sustain a national income that will assure full production and full employment under our democratic system of private enterprise, with Government encouragement and aid whenever and wherever that is necessary.

The keynote back of all this literature that we read, the keynote of all that we propose to do in reconversion can be found in the one word JOBS.

We shall lease or dispose of our Government-owned plants and facilities and our surplus war property and land, on the basis of how they can best be operated by private enterprise to give jobs to the greatest number. (cheers and applause)

We shall follow a wage policy that will sustain the purchasing power of labor—for that means more production and more jobs.

You and I know that the present policies on wages and prices were conceived to serve the needs of the great masses of the people. They stopped inflation. They kept prices on a relatively stable level. Through the demobilization period, policies will be carried out with the same objective in mind—to serve the needs of the great masses of the people.

This is not the time in which men can be forgotten as they were in the Republican catastrophe that we inherited. The returning soldiers, the workers by their machines, the farmers in the field, the miners, the men and women in offices and shops, do not intend to be forgotten. (cheers and applause)

No, they know that they are not surplus. Because they know that they are America.

We must set targets and objectives for the future which will seem impossible—like the airplanes—to those who live in and are weighted down by the dead past.

And for months—and today and in the future we are working and will continue to put forth the logistics of the peace, just as Marshall and King and Arnold, MacArthur, Eisenhower and Nimitz are organizing the logistics of this war.

I think that the victory of the American people and their Allies in this war will be far more than a victory against fascism and reaction and the dead hand of despotism of the past. The victory of the American people and their Allies in this war will be a victory for democracy. It will constitute such an affirmation of the strength and power and vitality of government by the people as history has never before witnessed.

And so, my friends, with that affirmation of the vitality of democratic government behind us, that demonstration of its resilience and its capacity for decision and for action—with that knowledge of our own strength and power—we move forward with God's help to the greatest epoch of free achievement by free men that the world has ever known or imagined possible.


## LETTER TO HAMILTON HOLT

*The White House. November 20, 1944*

*Re-elected, he wrote to an old friend, the President of Rollins College, a few meditations.*

Dear Hammy:

I have not had a chance before this to thank you for that nice letter of October twenty-eighth for, as you know, I have been over the hills and far away most of the time since.

I really feel that if we can continue our foreign policy we

may arrive at an era and a method of peace that will last as long as you and I live. I will, as you know, avoid the political angle that cropped up in 1919, if it is possible to do so.

I hate the fourth term as much as you do—and the third term as well—but I do not worry about it so much as a matter of principle. It would be a mistake, of course, to establish it as a tradition but I think I can well plead extenuating circumstances! The real meat of the question is not the length of term, but the continued opportunity of the voters of the country freely to express themselves every four years. And there is the further question of the personality of the individual. You and I know plenty of people who love power of a certain type and who, with perfectly good intentions, would hate to give it up. I am not one of this type, as you know. For as far as individual preference goes I would, quite honestly, have retired to Hyde Park with infinite pleasure in 1941.

Then there is the other question of the alternative. Willkie was an anomaly who improved greatly in his general thinking after 1940. But, although I liked him personally, I did not feel that he had much knowledge of the world and that he would had to have learned about the world in the school of hard experience. This would have been a rather dangerous experiment in 1940.

As to the last gentleman who was the alternative [Governor Thomas E. Dewey of New York], I say nothing.

I do hope to have a chance of seeing you one of these days.

Always sincerely yours,


## LETTER TO SIDNEY HILLMAN

*The White House. November 25, 1944*

*The President had been accused of ordering his henchmen at the 1944 Chicago Convention, when opposition rose among conservative Democrats to the renomination of Vice President Wallace, to "clear everything with Sidney"—meaning that he would agree to any nominee who was acceptable to organized labor.*

Dear Sidney:

One thing I want to make perfectly clear to Sidney is my appreciation.

It was a great campaign and nobody knows better than I do how much you contributed to its success. I was glad to hear that the CIO in Chicago authorized the continuation of the Political Action Committee. I can think of nothing more important in the years to come than the continuing political education and political energy of the people, who do the jobs of this land, in determination that the American nation shall do the great job it can do for all.

I send you no condolences for the licks you took in the campaign. You and I and Fala have seen what happened to the people who gave them.

Very sincerely yours,


## LETTER TO JESSE H. JONES

*The White House. January 20, 1945*

*On his Fourth Inauguration Day with great frankness and doubt-less some relish, Roosevelt in this manner rewarded Wallace for the drubbings he had taken at the hands of conservatives.*

Dear Jesse:

This is a very difficult letter to write—first, because of our long friendship and splendid relations during all these years and also because of your splendid services to the Government and the excellent way in which you have carried out the many difficult tasks during these years.

Henry Wallace deserves almost any service which he believes he can satisfactorily perform. I told him this at the end of the campaign, in which he displayed the utmost devotion to our cause, traveling almost incessantly and working for the success of the ticket in a great many parts of the country.

Though not on the ticket himself, he gave of his utmost toward the victory which ensued.

He has told me that he thought he could do the greatest amount of good in the Department of Commerce, for which he is fully suited, and I feel, therefore, that the Vice President should have this post in the new Administration.

It is for this reason only that I am asking you to relinquish this present post for Henry, and I want to tell you that it is in no way a lack of appreciation for all that you have done, and that I hope you will continue to be a part of the Government.

During the next few days I hope you will think about a new post—there are several Ambassadorships which are vacant—or about to be vacated. I make this suggestion among many other posts and I hope you will have a chance, if you think well of it, to speak to Ed Stettinius, who will not leave to join me for several days.

Finally, let me tell you that you have my full confidence and that I am very proud of all that you have done during these past years.

With my warm regards,

Always sincerely,

## PRESS CONFERENCE #991

*Aboard* U.S.S. Quincy, *Algiers to Newport News.*

*February 19, 1945*

*Returning from the Yalta Conference hopeful that Big Three unity assured victory over Germany and Japan and successful establishment of the United Nations, the President gossiped about his experiences and plans.*

THE PRESIDENT: Three years ago, when I was first talking about the United Nations, Winston (Churchill) said to me, "Where will you put it?"

I said, "Not Geneva. Geneva's unlucky, has an unlucky record. I don't want to hold it in any location. I want everybody pleased."

Although I don't think I will get it, I want to get a building like Al Smith's Empire State Building, just for the records and the records staff, and then have the conferences meet half the time in one of the Azores Islands. I was there once. In front of my house—I knew a Portuguese on San Miguel—had a great big house. He used to like to take me out on the front steps. There, right in front of me, were royal palms and Norwegian spruce, growing side by side. It's a wonderful climate.

Q: Wouldn't it turn into a resort after a while?

THE PRESIDENT: Not on the little island. I wouldn't let anybody on it. Not even the press.

Q: How did you like Russia?

THE PRESIDENT: Very much. I will give you a story on that.

Yalta was Hollywood and our South all rolled into one. We lived in what used to be the Czar's palace. He and his family had any number of very beautiful villas in the Crimea. And when the Czar went out in 1917, the Soviets took over all the properties, and they turned them into a series of sanatoria and rest places. And if you were a Communist—if you needed a rest—had a bad cold—you made application, you were sent down there and you would be given a rest period there. The place was always apt to be filled with people. They ran from the Imperial Palace down to the small villas.

Town of Yalta itself is filled with villas, and when the Germans came in and put their bombs inside the villas, and blasted everything inside and then set fire to everything, the buildings were all gutted.

Q: Did that indicate that when they did it they felt they would not stay?

THE PRESIDENT: Yes.

Q: Did they do that when they came in?

THE PRESIDENT: No, when they got out.

Q: What can they do about getting reparations in kind from the Germans?

THE PRESIDENT: Get all they can.

Q: Will they have much to pay off with?

THE PRESIDENT: Yes, I think so. Got a lot of German prisoners.

Q: While you were over there, did you pick up any news of Hitler, how he was, what he was doing?

THE PRESIDENT: Nothing. I talked with a lot of newspaper men. They were disguised as secret service men—OGPU. They told me they had no information on him.

THE PRESIDENT: The Czar's palace was full of poor people, as everybody is in a sense poor in Russia. It was full of them up to the time the Germans took over. And then the Germans, before they went out, looted the whole palace. There was nothing left except two pictures in my bedroom.

Apparently the Czar, way back before 1917, was afraid that he would be murdered. He had numerous bedrooms which he occupied, and he used to change bedrooms almost every night —sometimes in the middle of the night.

The Czarina's bedroom was up one flight. You have probably seen the little pamphlet made up by Kathleen Harriman. One part in this pamphlet proved to be untrue, the part about a secret stairway for Rasputin to go up at any time. There's been quite a discussion between Admiral King and General Marshall as to who was occupying Rasputin's room. The Rasputin story was apparently all blown up. She was just spiritualistic.

Q: Did the Judge (Samuel I. Rosenman) tell you how he had become a denizen of the Casbah—the Casbah at Algiers?

THE PRESIDENT: Yes, I think he said something about it.

Q: He took in all parts of the town.

THE PRESIDENT: He did.

I would give anything in the world to write a funny story about Farouk and Haile Selassie and, on the second day, Ibn Saud, but I don't dare do it.

Q: We have heard stories of that, about the tents and so forth.

THE PRESIDENT: I hope they got some pictures showing the

destroyer coming alongside—with the guard lined up the length of the forecastle—the King, a great big whale of a man —big proportions—sitting in a Louis Quinze chair, up on the forward gun deck, upon a great pile of Turkish carpets. Yes, I believe we've got pictures of them.

Q: Do you think they could be released? Don't you think it would be a good idea to show the movies at our annual dinner? They would be the hit of the show.

THE PRESIDENT: Yes, I think it would be all right. I think we have gotten a movie in color.

Q: What did he seem to think of everything?

THE PRESIDENT: I have not even said to Sam (Judge Rosenman) what he said about the Jews. It was perfectly terrible. He doesn't mind the Jews there now, but he does mind the situation of the Jews that come there from Paris, London and New York. He makes all the difference in the world between them. The general feeling is that the Arabs want to be let alone. Do not interfere with the Arabs. Very interesting point of view. He is afraid that the Arabs will be controlled by the foreign Jews that come in. Says there's no way of keeping them in the bounds of Palestine.

Q: What is his conception of the outside world?

THE PRESIDENT: Pretty clever old boy.

Q: How did you lure him out of his country?

THE PRESIDENT: I just sent him a telegram asking him to meet me.

Q: How old is he?

THE PRESIDENT: Seventy-five, but don't print that. He said to me, "An Arab has no age. You and I are the same age." Now there's no secret about my age. He appears to be, and I think he is, well over seventy. The Minister, Colonel Eddy, thinks he is seventy.

Q: Did you smoke in front of him?

THE PRESIDENT: No, no liquor nor smoking, and I sent Anna ashore before he came aboard. It was a chance for her to see Cairo.

Q: Someone told us in Algiers the other day that you never

say how is your daughter or your mother. You say how is your house.

THE PRESIDENT: He started off from Jidda on the destroyer, appropriately called the *Murphy*.

Q: Has any ship ever had a cruise like the *Murphy* had, with the tents and sheep aboard?

THE PRESIDENT: No. It was perfectly amazing.

I think you can work up some kind of story that won't give offense. Women are taboo. The fact that this was the first time he ever left Arabia is all right. He was wounded nine times in battle. He's quite lame. I gave him one of my wheelchairs. I honestly don't know whether you should mention that. It might be taboo.

Q: Did he ask you for it?

THE PRESIDENT: No, he saw me in it—said it would save him many steps at home.

Q: I think that it will do him a lot of honor to mention it.

THE PRESIDENT: Yes, I think so too.

This ship was a busy place for two days, with visits by the King of Egypt, Haile Selassie and Ibn Saud.

Q: Was Haile Selassie as colorful and impressive as Ibn Saud?

THE PRESIDENT: Yes.

Q: Did Ibn Saud have his ceremonial coffee server and food taster at work on the food you served him?

THE PRESIDENT: I didn't see him, but he may have done his work in the galley. After we got through with my coffee, he asked me if I would mind having his ceremonial coffee. So, in came his ceremonial coffee server. I tasted it. It was "Godawful." I drank two cups, but they were very small, tiny cups.

Q: Did you sweeten it?

THE PRESIDENT: Yes, I think so.

Q: The coffee in Algiers now is nothing but charred date seeds.

THE PRESIDENT: Why don't they get real coffee?

Q: The American messes had it, but the native people themselves have great difficulty getting it.

Q: Can you tell us something about your plans when you get back?

THE PRESIDENT: I haven't decided yet. I have only just started to write. Sam has done some, and I have dictated a part of it. When I get back I am thinking of going up to Congress, to the well of the House, sit at a table in the well and have the broadcast from there. That would save time. I wouldn't have to do it again in the evening.

Q: That would be a rather dramatic thing to do, sir. Congress would love that.

THE PRESIDENT: I haven't got any date, because I haven't the faintest idea of what we are running into. We might run into some bad weather that would delay us.

Q: Will we pass between Africa and Madeira?

THE PRESIDENT: Yes.

Q: How about the Canaries?

THE PRESIDENT: I don't know about them.

Q: South of Bermuda? Will we go south of Thirty Degrees?

THE PRESIDENT: About that.

Q: Do you think the submarines that were forced down today were laying for us?

THE PRESIDENT: It might well be, but I have no way of knowing. They got two ships out of a convoy yesterday.

Q: As a result of this latest conference, do you think that there is any real assurance that you can give the American people and the rest of the world?

THE PRESIDENT: Yes, I think so, but we have to win the war first. That is tacked into everything we say: that we have to win the war first.

Q: Do you feel that the machinery you have provided is such that it will prevent any repetition of any other general war?

THE PRESIDENT: I cannot tell how many nations will continue as members. If they all continue and abide by it, there won't be another war. This will take care of that.

Q: Do you think that these continuing Russian successes will hurt that work-or-fight legislation?

THE PRESIDENT: I haven't been home in more than a month. You know more about that than I do.

Q: Won't it take a pretty big job of salesmanship, once Germany collapses, to keep things going?

THE PRESIDENT: Yes.

Q: In view of the progress made at this conference, do you think it will be necessary to have any further Big Three conferences?

THE PRESIDENT: That depends a good deal on the (San Francisco) conference on the 25th of April, which is not a conference to do the necessary work, but only to organize. Then we've got to go to Congress to get whatever we need. England can do it by Cabinet action. After that, I think they will have to go to work organizing. Might take a couple of months. We will provide the machinery. Then they will have the first meeting of the United Nations. When or where, I haven't the faintest idea.

Q: Then do you think the Big Three will meet?

THE PRESIDENT: First, we've got to get the authority. We will try to get authority to be a member.

Q: You have probably heard most of the Congressional reaction to the Crimea Conference. How does it look to you?

THE PRESIDENT: I haven't seen any more than you have, but it's a generally favorable press.

Q: We saw one—Wallace White's. It was good—ran pretty true to form.

THE PRESIDENT: I got one exception. I think I've got it right here. No, I can't find it. Vandenberg agrees to go, but on the condition that he could not be bound by anything that was done.

Q: Would there be any action by which he could be bound?

THE PRESIDENT: He wants to be free to saw his head off.

Q: Stassen didn't put any strings on his acceptance, did he?

THE PRESIDENT: No, sir; Stassen will come back for the meeting.

Q: Maybe you will want to fire Vandenberg and put Dewey on? (laughter)

Q: Do you think Dewey would accept?
THE PRESIDENT: I don't know. . . .

# ADDRESS TO CONGRESS ON
# YALTA CONFERENCE

*The Capitol. March 1, 1945*

*This was the last important address Franklin D. Roosevelt de-*
*livered. His weariness is suggested in the first paragraph—the*
*only time he asked for special consideration because of his crip-*
*pled legs. He did not live to help carry out the policies formu-*
*lated at Yalta which he pleaded for in this Address. They pro-*
*duced controversy that continues in our day. The death of his*
*hope that Stalin would collaborate in the peace made Roose-*
*velt's commitments seem very mistaken to many observers. The*
*worst accusations are that in a secret protocol he promised Stalin*
*to influence China to make concessions to Russia in return for*
*a promise by Stalin that Russia would enter the war against*
*Japan, and that he was taken in by Stalin's promises to support*
*democratic regimes in eastern Europe. Still the facts are that vic-*
*tory against all the Axis nations was won; no one could foresee*
*that Russia's aid against Japan would be unnecessary; the United*
*Nations was established; the United States Senate did give its*
*consent to entry into the United Nations; and no third world war*
*has occurred. These aims were primary in Roosevelt's mind dur-*
*ing his last days.*

I hope that you will pardon me for this unusual posture of
sitting down during the presentation of what I want to say,
but I know that you will realize that it makes it a lot easier for
me not to have to carry about ten pounds of steel around on
the bottom of my legs; and also because of the fact that I have
just completed a fourteen-thousand-mile trip.

First of all, I want to say, it is good to be home.

It has been a long journey. I hope you will also agree that
it has been, so far, a fruitful one. . . .

I come from the Crimea Conference with a firm belief that
we have made a good start on the road to a world of peace.

There were two main purposes in this Crimea Conference. The first was to bring defeat to Germany with the greatest possible speed, and the smallest possible loss of Allied men. That purpose is now being carried out in great force. The German Army, and the German people, are feeling the ever-increasing might of our fighting men and of the Allied armies. Every hour gives us added pride in the heroic advance of our troops in Germany—on German soil—toward a meeting with the gallant Red Army.

The second purpose was to continue to build the foundation for an international accord that would bring order and security after the chaos of the war, that would give some assurance of lasting peace among the Nations of the world.

Toward that goal also, a tremendous stride was made. . . .

In addition . . . there were other problems of vital political consequence.

For instance, first, there were the problems of the occupation and control of Germany—after victory—the complete destruction of her military power, and the assurance that neither the Nazis nor Prussian militarism could again be revived to threaten the peace and civilization of the world.

Second—again for example—there was the settlement of the few differences that remained among us with respect to the International Security Organization [United Nations] after the Dumbarton Oaks Conference. As you remember, at that time, I said that we had agreed ninety per cent. Well, that's a pretty good percentage. I think the other ten per cent was ironed out at Yalta.

Third, there were the general political and economic problems common to all the areas which had been or would be liberated from the Nazi yoke. This is a very special problem. We over here find it difficult to understand the ramifications of many of these problems in foreign lands, but we are trying to.

Fourth, there were the special problems created by a few instances such as Poland and Yugoslavia.

Days were spent in discussing these momentous matters

and we argued freely and frankly across the table. But at the end, on every point, unanimous agreement was reached. And more important even than the agreement of words, I may say we achieved a unity of thought and a way of getting along together.

Of course, we know that it was Hitler's hope—and the German war lords'—that we would not agree—that some slight crack might appear in the solid wall of Allied unity, a crack that would give him and his fellow gangsters one last hope of escaping their just doom. That is the objective for which his propaganda machine has been working for many months.

But Hitler has failed.

Never before have the major Allies been more closely united—not only in their war aims but also in their peace aims. And they are determined to continue to be united with each other—and with all peace-loving Nations—so that the ideal of lasting peace will become a reality. . . .

Provision was made for daily exchange of information between the armies under the command of General Eisenhower on the western front, and those armies under the command of the Soviet marshals on that long eastern front, and also with our armies in Italy—without the necessity of going through the Chiefs of Staff in Washington or London as in the past.

You have seen one result of this exchange of information in the recent bombings by American and English aircraft of points which are directly related to the Russian advance on Berlin. . . .

Details of these plans and arrangements are military secrets, of course: but this tying of things in together is going to hasten the day of the final collapse of Germany. The Nazis are learning about some of them already, to their sorrow. And I think all three of us at the Conference felt that they will learn more about them tomorrow and the next day—and the day after that!

There will be no respite for them. We will not desist for one moment until unconditional surrender. . . .

We made it clear again at Yalta, and I now repeat that un-

conditional surrender does not mean the destruction or enslavement of the German people. The Nazi leaders have deliberately withheld that part of the Yalta declaration from
the German press and radio. . . .

Our objective in handling Germany is simple—it is to secure
the peace of the rest of the world now and in the future. Too
much experience has shown that that objective is impossible
if Germany is allowed to retain any ability to wage aggressive
warfare.

These objectives will not hurt the German people. On the
contrary, they will protect them from a repetition of the fate
which the General Staff and Kaiserism imposed on them before, and which Hitlerism is now imposing upon them again a
hundredfold. It will be removing a cancer from the German
body politic which for generations has produced only misery
and only pain to the whole world.

During my stay in Yalta, I saw the kind of reckless, sense-
less fury, the terrible destruction that comes out of German
militarism. . . .

I had read about Warsaw and Lidice and Rotterdam and
Coventry—but I *saw* Sevastopol and Yalta! And I know that
there is not room enough on earth for both German militarism
and Christian decency. . . .

I—as you know—have always been a believer in the document called the Constitution of the United States. And I spent
a good deal of time in educating two other Nations of the
world in regard to the Constitution of the United States. The
[United Nations] Charter has to be—and should be—approved by the Senate of the United States, under the Constitution. I think the other Nations all know it now. . . .

The Senate and the House of Representatives will both be
represented at the San Francisco Conference. The Congressional delegates to the San Francisco Conference will consist
of an equal number of Republican and Democratic members.
The American Delegation is—in every sense of the word—bipartisan.

World peace is not a party question. I think that Republicans want peace just as much as Democrats. It is not a party question—any more than is military victory—the winning of the war. . . .

The structure of world peace cannot be the work of one man, or one party, or one Nation. It cannot be just an American peace, or a British peace, or a Russian, a French, or a Chinese peace. It cannot be a peace of large Nations—or of small Nations. It must be a peace which rests on the cooperative effort of the whole world.

It cannot be a structure of complete perfection at first. But it can be a peace—and it will be a peace—based on the sound and just principles of the Atlantic Charter—on the concept of the dignity of the human being—and on the guarantees of tolerance and freedom of religious worship. . . .

The three most powerful Nations have agreed that the political and economic problems of any area liberated from Nazi conquest, or of any former Axis satellite, are a joint responsibility of all three Governments. They will join together, during the temporary period of instability—after hostilities—to help the people of any liberated area, or of any former satellite state, to solve their own problems through firmly established democratic processes. . . .

One outstanding example of joint action by the three major Allied powers in the liberated areas was the solution reached on Poland. The whole Polish question was a potential source of trouble in postwar Europe—as it has been sometimes before. . . . Our objective was to help to create a strong, independent, and prosperous Nation. . . . To achieve that objective, it was necessary to provide for the formation of a new government much more representative than had been possible while Poland was enslaved. There were, as you know, two governments—one in London, one in Lublin—practically in Russia. Accordingly, steps were taken at Yalta to reorganize the existing Provisional Government in Poland on a broader democratic basis, so as to include democratic leaders now in Poland and those abroad. . . .

The decision with respect to the boundaries of Poland was,

frankly, a compromise. I did not agree with all of it, by any means, but we did not go as far as Britain wanted, in certain areas; we did not go as far as Russia wanted, in certain areas; and we did not go as far as I wanted, in certain areas. It *was* a compromise. . . .

Quite naturally, this Conference concerned itself only with the European war and with the political problems of Europe —and not with the Pacific war. . . .

It is still a long, tough road to Tokyo. It is longer to go to Tokyo than it is to Berlin, in every sense of the word. The defeat of Germany will not mean the end of the war against Japan. On the contrary, we must be prepared for a long and costly struggle in the Pacific.

But the unconditional surrender of Japan is as essential as the defeat of Germany. I say that advisedly, with the thought in mind that that is especially true if our plans for world peace are to succeed. For Japanese militarism must be wiped out as thoroughly as German militarism. . . .

On my voyage, I had the benefit of seeing the Army and Navy and Air Force at work.

All Americans, I think, would feel as proud of our armed forces as I am, if they could see and hear what I saw and heard.

Against the most efficient professional soldiers and sailors and airmen of all history, our men stood and fought—and won.

This is our chance to see to it that the sons and the grandsons of these gallant fighting men do not have to do it all over again in a few years.

The Conference in the Crimea was a turning point—I hope in our history and therefore in the history of the world. There will soon be presented to the Senate of the United States and to the American people a great decision that will determine the fate of the United States—and of the world—for generations to come.

There can be no middle ground here. We shall have to take the responsibility for world collaboration, or we shall have to bear the responsibility for another world conflict.

I know that the word "planning" is not looked upon with favor in some circles. In domestic affairs, tragic mistakes have been made by reason of lack of planning; and, on the other hand, many great improvements in living, and many benefits to the human race, have been accomplished as a result of adequate, intelligent planning—reclamation of desert areas, developments of whole river valleys, and provision for adequate housing.

The same will be true in relations between Nations. For the second time in the lives of most of us this generation is face to face with the objective of preventing wars. To meet that objective, the Nations of the world will either have a plan or they will not. The groundwork of a plan has now been furnished, and has been submitted to humanity for discussion and decision.

No plan is perfect. Whatever is adopted at San Francisco will doubtless have to be amended time and again over the years, just as our own Constitution has been.

No one can say exactly how long any plan will last. Peace can endure only so long as humanity really insists upon it, and is willing to work for it—and sacrifice for it. . . .

I am confident that the Congress and the American people will accept the results of this Conference as the beginnings of a permanent structure of peace upon which we can begin to build, under God, that better world in which our children and grandchildren—yours and mine, the children and grandchildren of the whole world—must live, and can live.

And that, my friends, is the principal message I can give you. But I feel it very deeply, as I know that all of you are feeling it today, and are going to feel it in the future.

## UNFINISHED ADDRESS PREPARED FOR THOMAS JEFFERSON DAY

*April 13, 1945*

*When the President died on April 12 at Warm Springs, he had been working on this address for delivery over the radio to the*

*Jefferson Day Dinner. On the typescript he had made various
changes and had added the final sentence in his own handwriting.*

Americans are gathered together this evening in communities all over the country to pay tribute to the living memory of Thomas Jefferson—one of the greatest of all democrats; and I want to make it clear that I am spelling that word "democrats" with a small "d".

I wish I had the power, just for this evening, to be present at all of these gatherings.

In this historic year, more than ever before, we do well to consider the character of Thomas Jefferson as an American citizen of the world.

As Minister to France, then as our first Secretary of State and as our third President, Jefferson was instrumental in the establishment of the United States as a vital factor in international affairs.

It was he who first sent our Navy into far distant waters to defend our rights. And the promulgation of the Monroe Doctrine was the logical development of Jefferson's far-seeing foreign policy.

Today this nation which Jefferson helped so greatly to build is playing a tremendous part in the battle for the rights of man all over the world.

Today we are part of the vast Allied force—a force composed of flesh and blood and steel and spirit—which is today destroying the makers of war, the breeders of hatred, in Europe and in Asia.

In Jefferson's time our Navy consisted of only a handful of frigates headed by the gallant *U.S.S. Constitution*—"*Old Ironsides*"—but that tiny Navy taught nations across the Atlantic that piracy in the Mediterranean—acts of aggression against peaceful commerce and the enslavement of their crews was one of those things which, among neighbors, simply was not done.

Today we have learned in the agony of war that great power involves great responsibility. Today we can no more escape the consequences of German and Japanese aggression than could we avoid the consequences of attacks by the Barbary Corsairs a century and a half before.

We, as Americans, do not choose to deny our responsibility.

Nor, do we intend to abandon our determination that, within the lives of our children and our children's children, there will not be a third world war.

We seek peace—enduring peace. More than an end to war, we want an end to the beginnings of all wars—yes, an end to this brutal, inhuman and thoroughly impractical method of settling the differences between governments.

The once powerful, malignant Nazi state is crumbling. The Japanese war lords are receiving, in their own home-land, the retribution for which they asked when they attacked Pearl Harbor.

But the mere conquest of our enemies is not enough.

We must go on to do all in our power to conquer the doubts and the fears, the ignorance and the greed, which made this horror possible.

Thomas Jefferson, himself a distinguished scientist, once spoke of "the brotherly spirit of Science, which unites into one family all its votaries of whatever grade, and however widely dispersed throughout the different quarters of the globe."

Today, science has brought all the different quarters of the globe so close together that it is impossible to isolate them one from another.

Today we are faced with the pre-eminent fact that, if civilization is to survive, we must cultivate the science of human relationships—the ability of all peoples, of all kinds, to live together and work together, in the same world, at peace.

Let me assure you that my hand is the steadier for the work that is to be done, that I move more firmly into the task, knowing that you—millions and millions of you—are joined with me in the resolve to make this work endure.

The work, my friends, is peace. More than an end of this war—an end to the beginnings of all wars. Yes, an end, forever, to this impractical, unrealistic settlement of the differences between governments by the mass killing of peoples.

Today, as we move against the terrible scourge of war—as we go forward toward the greatest contribution that any generation of human beings can make in this world—the contribution of lasting peace, I ask you to keep up your faith. I measure the sound, solid achievement that can be made at this time by the straight-edge of your own confidence and your resolve. And to you, and to all Americans who dedicate themselves with us to the making of an abiding peace, I say:

The only limit to our realization of tomorrow will be our doubts of today. Let us move forward with strong and active faith.